HAUSA

Hausa is one of the most important languages of West Africa. It is the mother-tongue of some fifteen to twenty million people, living mainly in the northern states of Nigeria and the neighbouring Niger Republic. In addition, there are approximately ten million non-native Hausa speakers. This book has been specially prepared for students working by themselves who wish to learn to speak, read and write Hausa. It is based on the Kano dialect which is normally accepted as 'standard' Hausa for teaching purposes. The grammar of the language is introduced step-by-step in a series of graded lessons, supported by numerous test sentences, lively dialogues, typical conversation pieces and, later on, traditional fables and proverbs. A bibliography to guide those who wish to proceed further, quick-look tables of grammatical synopsis and a two-way vocabulary of some 2000 words are also included. Special attention is given to marking tone and vowel length, two essential aids to acquiring fluency often ignored in other published texts used for teaching Hausa.

TEACH YOURSELF BOOKS

HAUSA

Charles H. Kraft, Ph.D.

Department of Linguistics, University of California

in association with

A. H. M. Kirk-Greene, M.A.(Cantab.)

*Senior Research Fellow in African Studies, St. Antony's College,
Oxford University*

*Formerly Head of the Department of Languages,
Ahmadu Bello University, Zaria, Nigeria
Sometime Member of the Hausa Language Board and
Chairman of the Higher Standard Hausa Board of Examiners*

ST. PAUL'S HOUSE   WARWICK LANE   LONDON EC4P 4AH

First printed 1973

Copyright © 1973
The English Universities Press Ltd.

ISBN 0 340 05958 3

Made and printed in Great Britain for The English Universities Press Ltd., by Stephen Austin and Sons, Limited, Hertford

Contents

Preface

Were it not for the fact that we have three matters to record, no prefatory note would be necessary in a volume in the well-established Teach Yourself series.

First, a note on the history of the materials in this Hausa grammar. The original lessons were used from 1962–1968 by Mr. Kirk-Greene in regular African language courses in the Summer Schools at the University of California, Los Angeles, and for faculty and post-graduate classes at Ahmadu Bello University. A parallel and advanced version was used by Dr. Kraft in his credit-earning courses at Michigan State University between 1964 and 1968, and at UCLA from 1968 to the present. On the experience gained from this considerable testing period we have combined and revised our course materials. Since 1966, Dr. Kraft has worked on the task of incorporating them into the eventual text of *Teach Yourself Hausa*. If the foundations of this volume lie in the original work of one of us, the credit for the final version is essentially that of the other.

Secondly, a reference to some of the distinctive features of this Hausa grammar. In most existent grammars, insufficient attention has been paid to the questions of marking tone and vowel length; we have given special attention to these essential aids to acquiring fluency. The supplementary sections of the book, such as the bibliographical guide to further reading, referential lessons, quick-look tables of grammatical synopsis and a two-way vocabulary of some 2000 words will place the student who completes this course in a promising position to sit formal examinations in Hausa and then, hopefully, move to the field to put into practice what he has learned at home. Again, we have sought to support

the morphological and syntactical analysis by a series of
lively dialogues and typical situational conversations,
and, later on, of traditional fables, proverbs and stories.
Where the student has the advantage of working with a
Hausa informant, he may conveniently have these
conversation-pieces read or recorded. But since we are
aware that, in the nature of the Teach Yourself series,
many students will initially be faced with the problem of
literally teaching themselves, we have here and there
eschewed an approach that holds that grammars should
be purely descriptive and never prescriptive, and have
taken advantage of our class experience where we have
found that a didactic ' laying down of the basic rules '
is very often a helpful and appreciated framework for
those beginning to learn an African language.

Thirdly, and most importantly, the acknowledgement
of our debts of gratitude. To name all those—scholars,
informants, research assistants, students—who have so
readily co-operated in our work on this new Hausa
course would be impossible. But we hope that if we
specify those to whom our greatest thanks for information, explanation and clarification goes, and happily
dedicate our book to all students of Hausa, be they
Nigerian or otherwise, past or future, we shall have
achieved our aim of due acknowledgement. Those to
whom our special thanks are due include Mr. F. W.
Parsons, Reader in Hausa at the School of Oriental and
African Studies, University of London, whose exhaustive
comments on the text were so helpful and upon whose
scholarly analyses of Hausa verbs and noun plurals we
have leaned so heavily ; Dr. D. W. Arnott, Professor of
West African Languages at the University of London,
for his suggested improvements ; Messrs. G. P. Bargery
and R. C. Abraham, whose monumental dictionaries we
rarely turned to in vain ; the numerous and enthusiastic
students registered for our respective courses over the

years ; our various research assistants, Yahaya Aliyu,
Benjamin Ishaku, Salisu Abubakar, Ibrahim Wada, Sani
Abdullahi, Katherine (Powers) de Blij and Marguerite
G. Kraft ; and our typists, Jean Gorman and Dorothy
Pelton, who have dealt so nobly with a language quite
strange to them. In hoping that this book may be a
helpful contribution to the learning of one of the two
most important languages of Africa, we conclude by
reminding our readers of the Hausa proverb **Kàràtū,
farkonkà maɗàcī, ƙarshenkà zumà**: *it may be bitter to
begin study but the end is sweet.*

CHARLES H. KRAFT, Ph.D.

Department of Linguistics,
University of California at Los Angeles

in association with

A. H. M. KIRK-GREENE, M.A.

St. Antony's College, Oxford

1973

Part One

Introduction

Lesson 1

The Hausa Language

1. Hausa historically is primarily the name of a language rather than of a people. By extension, it has come to be used to describe the majority group of northern Nigerians, linked by a sense of unity based on a common language, history and customs. Ethnically, however, there exists some heterogeneity within this group, and religion-wise there are a few Christian and animist Hausa as well as Muslim Hausa.

2. The present-day Hausa people originate from the **Hausā Bakwài,** the seven historical states of Kano, Katsina, Daura, Zazzau (Zaria), Biram, Gobir and Rano, which form the nucleus of the Kano, North Central and North-western states of Nigeria and of the contiguous portion of Niger Republic. These states flourished some 400 years ago ; Kano city is reputed to be a thousand years old. At the beginning of the nineteenth century, the Fulani of Sokoto incorporated the governments of the **Hausā Bakwài** into the Sokoto empire, the foundation of the political entity recognized up to 1966 as the Northern Region of Nigeria. The kingdom of Bornu, along with the remainder of present-day North-eastern, Benue-Plateau and Kwara states, remained outside the mainstream of Hausa and later Fulani influence.

Those ancient states where Hausa was spoken, but not as a mother tongue, were known as the **Banzā Bakwài,** the seven ' illegitimate ' ones. They included such areas as Ilorin (Yoruba), Nupe, Yauri, Kebbi, Kwararafa (Jukun), Gwari and Zamfara. **Gwārī** is a term still used to refer contemptuously to one who haltingly stammers out

pidgin-Hausa : **Bàgwārī nè.** Its opposite, the flattery
given to a foreigner who speaks fluent Hausa, is **yā iyà
Hausā kàmar jàkin Kanò,** literally *he speaks Hausa like
a Kano donkey.* The Kano dialect is that normally
accepted as ' standard ' Hausa for teaching purposes, and
is the one preferred in this book.

3. The Hausa language is generally recognized to be the
largest West African language. Fifteen to twenty million
people can claim Hausa as their mother-tongue with
some ten million non-native speakers demonstrating
varying degrees of competence in the language. It is the
predominant language of the northern states of Nigeria
and of neighbouring Niger Republic. Sizable Hausa-
speaking communities (often itinerant and trading) are
also found in many of the major cities of West, North and
Equatorial Africa.

In the former Northern Region of Nigeria up to 1966,
Hausa shared with English the status of ' official '
language and both were written into the constitution. In
1964 the Northern House of Assembly considered the
adoption of Hausa as the only language of business
throughout the Government and in the legislature.
Regulations towards implementing this were introduced
but were rescinded in early 1966. Without a knowledge
of Hausa, however, it is awkward to move very far from
northern Nigeria's urban circles and difficult to communi-
cate effectively with any but the English-speaking elite.

4. Hausa is classified by Greenberg as a member of the
Chàdic group of the Afroasiatic family of languages.[1] It
is, therefore, more closely related genetically to Arabic,
Hebrew, Berber and other members of the Afroasiatic

[1] See Greenberg, J. H., *The Languages of Africa.* Bloomington,
Indiana : Indiana University, 1963.

family than are most of the rest of the languages of sub-Saharan Africa. To this extent Hausa is not a ' typical ' African language.

The conceptual framework of the Hausa-speaking peoples expressed through the language is, however, definitely African and bears a close relationship to that expressed through more ' typically ' African Niger-Kordofanian languages to the south of Hausa.

The cultural influence of the Near East upon the Hausa people is, however, quite prominent and is reflected in the language. The influence of Muslim thought and culture may be said to permeate many aspects of Hausa life and language. Borrowings of concepts (especially religious and philosophical) and vocabulary are recognizable at every turn.

As one result of early Muslim influence, Hausa has a literary tradition extending back several centuries before contact with Western culture. Hausa was first written in an Arabic script known as **àjàmì**. Today this representation of the language is largely restricted to Muslim scholars, divines (**màlàmai**) and their Koranic schools, having been superseded for most purposes by the Roman script (minus the diacritics) which is used in this book.

A large amount of printed literature is available in Hausa, and a variety of periodicals have appeared over the years, at least two of which are still produced regularly. Foremost among the secular producers of Hausa literature has been the Gaskiya Corporation, Zaria. In recent years, however, the Northern Nigeria Publishing Corporation at Zaria has emerged as the principal publisher of Hausa texts. The weekly newspaper *Gaskiya Ta Fi Kwabo* is the most prominent of the Hausa periodicals, and is supported by a relatively large number—when compared to the number of publications in other vernaculars—of books printed in Roman script and published by various commercial and mission groups in Northern Nigeria. Since its removal to Kaduna in 1966, however, it has failed to retain the standard orthography (especially with respect to the ' hooked ' letters), and should not, therefore, be imitated by those sitting for formal Hausa language examinations.

Lesson 2

Hausa Pronunciation I : Consonants and Vowels

1. Twenty-one written symbols will be employed to represent the twenty-four Hausa consonants (three of the consonants, **sh**, **ts** and **'y**, are represented by double letters).[1] The following chart provides a fairly accurate indication of the sounds of sixteen of these consonants :

b as in *big* : bābù, bàbba, bàkī [2]
c as the *ch* in *church* : can, cikà, màcè
d as in *dog* : don, bàdūkù, darē
g as in *good* (never as in *gist*) : gudù, gērō, dōgō
h as in *hat* : hūtà, habà, rahà
j as in *jot* : jāwō, kujèrā, jìkī
k as in *king* : kàrē, kūkā, kōwā
l as in *like* : lādā, lallē, lāfiyà
m as in *man* : mōtà, makòyī, dāmā
n as in *not* : nāmà, hannū, nīsa
s as in *son* : sanyī, sanì, Hausā
sh as in *shut* : shìga, shā, tāshì
t as in *tin* : tàfì, tēbùr, fitō
w as in *win* : watà, wurī, rawā
y as in *yet* : yārò, hanyōyī, yunwà
z as in *zero* : zuwà, zāfī, kàzā

---

[1] The letters *q*, *v* and *x* are not used in Hausa except sometimes in the spelling of foreign names. The letter *p* is sometimes seen as a non-standard representation of the sound regularly written as *f*, which, however, often sounds more like English *p* than English *f*. The sound represented in English by *qu* occurs regularly in Hausa words, but is written **kw**.

[2] See pages 9–11 and 14 for explanations of the diacritical marks.

2. The remainder of the consonants require special treatment.

f sounds very much like the English *f*, but is produced between the lips rather than between the lower lip and upper teeth as in the English *f*. Often, too, Hausa f is pronounced nearer the English *p*, e.g. **fīlī, lāfiyà, fìta, fātà, farī**. In some words it is interchangeable with **h**, e.g. **fuɗu/huɗu, tsōfō/tsōhō**.

' is a glottal catch like that which precedes each vowel in English exclamations such as *oh-oh* or *uh-uh*. In Hausa **'** is written when it occurs in the middle of a word, e.g. **ā'à, nà'am**. Every word beginning with a vowel in Hausa actually starts with a glottal catch, but this, since it is predictable, is not written either in the official orthography or in this book, e.g. **aikì, àddā, ī.**

'y is a very rare Hausa sound which consists of *y* preceded by a glottal catch, e.g. **'yā'yā, 'yarsà.**

The consonants **ɓ, ɗ, ƙ** and **ts** are known technically as *glottalized consonants*. That is, each is produced with a simultaneous glottal catch and released with a rather explosive quality to it. The **ɓ** and **ɗ**, in addition, are often produced implosively, i.e. with the air stream pulled into the mouth rather than expelled from the mouth as with **ƙ** and **ts**. In the schools of Hausaland the letters representing these sounds are referred to as *hooked* letters.

ɓ is like **b**, but with a simultaneous glottal catch and an explosive quality to the release, e.g. **ɓērā, lēɓè, haɓà.**

ɗ is like **d** (though the tongue position is a bit farther back), but with a simultaneous glottal catch and an explosive quality to the release, e.g. **ɗākì, ɗaya, kuɗī.**

ƙ is like **k**, but with a simultaneous glottal catch and an explosive, click-like quality to the release, e.g. **ƙōfà, zāƙī.**

ts is like **s**, but with a simultaneous glottal catch, an explosive quality to the release and, for many speakers, an initial *t* sound, e.g. **tsāfì, yātsà, tsūtsà.**

r is either a short trill or a flap which often sounds

much like an **l**. Though many Hausa speakers will maintain a distinction between the two **r** sounds, consistently employing one in certain words and the other in other words, the processes of linguistic change have so affected the use of these sounds that it is often impossible to predict accurately which **r** will be employed in a given word. The majority of Hausa speakers employ a trilled **r** before most consonants (except labial and velar), e.g. **murnà** ; in final position, e.g. **har** ; regularly in words borrowed from other languages, e.g. **barkà, karàntā** ; and in a relatively small number of other words. The flap **r** occurs in most other contexts. The student is encouraged to discover what the pattern followed by his informant is, and to learn to employ that pattern in his own speech. He may find it convenient to add a tilde (ř) throughout these lessons to indicate when the trill occurs in his informant's speech. The present authors have weighed the relative merits of consistently indicating the difference between the two **r** sounds throughout these lessons and felt that it would be less confusing to omit such indication here.

3. Hausa makes use of five short and five long vowels. However, only five written symbols are used in Hausa literature to represent these ten sounds. It is, therefore, necessary to supplement the accepted writing system in order to enable the student to know which sound is to be employed in a given word. *Long vowels* will thus be indicated in these lessons by the presence of a macron (ā) above the letter. Vowels with no macron are therefore short.

Due to the wide dialectal differences in the pronunciation of English vowels, it is very difficult to illustrate Hausa vowels unambiguously by employing English words. The following attempt to do so is only a general guide and must not therefore be depended upon too heavily. The student must do his best to imitate his informant's production of the vowel sound carefully, whether or not the English illustration of the Hausa sound given below is accurate for his dialect. He may later find it profitable to substitute other English (or non-English) key-words for those given below. In any event, the long vowels (ā, ē, ī, ō, ū) are always ' pure ' vowels in Hausa, unlike English where they are usually phonetic diphthongs (technically known as glides).[3] The student should keep this basic difference between Hausa and English vowels in mind as he refers to the English ' key-words ' below.

a most frequently [4] similar to the *u* in *butter, cuff* : **habà, àllō, tàfi**

ā similar to *a* in *far, car, psalm* : **rānā, fātà, tàfī**

e similar to *e* in *bet, check* : **fensìr, màcè, gòbe**

---

[3] The student unaware of this characteristic of English pronunciation might profitably watch his lips in a mirror as he pronounces slowly a word such as *hope* or *loaf*. He will note that as he completes the vowel segment of the word his lips become more tightly pursed into a *w*-like position in anticipation of the final labial consonant. This process is technically known as a *vowel glide*, and these words are spelled phonetically *howp* and *lowf* to indicate the fact that the vowel segment in them is a complex of *o* plus *w*. Less easily observable but nonetheless real vowel glides occur on most other ' long ' vowels in English as well. The vowel in *feet*, for example, involves a sliding (gliding) forward of the tongue into a *y* position (phonetically spelled *fiyt*) as does that in *rate* (phonetically *reyt*). Likewise the vowel in *far* involves a tongue glide which may be phonetically represented by an *H* (e.g. *faH* or *faHr*). The point is that Hausa vowels are not characterized by this type of ' diphthongizing '. Hausa long vowels are, therefore, phonetically representable as *oo* rather than *ow*, *ii* rather than *iy*, *aa* rather than *aH*, *uu* rather than *uw*, *ee* rather than *ey*. The English learner of Hausa must, therefore, give some attention to keeping his lips still as he produces a Hausa ō or ū, and his tongue in its starting position when he produces Hausa ī, ē and ā, regardless of the consonant that follows.

[4] In proximity to **y** or **i**, **a** is often pronounced as short **e**, e.g. **yànzu, sai.** Other slight variations also occur in the pronunciation of **a**. The student should be on the lookout for them and seek to imitate the native speaker's production at all times.

ē similar to *a* in *rate, mate, date* : lēɓè, gēmǜ, tēbùr
i similar to *i* in *pin, bit* : cikì, gidā, idò
ī similar to *e* in *she, feet* : kīfī, shī, rìgā
o similar to *o* in *obey* (very short) : Bellò
ō similar to *o* in *open, goal* : dōkì, tuwō, mōtà
u similar to the vowel in *foot, put* : ukù, mùtûm, dubū
ū similar to *oo* in *boot, root, toot* : sūnā, tǜlū, hùlā

4. Short vowels are *quantitatively shorter* in duration than long vowels and very often differ in *quality* as well. That is, if a given short vowel requires a certain length of time to be produced, its long counterpart may require twice as much time. The fact that a given vowel is short rather than long may also be signalled (especially in closed syllables) by the fact that the short vowel *sounds* different from its long counterpart. Thus, the difference between tàfi, *go away*, and tàfī, *palm of the hand*, is signalled both by the differences in the actual length of the two a's and by the fact that they ' sound ' different (i.e. have a different phonetic quality).

5. In addition to the ten vowels, there are in Hausa two diphthongs. These are combinations of a short *a* plus *y* or *w* which occur in a single syllable. They are, however, written as ai and au:

ai usually approximates the *u* in *cuff* + *y* : kâi, nai ; or the *e* in *bet* + *y* : sai, zâi
au usually approximates the *u* in *cup* + *w* : ƙauyè, launì.

6. The student should always keep in mind the fact that a language is made up primarily of *sounds* rather than written symbols. Written symbols are used in this book only as guides to the spoken sounds of the Hausa language, not as an end in themselves.

The system of written symbols here employed is designed to be as true a guide as possible to the spoken language. Therefore, *each written symbol represents one, and only one, meaningful unit of sound in Hausa.*

Lesson 3

Hausa Pronunciation II : Tone and Intonation

1. No language is known to be spoken without the systematic use of pitch distinctions in addition to the distinctions between the various vowels and consonants. English, for example, is characterized by a very intricate intonational system (the specifics of the system vary from dialect to dialect) in which pitch distinctions play a major part.

A large proportion of the world's languages—including all but a very few African languages—employ pitch *tonally* rather than intonationally. This is a usage quite distinct from that of English. Such languages are known as *tone languages*. Hausa is a tone language.

Each Hausa syllable consists of a given set of consonants and vowels plus an assigned tone. Each word must, therefore, be learned and pronounced with its proper tone pattern as well as its proper vowels and consonants.[1] In order to facilitate proper learning, and to avoid ambiguity, we have considered it helpful to employ accent marks in this book to indicate the proper tone of each syllable. In the traditional orthography (which does not indicate either tone or vowel length), for

---

[1] It is important to observe that *tone* and *tone pattern* are terms employed to designate a system which employs pitch distinctions in a relative manner—not in an absolute manner like notes in music. Different speakers, e.g. men and women, have different voice pitches and these may be varied for emotional reasons. It is the *relative interval* between successive syllables of speech that determines the tonal (and intonational) patterns being employed in language, *not* the absolute pitch on which these speech segments fall.

example, the spelling **jibi** represent two distinct words
and the spelling **fito** represents three distinct words,
differing in tone (see below).

2. In Hausa there are two tone levels (termed *high* and
low), and a less frequent combination of high and low
resulting in a *falling* tone. These tones are not necessarily
assignable to absolute pitch levels such as those of a
musical scale, but rather are important because they
contrast with each other in a systematic way within the
language. That is, Hausa high tone is of importance
because it contrasts with low tone to account for the
difference in meaning between words like **jībi**, *day after
tomorrow*, and **jībì**, *a meal*, or between **fitō**, *come out*,
fitò, *ferrying*, and **fìtō**, *guinea corn beer*.

3. In this book the grave accent (`) is employed over the
vowel of the relevant syllable to indicate *low tone*. A
high-tone syllable is signalled by the *absence of any tone
mark* over the vowel. The circumflex (^) accent over a
vowel indicates a *falling-tone* syllable (i.e. one which
starts high and falls to low). A few examples of words
differing only in tone are:

a cry	**kūkā**	**kūkà**	baobab tree
inside	**cikī**	**cikì**	stomach
he went	**yā tàfi**	**yâ tàfi**	he will go
(particle of assent)	**na'àm**	**nà'am**	(reply to a call)

4. Hausa also has an *intonational system*. This system
involves the specifying and modification of the pitch
levels in the tonal system. Hausa intonation applies to
whole utterances, not to each syllable as is the case with
tone.

While every syllable has its own tone, the specific
pitch level of each syllable in an utterance is determined

by the intonational system in accordance with the position of the given syllable in the utterance. The tonal pattern of a word determines whether the pitch of the syllable is the same, higher or lower than the pitch of the immediately preceding and following syllables in the utterance. The intonational system specifies how much difference there will be between contiguous syllables with different tones.

The total pitch component (tone plus intonation) of a Hausa utterance can be conveniently described in terms of five pitch levels.[2] These can be numbered from 1 to 5, with 1 referring to the lowest and 5 to the highest pitch level.

5. The most characteristic type of Hausa intonation may be termed *declarative intonation*. This type of intonation has a generally descending pitch pattern and may be represented on a chart as follows :

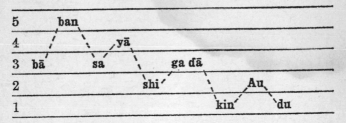

Bàbansà yā shìga dākìn Audù.   Father-his he entered
room-of Audu.

The first high tone in a declarative pattern is on pitch level 5. The next low is on pitch 3, the next high on 4,

[2] See also Hodge, Carleton T., *Hausa Basic Course*, pp. 3 ff., and Kraft, Charles H., and Marguerite G., *Spoken Hausa: Introductory Course*. An annotated bibliography will be found on pages 289 ff. (Lesson 43).

etc. The pattern, therefore, is to drop two steps from a high to a low, and to climb one step from a low to a high, but with two qualifications :

(i) An initial low tone will be on level 3 and the following high on level 5.

(ii) A final low will drop to level 1, even if the utterance is not long enough to force it there, but will go no lower than level 1.

6. *Interrogative intonation* is of two types :

(*a*) When the utterance includes no interrogative word, the last high tone will jump to a pitch level at least one step higher than the pitch level of the previous high-tone syllable. Often, in fact, the whole utterance is pitched on a higher level than in the corresponding statement. If the final syllable is high, it will slur from the very high level to a level at least one step lower. A following low tone (if present) will drop only one step rather than all the way down to level 1 as in the declarative pattern :

5	ka		fi		su			ne
4		lā		yā			ai		e
3	nā				nā				
2							kī		
1									

Kanà   lāfiyà ?   Sunà aikì nē ?
Are you well ?   Are they working ?

These utterances as statements (declarative intonation) would be as follows, in contrast with the interrogative patterns above :

5	ka			su	
4		lāfi			ai
3	nā			nā'	
2					nē
1		yā		kī	

Kanà lāfiyà.   **Sunà aikì nē.**
You are well.   They are working.

(b) When the utterance includes an interrogative word it
    employs the declarative pattern with two modifica-
    tions :

   (i) The whole utterance may be on a slightly higher
        pitch.

  (ii) A final high-tone syllable becomes a falling slur
        to a level at least one step lower. If the final
        syllable is a low tone, the second modification
        does not apply.

5	nā gida			zā			nā ai	
4		a				zo		
3	i		yaushe		ka'	o	i	
2								
1								kī

Ìnā gidā ?   **Yàushè zā kà zō ?**   **Ìnā aikì ?**
How's (your)   When will you   How's (your)
  family ?   come ?   work ?

7. *Vocative intonation*, employed when using a person's
name or title in addressing him, is the same as that
described under 6 (b) above :

5	nu Mūsa	Nā gaishē		nu Au
4	a		dā	
3	san		ka	bi	san
2			li	i	
1					du

Sànnu, Mūsā.	Nā gaishē kà, d̃ālìbì.	Sànnu, Audù.
Greetings, Musa.	I greet you, student.	Greetings, Audu.

8. *Stress* is also present in Hausa, but is not nearly as important in Hausa as in English. The student must, however, learn to recognize and imitate the stress as well as the pitch pattern of each utterance. The following generalizations concerning Hausa stress may be helpful:

(i) Differences in stress alone do not account for differences in meaning between words.

(ii) Stress generally, though by no means always, falls on syllables possessing high tone (as exceptions note the following—the underlined syllable takes the stress: màcè cē, *it is a woman*; kàwō àkwàtì, *bring the box*).

(iii) When a series of high-tone syllables is followed by a low tone, the high-tone syllable immediately preceding the low syllable carries greater stress than the preceding high syllables unless such a syllable is both word-final and possesses a short vowel (e.g. ita cè, *it is she*).

9. The importance of mastering the tone and intonation patterns of Hausa cannot be overemphasized. To ' learn ' Hausa words and longer utterances without taking the trouble to acquire the proper pitch pattern suggests an indifference by the speaker that indicates disrespect or

even ignorance. Foreigners have insulted Hausa-speakers too long by simply carrying their own intonational patterns over into Hausa. It is an everlasting tribute to the patience and kindness of the Hausa people that they have not only put up with such carelessness but even learned to understand some of the things we have attempted to say in our bastardized form of their language !

The tone pattern of each word is fully as integral to it as are the vowels and consonants, and it must be as completely mastered. It is for this reason that the effort has been made to indicate the tone and vowel length of each Hausa syllable in this book.

Part Two

Grammar

Lesson 4

Greetings I

1. In Hausa society, greetings are usually more than a casual ' hello ' or nodded ' morning '. They are the hallmark of courtesy and good manners. Different greetings exist for different times of the day and for different activities. The more common of these greetings are given below. Other important greetings are given in Lesson 31.

2. The following greetings can be used with anyone, at any time.

Greeting		*Reply*	
hello	sànnu	yâuwā, sànnu (kàdai)	hello
are you well ?	lāfiyà ?	lāfiyà lau	I'm fine
how's (your) tiredness ?	ìnā gàjiyà ?	bâ gàjiyà	there is no tiredness
how's (your) work ?	ìnā aikì ?	aikì da gòdiyā	I'm thankful for it
how's (your) family ?	ìnā gidā ?	lāfiyà	fine
what's the news ?	ìnā làbārì ?	(làbārì)sai àlhērì	all is well
fine	tò mādàllā		
see you later	sai an jimà	yâuwā, sai an jimà	okay, see you later

3. A typical greeting situation will include some such sequence as that listed in section 2 above. The following more specialized greetings are substitutable for the first (lines 3 and 4) or the last (line 5) greeting in the above list when appropriate :

C

(a) Morning greetings

Greeting		Reply	
how did you sleep ?	inā kwānā ?	lāfiyà	fine
did you sleep well ?	kwal lāfiyà ?	lāfiyà	fine

(b) Midday and afternoon greetings :

Greeting		Reply	
how's (your) day ?	inā wunì ?	lāfiyà	fine

4. Greetings for special situations :

Greeting		Reply
greetings at (your) work	sànnu dà aikì	yâuwā, sànnu
greetings at (your) coming	sànnu dà zuwà	yâuwā, sànnu
greetings (on entering a home)	sàlāmù àlaikùn	yâuwā, àlaikà sàlāmù

5. Parting greetings :

Greeting		Reply
see you later	sai an jimà	yâuwā, mù jimà dà yawà
see you tomorrow	sai gòbe	yâuwā, sai gòbe
see you sometime (soon)	sai wani lōkàcī	yâuwā, sai wani lōkàcī
until morning	sai dà sāfē	yâuwā, sai dà sāfē
until evening	sai dà yâmmā	yâuwā, sai dà yâmmā
see you some day	sai wata rānā	yâuwā, sai wata rānā

A common alternative reply to any of these greetings is :

　　tò Allà yà kai mù　may God bring it about (*lit.* okay, may God take us [to that time])

to which one responds in turn :

　　àmin　may it be so

VOCABULARY

Nominals

aikì	work
Allà	God
an jimà	after a while (this is actually a verbal construction but often functions as a nominal)
gàjiyà	tiredness
gidā	home, household
gòbe	tomorrow
inā	where ?, how ?
kwānā	period of night
làbārì	news
lāfiyà	health, well-being
lōkàcī	time
sāfē	morning
yâmmā	early evening ; west
wani (*m.*),	
wata (*f.*)	a certain, a
wunì	period of daylight

Verbals   *Particles*

bâ, bābù	there is no/none	àmin	amen, may it be so
jimà	wait a while		
kai	carry, take, convey	dà	with, and
		mādàllā	splendid, thank you (*lit.* thanks be to God)
		sai	until, except
		sànnu	greetings
		tò ¹/tô	well, okay
		yâuwā/ yâuwa ¹	fine, okay

¹ The low-tone form **tò** and the form **yâuwa** (with the short final vowel) only occur if no pause (indicated in these lessons by a comma) occurs between these particles and a following word.

Dialogue

Bellò :   Sànnu dà zuwà, Ìsā.
Ìsā :   Yâuwā, sànnu.
Bellò :   Ìnā gàjiyà ?
Ìsā :   Bâ gàjiyà.
Bellò :   Ìnā aikì ?
Ìsā :   Aikì dà gòdiyā.
Bellò :   Ìnā làbārì ?
Ìsā :   Làbārì sai àlhērì.
Bellò :   Tò mādàllā.
Ìsā :   Kwal lāfiyà ?
Bellò :   Lāfiyà.
Ìsā :   Ìnā gidā ?
Bellò :   Lāfiyà lau [2]
Ìsā :   Tò mādàllā. Sai gòbe.
Bellò :   Tò Allà yà kai mù.
Ìsā :   Àmin

---

[2] **Lau** is an emphasizing particle equivalent to ' very well '.

Lesson 5

Gender of Nouns

1. All singular nouns are either masculine or feminine. There is no neuter in Hausa.

2. Most nouns ending in -a are feminine. Many, however, are masculine. Following are some of the more common nouns which have a final -a but are masculine:

gidā	home, compound	sūnā	name
ruwā	water	gùgā	bucket
wàsā [1]	game	ɓērā	mouse
watà	moon, month	nāmà	meat

3. Words for acceptedly male and female things, regardless of their final vowels, express the expected gender. (See Lesson 6 for use of nē with masculine nominals, cē with feminine.)

Mùtûm nē.	It is a man.
Màcè cē.	It is a woman.
Sâ nē.	It is a bull.
Zàkarà nē.	It is a rooster.

4. No gender distinction is made in the plural. Nē is used with all plural nominals, even if they refer to females.

Mātā nè.	They are women.
Bēràyē nè.	They are mice.
Jākunà nē.	They are donkeys.

[1] But this is feminine in some areas.

5. The common names of most animals, though grammatically either masculine or feminine, refer to either sex.

Bērā nè.	It is a rat (either sex).
Giwā cè.	It is an elephant (either sex).
Àkwiyà cē.	It is a goat (either sex).[2]
Tunkìyā cè.	It is a sheep (either sex).[2]

6. The names of towns, countries and rivers are feminine.

Nījēriyà	Nigeria	**Bīnuwài**	River Benue
Fàransà	France	**Ìkko**	Lagos
Ingìlà	England	**Kanò**	Kano
Amirkà	America	**Sakkwato**	Sokoto
Kwârà	River Niger	**Baucī**	Bauchi

7. A feminine of many nouns referring to persons or animals and of many adjectival nominals may be formed by changing the masculine ending as follows :

(a) A final -ō or -ū to -uwā :

tsōfō (*m.*)	old person	**tsōfuwā** (*f.*)
dōgō (*m.*)	tall person	**dōguwā** (*f.*)
tsuntsū (*m.*)	bird	**tsuntsuwā** (*f.*)

(b) A final -ē to -ìyā :

Bàhaushè (*m.*)	Hausa person	**Bàhaushìyā** (*f.*)
Bàlārabè (*m.*)	Arab	**Bàlārabìyā** (*f.*)
Bàtūrè (*m.*)	white man	**Bàtūrìyā** (*f.*)
shēgè (*m.*)	bastard	**shēgìyā** (*f.*)

(c) A final -ī to -ìyā :

majēmī (*m.*)	tanner	**majēmìyā** (*f.*)
ɗālìbī (*m.*)	student	**ɗālibìyā** (*f.*)
mahàifī (*m.*)	parent	**mahaifìyā** (*f.*)

---

[2] Unless the animal referred to is known to be male, in which case the words **ràgō**, *ram*, and **bùnsurū**, *he goat*, are used.

or to a high tone -ā :

jàkī (m.)	donkey	jàkā (f.)
jārùmī (m.)	brave person	jārùmā (f.)
gwànī (m.)	expert	gwànā (f.)
mālàm(ī) (m.)	teacher	mālàmā (f.)
ɗālìbī (m.)	student	ɗālìbā (f.)

8. Some nouns, especially kinship terms, may be either masculine or feminine :

kàkā	grandfather *or* grandmother
jikà	grandson *or* granddaughter
àutā	youngest brother *or* sister

VOCABULARY

Nominals

àkwiyà (f.)	goat
Amirkà (f.)	America
Bàtūrè	white man
ɓērā	mouse, rat
ɗālìbī (pl. ɗàlìbai)	student
gīwā (f.)	elephant
gùgā	bucket
Ingìlà (f.)	England
jàkī	donkey
kàkā	grandparent
Kanò (f.)	Kano
màcè (f.) (pl. mātā)	woman, wife
màcè + -r = màtar . . .	wife of . . .
mālàm	teacher, Mr.
mè/mènē/ mènēnè	what ?
mùtûm (pl. mutànē	man, person (pl. people)

Nījēriyà (f.)	Nigeria
ruwā	water
sâ	bull
sūnā	name
tsuntsū	bird
tunkìyā (f.)	sheep
wannàn	this
wàsā	game, play
watà	moon, month
zàkarà	rooster, cock

Particles

nē (f. cē)	is, are, were

EXERCISES

Translate into English :

1. **Ruwā nè.**
2. **Jākunà nē.**
3. **Giwā cè.**
4. **Tsōfuwā cè.**
5. **Bàtūrè nē.**
6. **Tsuntsū nè.**
7. **Kàkā nè.**
8. **Bērā nè.**
9. **Dālìbī nè.**
10. **Mùtûm nē.**

Translate into Hausa with either **nē** (*m.*) or **cē** (*f.*) :

1. It's a name.
2. It's a bull.
3. They are mice.
4. He's a Hausa person (*m.*).
5. They are women.
6. She's a woman
7. It's a game.
8. It's a rooster.
9. It's a home.
10. It's the moon.

Dialogue

Mūsā : **Sànnu ɗālìbī.**
Audù : **Yâuwā, sànnu mālàm.**
Mūsā : **Mènēnè wannàn ?**
Audù : **Wannàn jàkī nè.**
Mūsā : **Tò, mènēnè wannàn ?**

Audù : Tsuntsū nề.
Mūsā : Mềcēcề wannàn ?
Audù : Àkwiyà cē.
Mūsā : Tồ, mềcēcề wannàn ?
Audù : Wannàn tunkìyā cề.
Mūsā : Tồ mādàllā, sai gồbe.
Audù : Yâuwā, Allà yà kai mù.

Lesson 6

'To be' : N̄e, Cē and Kè nan [1]

1. The sense of *am/is/are/was/were* is, regardless of aspect (or 'tense'), expressed by **nē** if the subject is masculine or **cē** if it is feminine. As no gender distinction is made in noun plurals, **nē** is always used with plural forms. (See Lesson 5, section 4.)

2. **Nē/cē** typically occurs at the end of a phrase or clause and its tone is always opposite to the tone of the preceding syllable.

Sarkī nè.	It is a chief.
Yārò nē.	It is a boy.
Makarantā cè.	It is a school.
Yārinyà cē.	It is a girl.
Yârā nè.	They are children.
Yā tàfi gidā nè.	He went home (emphatic).

3. The construction **kè nan** can often be used to express the same meaning as **nē/cē**. The use of **kè nan**, however, typically implies greater emphasis than would the use of **nē/cē**.

Kuɗī kè nan.	It is money.
Sarkī kè nan.	It is the king!
Yā sàmi kuɗī kè nan.	He's become really wealthy!
Tô, mun dāwō gidā kè nan.	Well, we're back home.

[1] These forms are not, however, the only ways to render the English verb 'to be'. For other renderings, see Lessons 18 and 19.

4. The phrase **shī kè nan**, literally meaning *it is this,* is common in the Hausa language, and is used to express finality and, often, to signal transition to a new topic similar to the notion of *that's all, that's that, that's all there is to it, that's the end of the matter*.

> **Yā mutù. Shī kè nan. Bāyan wannàn ...** He died. That was that. After this ...

5. In the negative, **bà ... ba nè/cè** or **kè nan** is used.

Bà idò ba nè.	It is not an eye.
Bà kuɗī ba kè nan.	It is not money !
Bà giwā ba cè.	It is not an elephant.
Bà yârā ba nè.	They are not children.

6. The independent pronouns commonly occur with **nē/cē** and **kè nan**.

nī nè	it is I (*m.*)	**ita cè**	it is she
nī cè	it is I (*f.*)	**mū nè**	it is we
kai nè	it is you (*m.*)	**kū nè**	it is you (*pl.*)
kē cè	it is you (*f.*)	**sū nè**	it is they
shī nè	it is he (*m.*)		

Wànē nè ? Nī nè.	Who is it ? It's I.
Shī nè zâi tàfi.	It is he who will go.
Wà ya [2] zō ? Nī kè nan.	Who has come ? I.

VOCABULARY

Nominals

gàrī	town
idò	eye
kâi	head
kàsuwā (*f.*)	market

---

[2] The reason for a short vowel on this (and other) person-aspect pronouns when following an interrogative is explained in Lesson 20, section 7 (*b*) (ii).

kuɗī	money
kyâu	goodness
lâifī	fault, sin
makarantā (*f.*)	school
sānìyā (*f.*)	
(*pl.* shānū)	cow (*pl.* cattle)
sarkī	chief
yārinyà (*f.*)	girl
yārò (*pl.* yârā)	boy (*pl.* children)
wà, wànē,	
wànēnè ?	who ?

Verbals

dāwō	return (here), come back
shìga	enter, go in
tàfi	go (away), go (to)

Particles

ā'à	no
ī	yes
ƙalau	very

Important Phrases

bâ lâifī	that's okay (*lit.* there's nothing wrong), never mind
dà kyâu	good !
shī kè nan	that's that

EXERCISES

Translate into English :

1. Wànē nè ?
2. Gàrī kè nan.
3. Bà sarkī ba nè.
4. Makarantā cè.
5. Gùgā nè.

6. Bà gidā ba nè.
7. Bà yârā ba nè.
8. Nī nè.
9. Ita cè.
10. Mū nè.

Translate into Hausa :

1. It is a school
2. He is a man.

3. They are boys.
4. He is a chief.

5. That's all.   8. It is money.
6. It is not a bull, it is a cow. 9. It is not an eye.
7. They are not children.   10. It is not a market.

Dialogue

Yūsufù : **Sànnu dà zuwà, Daudà.**

Daudà : **Yâuwa sànnu.**

Yūsufù : **Kwal lāfìyà ?**

Daudà : **Lāfìyà ƙalau.**

Yūsufù : **Wànē ya tàfi gàrī ?**

Daudà : **Audù nē.**

Yūsufù : **Yā dāwō nè ?**

Daudà : **Ā'à, sai gòbe.**

Yūsufù : **Tò dà kyâu**

Lesson 7

Completed Action

1. In Hausa, the *aspect* (termed aspect rather than tense since it denotes kind of action rather than time of action) of verbs is shown by changes in the *person-aspect pronoun*, not in the verb itself. This precedes the verb.

2. The *completive aspect* indicates action regarded as completed or as occurring at a specific point (rather than as a process) in time. This point in time may be past, present or future as indicated by the context. In the absence of contextual evidence to the contrary, however, it is usually possible to assume that the reference is to a point in time in the past.

3. There are two forms of the completive aspect. The first set of *person-aspect pronouns* here listed with the verb **zō**, *come*, is the most commonly used.[1] Note the feature in Hausa of distinct masculine and feminine forms in the second person singular as well as the third person singular.

nā zō	I have come	**mun zō**	we have come
kā zō	you (*m*.) have come	**kun zō**	you (*pl*.) have come
kin zō	you (*f*.) have come		
yā zō	he has come	**sun zō**	they have come
tā zō	she has come		
an zō	one has come		

---

[1] See Lesson 20, section 2, for the other set.

4. In every aspect in Hausa, except the imperative, the verb must, unlike English, be preceded by a *person-aspect pronoun* (henceforth abbreviated *p-a* or *p-a pronoun*), regardless of whether there is already a noun subject or not.

Examples :

Audù yā zō.	Audu (he) has come.
Yârā sun tàfi.	The boys (they) have gone.

5. The impersonal p-a pronoun **an** is used in translating the English passive :

An kāwō àbinci.	Food has been brought.	(*Lit.* one has brought food.)
An kashè fìtilà.	The lamp has been extinguished.	(*Lit.* one has killed the lamp.)

This difference from English may be easier to remember if one adapts the English passive into Hausa thought patterns—substituting *someone brought the food* for *the food was brought.*

6. The *negative of the completed aspect* is formed by placing **bà** (low tone, short vowel) immediately before the p-a pronoun, and **ba** (high tone, short vowel) at the end of the utterance. The construction thus becomes :

    bà + p-a pronoun + verb + **ba**

bà	**tà**	**zō**	**ba**
not	she	has come	not

She has/did not come.

7. The negative form of the completed aspect used with the verb **zō** :

Singular   *Plural*
bàn zō ba   bà mù zō ba
bà kà zō ba   bà kù zō ba
bà kì zō ba
bài zō ba   bà sù zō ba
bà tà zō ba
bà à zō ba

8. Note three differences between the p-a pronouns employed in the affirmative completive and those employed in the negative completive :

(a) The negative p-a pronouns have a low (rather than high) tone and a short (rather than long) vowel.

(b) In all plural forms, in the second person singular feminine, and in the impersonal **an,** the negative forms have no final **-n.**

(c) In the first and third persons singular, the p-a pronoun elides with the first **bà,** so that **bà nà** becomes **bàn** and **bà yà** becomes **bài.** This is virtually always so in spoken and usually so in written Hausa.

Examples :

Bà kà kāwō àbinci ba.   You did not bring food/You
                              have not brought food.

Bài shā ruwā ba.   He did not drink water/He has
                              not drunk water.

9. When the verb is followed by an object or other sentence material, the final **ba** usually (but by no means invariably) occurs at the end of the sentence. An important exception to this rule is the word **tùkùna** (*not*) *as yet*, which regularly comes after the final **ba.** The first negative word **bà** must never be separated from its p-a pronoun.

bà + p-a pronoun + verb + ... + **ba**

bà	**kà**	**zō**	**gidā**	**ba**
not	you	came	home	not

You did not come home.

bà	**sù**	**zō**	**ba**	**tùkùna**
not	they	came	not	(not) as yet

They have not come yet.

VOCABULARY

Nominals

àbinci	food
àbōkī	friend
darē	night
fìtìlà (*f.*)	lantern, lamp
gōnā (*f.*)	farm, garden
kōmē	anything
kujèrā (*f.*)	stool, chair
littāfì	book
nōmā (*f.*)	farming
ùbā	father
uwā (*f.*)	mother
yâu	today

Verbals		*Particles*	
bi [2]	follow	**ɗàzu**	just now
ci [2]	eat	**tùkùna,**	
ji [2]	hear, understand, feel	**tùkùn**	(not) yet
kāwō	bring		
shā	drink		
yi [2]	do, make		
zō	come		

[2] Monosyllabic verbs ending in -i (**bi, ci, fi, ji ƙi, yi**) have a *long* -i before a pronoun direct or indirect object, and a *short* -i before a noun object or when they stand without an object following. The verbal noun has a long -i with falling tone.

D

Important Phrases

bâ kōmē   there is nothing (wrong), it does not matter,
                never mind

EXERCISES

Translate into English :

1. **Bà sù tàfi ba.**
2. **Bàn ci àbinci ba tùkùna.**
3. **Bà sù kāwō littāfì ba.**
4. **Yārinyà bà tà dāwō ba.**
5. **Audù bài zō makarantā ba.**

Translate into Hausa :

1. The man did not make a farm.
2. He did not come this morning.
3. The girl did not go to [3] the farm.
4. I have not yet done the work.
5. The chair was not brought.

Dialogue

Bàƙo :   Ìnā wunì ?
Garbà :   Lāfiyà.
Bàƙo :   Ìnā gàjiyà ?
Garbà :   Bābù gàjiyà.
Bàƙo :   Tò mādàllā.
Garbà :   Kā zō lāfiyà ?
Bàƙo :   Lāfiyà, bâ kōmē.
Garbà :   Gidā lāfiyà ?
Bàƙo :   Lāfiyà ƙalau.
Garbà :   Ìnā Bellò ?
Bàƙo :   Ya tàfi Kanò.
Garbà :   Tò dà kyâu. Yā tàfi kàsuwā ?
Bàƙo :   Ā'à, bài tàfi kàsuwā ba.
Garbà :   Tò bâ lâifì. Sai an jimà.
Bàƙo :   Yâuwa sai an jimà.

[3] **tàfi** = *go (to).*

Lesson 8

Genitival Link

1. In understanding the possessive construction in Hausa, it is helpful to rephrase the English *the chief's house* as *the house of the chief*. *Of* is expressed by **na** if the noun possessed is masculine, or **ta** if it is feminine. The gender of the possessing noun is immaterial.

2. Usually this genitival link is shortened and suffixed to the noun. **Na** contracts to **-n** and **ta** becomes **-r** (except after the few feminine nouns which do not end in **-a,** when the **ta** becomes **-n**). Note that the final vowel of the possessed noun is always short before the **-n/-r** suffix.[1]

	gidā na sarkī = gidan sarkī	the chief's house
Masculine noun possessed	kàrē na Daudà = kàren Daudà	David's dog
	àbinci na kyânwā = àbincin kyânwā	cat's food
Feminine noun possessed	sānìyā ta Audù = sānìyar Audù	Audu's cow
	rìgā ta Garbà = rìgar Garbà	Garba's gown

3. The shorter, suffixed forms (**-n/-r**) are far more frequent than the longer forms. **Na/ta,** however, is preferred (or required):

---

[1] This is because Hausa does not admit a long vowel (or a diphthong) in a closed syllable.

(a) With any noun to indicate possession of something previously referred to but not re-specified (see Lesson 9, section 5, for the use of related forms before pronouns) :

na Audù nē	it (masculine thing) is Audu's
ta Bellò cē	it (feminine thing) is Bello's
bà sù kāwō na Daudà ba	they did not bring David's
na Kànde yā yi kyâu	Kande's is nice

(b) When the **na/ta** phrase is the complement of **nē/cē** :

gidā na Audù nē	the house belongs to Audu/is Audu's
rìgā ta Audù cē	the gown belongs to Audu/is Audu's

(c) As a substitute for a possessed word already mentioned to avoid the necessity of repeating it :

Ìnā gidan Bellò dà na Audù ?	Where is Bello's home and that of Audu ?
An kāwō rìgar Garbà dà ta Daudà.	Garba's and Dauda's gowns were brought

(d) When one or more words intervene between the word modified and the modifying noun or noun phrase introduced by **na** :

dōkìn nân na Bellò	this horse of Bello's
kèkē biyu na Garbà	Garba's two bicycles

(e) With numbers to form ordinal numbers :

na biyu nè	it is the second (one)
makarantā ta huɗu cè	it is the fourth school

4. There is no gender distinction in Hausa plurals. The form of the referential used in the plural is always **-n (na)**:

mātan Audù	Audu's wives
mutànen Sarkin Kanò	the Emir of Kano's people

5. Nouns ending in diphthongs **-ai** and **-au** usually drop the second vowel before the referential, and affix the **-n** to the **-a** : [2]

mâi	oil
mân shānū	butter (*lit.* oil of the cow)
kyâu	(visual) goodness
kyânsà	its goodness

6. Many nouns (chiefly Arabic and English loans) ending in a consonant add **-i** before the referential.

mālàm	teacher
mālàmin makarantā	schoolteacher
mùtûm	man
mùtumìn sarkī	the chief's man

VOCABULARY

Nominals

cikī, cikin	inside, in . . .
dōkì	horse
ɗā	son
ɗākì	hut, room
ìyālì	one's family (wife and children)
iyàyē	parents
kàrē	dog
kèkē	bicycle
kyânwā (*f.*)	cat
mâi	oil
mālàmin	
makarantā	schoolteacher
mân shānū	butter, cream
nân/nan/nàn	here, this
rìgā (*f.*)	gown, coat
tàimakō	help, aid
Tūrancī	English language

[2] See footnote on section 2 above.

Verbals

gà	here is/are, there is/are (pointing to object)
gōdè [3]	thank
karàntā	read
rubùtā	write
tàmbayà [4]	ask, ask for

EXERCISES

Translate into English :

1. Ìnā gidan sarkī ?
2. Yàròn sarkī nè.
3. Nā kāwō fìtilàr Garbà.
4. Àbincin kyânwā nè.
5. Yārinyà tā tàfi gōnar mālàmin makarantā.

[3] Only now are scholars paying the close attention to the **correct** length of final vowels in Hausa that the phenomenon **deserves**. There is still some way to go before a definitive set of rules governing final vowel length can be formulated, but we are grateful **to** Professor Arnott and his colleagues at S.O.A.S. for allowing **us to** quote this provisional summary of the rules for polysyllabic **verbs.** In brief it may be said that :

A. Transitive and intransitive verbs with high-low **and high-low-** high tone pattern :

    1. Those ending in **-a** and **-e**

        (*a*) have the final vowel long when

            (i) they are not followed by an object

            (ii) they are followed by a direct object pronoun or **by** an indirect object

        (*b*) have the final vowel short when they are followed **by a** noun object.

    2. Those ending in **-i** and **-u** (high-low pattern)

        (*a*) have the final vowel short when the verb is intransitive

        (*b*) have the final vowel long when the verb is transitive.

B. Intransitive verbs with low-high and low-high-low tone pattern always have the final vowel short, except when they are followed by an indirect object. The verbal noun has a long final vowel.

C. The vowel length of monosyllabic verbs ending in **-i** has been dealt with at page 39, note 2.

[4] The student should not attempt to use this word with an object until he has covered the material in Lesson 15.

Translate into Hausa :

1. Is this the chief's house ?
2. The boy's father has gone to Kano.
3. The schoolteacher did not eat food.
4. Where is the horse's food ?
5. There is Audu's cow.

Dialogue

Ûmarù : Mènē nè sūnan wannàn ?
Àlī : Kèkē nè.
Ûmarù : Na wànē nè ?
Àlī : Wannàn kèken ɗan sarkī nè.
Ûmarù : Tô, ìnā kèken Audù ?
Àlī : Gà shi cân cikin ɗākì.
Ûmarù : Tò dà kyâu, nā gōdè.
Àlī : Tò bâ lâifī.

Lesson 9

Possessive Pronouns

1. There are two forms of the possessive pronoun : inseparable and separable.

2. The *inseparable*, which corresponds to the English *my, his,* etc., is formed in all persons, except the first person singular, by adding the genitival link **-n** or **-r** plus a pronominal suffix to the object possessed. The final vowel of the noun is shortened as in Lesson 8.

yārò̠	+ -n	+ sà	= yārònsà	his boy
yārò̠	+ -n	+ tà	= yāròntà	her boy
gōnā	+ -r	+ sà	= gōnarsà	his farm
gōnā	+ -r	+ tà	= gōnartà	her farm

3. The formation of the inseparable possessive pronoun differs in the *first person singular*. Here the suffix **-na** or **-ta** is suffixed directly to the thing possessed (**-na** to a masculine noun, **-ta** to a feminine—the gender (sex) of the speaker is irrelevant). The final vowel of the noun remains or becomes long.

yārò̠ + na = yārò̠na	my boy (said by male or female)
gōnā + ta = gōnāta	my farm (said by male or female)
àbinci + na = àbincīna	my food (said by male or female)

4. The complete table of inseparable possessive pronouns is :

Masculine noun		*Feminine noun*	
my boy	yārŏna [1]	gōnáta [1]	my farm
your (*m.*) boy	yārònkà	gōnarkà	your (*m.*) farm
your (*f.*) boy	yārònkì	gōnarkì	your (*f.*) farm
his boy	yārònsà	gōnarsà	his farm
her boy	yāròntà	gōnartà	her farm
our boy	yāròmmù	gōnarmù	our farm
your (*pl.*) boy	yārònkù	gōnarkù	your (*pl.*) farm
their boy	yārònsù	gōnarsù	their farm

Note that, except for the first person singular, all the inseparable possessive pronouns have a low tone and a short vowel. Note also that where the genitival link -n precedes -m (first person plural) it becomes -m for euphony. Especially in the western dialects of Sokoto and Katsina, the feminine -r may also assimilate in this way to any following consonant (e.g. gōnakkà, gōnassà, gōnammù). This assimilation is not always represented in written Hausa (thus the spelling gōnarmù is ordinarily pronounced gōnammù). (See footnote to section 7 below.)

5. To form the *separable* possessive pronouns, either nā- or tā-, depending on the gender of the thing possessed, is prefixed to the inseparable pronouns.

Nāsà nē.	It is his.
Gidā nākà nē.	The house is yours (*m.*).
Kyânwā tākà cē.	The cat is yours (*m.*).
Kyânwā tākì cē.	The cat is yours (*f.*).

6. As with the inseparable forms, an exception to the general pattern is found in the first person singular.

---

[1] The length of the vowel of the first person singular suffix (-na/-ta) is short only when utterance final (e.g. bā̀ ni àbincîna, *give me my food*). When another word follows, the vowel of the -na/-ta becomes long (e.g. àbincīnā nè, *it is my food*).

Here **nà-** or **tà-** is prefixed to **-wa**. This **-wa** suffix is invariable and disregards the gender of the possessor.

Gidā nàwa nè.   The house is mine (said by male or female).

Gōnā tàwa cè.   The farm is mine (said by male or female).

Note that the tones of these forms are low-high, just the opposite of the rest of the separable forms (and of the similar sounding word **nawà**, *how many* ?, see Lesson 11).

7. The complete table of the separable possessive pronouns is :

Singular	*Plural*
nàwa, tàwa	nāmù, tāmù
nākà, tākà	nākù, tākù
nākì, tākì	
nāsà, tāsà	nāsù, tāsù
nātà, tātà	

A short-vowel form of the feminines is usual when the separable possessives are used to modify other nouns, e.g. **gōnā tasà**, *his farm* ; **uwā takà**, *your mother*.[2]

8. The plural possessive pronoun is generally used in referring to a town or household. Only the chief of the town or head of the house would use the personal ' my ' : **gàrīna** or **gidāna**. Others would say **gàrimmù** or **gidammù**.

VOCABULARY

Nominals
àbù (+ -n
  = **àbin**)   thing

---

[2] Some Hausa scholars explain the use of the short-vowel forms, mostly in the third person singular, as a substitute for the inseparable possessive form in order to avoid the non-favoured combinations like **-rs, -rt.**

cân/can/càn	there ; that
farkō	first
gōrò	kolanut
hanyà (*f.*)	path, road, way
jiyà	yesterday
sàbulù	soap
shūkà	planting, sowing
tàre	together
yànzu	now
yàushè,	
yàushe	when ?

Verbals [3]

fārà	begin		
fita	go out (of)		
fitō	come out		
gamà	finish		
jē	go		
sâ	put, place		
shigō	come in		
shūkà	sow (seed)		

Particles

à	at, in
dòmin, don	because, in order to

Important Phrases

à kân	on (top of)
dà sāfē	in the morning
dom mè	why ?
nā tàfi	I'm going (now)
tàre dà	together with

EXERCISES

Translate into English :

1. Yārò yā tàfi Kanò tàre dà uwarsà.
2. Màlàminkù yā jē gōnarsà yâu dà sāfē.

[3] See footnote 3, page 44, concerning the final vowel length of verbs before objects.

3. Dom mè ka sâ littāfìnkà à kân kujèrāta ?
4. Dōkìnā yā shìga gàrin àbōkinkù.
5. Yā kāwō kèkēna. Bài kāwō nākà ba.

Translate into Hausa :

1. My mother and my father went to your house
   yesterday.
2. Where is my soap ? I put it in my room. Here is yours.
3. Our home is in Kano. Where is yours ?
4. Her father went out of town on the Kano road.
5. When did my friend eat his food ? In the morning.

Dialogue

Àdàmū :   Wannàn gidā nākà nē ?
Àbūbakàr :   Ī, nàwa nè.
Àdàmū: Ìnā gōnarkà ?
Àbūbakàr :   Gà gōnātā cân.
Àdàmū :   Tò dà kyâu.
Àbūbakàr :   Nā gamà shūkà jiyà.
Àdàmū :   Tô, yàushè ka fārà ?
Àbūbakàr: À farkon watàn nân.
Àdàmū :   Nī, bàn gamà tàwa ba tùkùna.
Àbūbakàr :   Tò bâ lâifī. Nā tàfi yànzu.
Àdàmū :   Tò sai wani lōkàcī.
Àbūbakàr :   Yâuwā, Allà yà kai mù.
Àdàmū :   Āmin.

Lesson 10

Specifiers—'This', 'That', 'These', 'Those'

1. *Specifiers* are a group of nouns which modify other nouns to make them more specific or less specific. This class of words includes the words often termed *demonstratives*.

Singular	*Plural*	
wannàn (*m.* and *f.*)	waɗannân	this, these
wancàn (*m.*), waccàn (*f.*)	waɗancân	that, those
wani (*m.*), wata (*f.*)	waɗansu, wasu	a, a certain, some (*pl.*)

wannàn yārò	this boy	waɗannân mutằnē	these people
wancàn gōnā	that farm	wani mùtûm	a certain man

2. The specifiers **nân**, *this, these,* and **cân**, *that, those,* follow the nouns they modify. The **-n/-r** referential is suffixed to the preceding noun. The tones on **nân** and **cân** may be high, falling or low, with or without slight differences in meaning. The following are the most typical ways in which these specifiers occur:

(*a*) A falling-tone **nân/cân** following a low-tone syllable or a low-tone **nàn/càn** following a high-tone syllable is the most common way in which these words occur. The meaning is typically non-emphatic, e.g.:

ɗākìn nân	this hut	mùtumìn cân	that man
àbincin nàn	this food	gōnar càn	that farm

(*b*) A high-tone **nan/can** may be employed to indicate

previous reference.   If the tone of the syllable
preceding the specifier is high, it becomes falling, e.g. :

rìgân nan [1]   this gown (previously referred to)
aikìn nan   this work (previously referred to)
kujèrâr can   that chair (previously referred to)

3. The specifier **nân** can optionally precede the noun it
modifies when the reference of such a noun is locative :

Nā gan shì nân gàrī.   I saw him (here) (in) this town.

4. **Nân** and **cân** may also occur alone (i.e. not as modifiers), meaning *here* and *there* respectively. Only high- and
falling-tone forms occur in this usage. The high-tone
forms typically indicate a greater distance from the
speaker than do the falling-tone forms, e.g. :

Gà Audù nân.   Here's Audu here (nearby).
Gà Audù nan.   Here's Audu here (in the vicinity).
Gà Audù cân.   There's Audu over there.
Gà Audù can.   There's Audu in the distance.

5. An **-n/-r** suffix may be used without a following noun
to specify that reference is to something previously
referred to or implied from the context, e.g. :

Gà rìgā, àmmā ìnā wàndôn ? There is a/the coat, but
where are the trousers (that go with it) ?

If the final syllable of the suffixed noun is high, it
becomes falling before **-n/-r** in this usage.[2] The suffixed

---

[1] Before **nân/nan/nàn** the feminine **-r** suffix usually becomes **-n**,
but such assimilation does not, as a rule, take place before **cân/can/**
càn, though it does in the compound **waccàn** (see above).

[2] We have sought to avoid the technical issue of whether *conso-*
nants can properly carry tone. But in this case, the falling tone
may be explained by the fact that this **-n/-r** suffix has a low tone,
and therefore a high final vowel + low **-n/-r** gives a falling tone
over the whole syllable $C\hat{V}n/C\hat{V}r$, whereas a low final vowel + low
-n/-r remains low.

form may usually be translated by the English definite article *the*, e.g. :

Audù yā kāwō àbinci.	Audu brought some food.
Àbincîn bâ kyâu.	The food was not good.
Gà kujèrâr.	Here is the chair (that we talked about previously).

6. The word **dîn,** usually meaning *the one previously referred to*, is usable in place of the **-n/-r** described in section 5 above and with essentially the same meaning. It is particularly used with borrowed words, especially those ending in a consonant.

       Inà sôn fensìr dîn.   I want the pencil.

Note that **nan** may accompany **dîn.**

Yārò dîn nan, bài dāwō ba.   That boy has not returned.

A possessive pronoun may also be suffixed to **dîn.** In the first person singular the form is **dīna.**

Nā kāwō kèkē dînkà.	I brought your bicycle (the one we were discussing).
Ìnā fensìr dîna ?	Where is my pencil ?

7. Rules for the employment of the English definite (*the*) and indefinite (*a, an*) articles in translating Hausa are not as simple as they appear at first sight. The rendering of the Hausa nominal without either the referential suffix **-n/-r** (see section 5, above) or the qualifying **wani/wata** (see section 1, above) is a complex question that is, unfortunately, not so cut and dried as the *the/a* dichotomy in English. Of the three grammatical sentences

   (i) **yārò yā zō**
  (ii) **yāròn yā zō**
 (iii) **wani yārò yā zō**

(ii) and (iii) are quite clear. **Yāròn yā zō** is best translated by *the boy has come*, a reference to some specified or implied boy being unambiguously understood. Similarly, **wani yārò yā zō** is best rendered by *a (certain) boy has come*. But what of (i) ? Standard Hausa grammars have rightly translated **yārò yā zō** as *the boy has come*, since, though English speakers might expect the more specific **yāròn yā zō** to indicate this meaning every time it is intended, Hausa rules do not correspond to English rules, and in Hausa, where there is no doubt of, or no significance attached to, which ' boy ' is meant, **yārò yā zō** does carry much of the specificity which English expresses by means of the definite article. This definiteness is plainly illustrated by such acceptable sentences as **sarkī yā zō**, *the chief has come* ; **bùɗè ƙōfà**, *open the door* ; **Bàhaushè yā zō**, *the Hausa man has come*—in none of which examples is there any question of choice over which *chief/door/Hausa man* is referred to.

While recognizing the area of uncertainty and the difficulty of formulating watertight rules for this issue, we do not go as far as Abraham, who is content to recognize no difference in Hausa between the English *the/a*. As basic rules of thumb, we recommend the following when translating into Hausa :

(a) Where the noun clearly refers back to a previous referent (stated or implied), *the* should ordinarily be rendered by means of the **-n/-r** suffix described above (section 5) : **yāròn yā zō**, *the boy (you were expecting) has come.*

(b) Where the sense requires *a certain*, **wani/wata** should be used : **wani yārò yā zō**, *a certain boy has come.*

(c) Where the specificity is immaterial or unmistakable, the unqualified noun should be used : **yārò yā zō**, *the boy has come.* When in doubt, this is the construction most likely to be right since it is the most frequent.

VOCABULARY

Nominals

àkwàtì	box
àlmājìrī	pupil, student
bàbba	big (thing)
cōkàlī	spoon
hakà	thus, so
kògī	river
ƙàramī	small (thing)
mōtà (*f.*)/	
mātò	car, lorry
tēbùr	table
wancàn (*pl.*	
waɗàncân)	that (*pl.* those)
wata (*f.*) (*pl.*	
waɗansu)	a certain, a (*pl.* some, certain)
wuƙā (*f.*)	knife
yawà	muchness, quantity, number

Verbals

àkwai	there is, there are
fāɗì	fall
hau	mount, climb
sanì ³	know

Particles

àmmā	but
dàgà	from
ɗîn	that previously referred to
kumā	also, further, and

Important Phrases

bàn sanì ba	I don't know
dà yawà	much, many
hakà nē	it is so, indeed
nā sanì	I know (it)
ruwan shâ	drinking water

³ The student should not attempt to use this word with an object until he has covered the material in Lesson 15.

E

EXERCISES

Translate into English :

1. Wani yārò yā fāɗì cikin ruwā.
2. Kògin nàn, Kwârà cē.
3. Kā sâ cōkàlin nàn cikin àkwàtìn nân.
4. Ìnā kujèrā ? Gà kujèrâr.
5. Waɗànnân mutànē sun tàfi wani gàrī.

Translate into Hausa :

1. This boy is my friend.
2. You (*f.*) (have) put that chair here.
3. These boys. Those boys.
4. I don't know yet.
5. I went to that town.

Dialogue

Kànde :   Waɗansu mutànē sun zō gidammù.
Maryamù :   Mādàllā, nā kāwō àbinci dàgà kàsuwā yâu.
Kànde :   Dà kyâu. Àkwai ruwan shâ dà yawà kumā.
Maryamù :   Sarkin gàrī nè ya zō.
Kànde :   Hakà nē. Yā zō tàre dà wani bàbban mùtûm.
Maryamù :   Mùtumìn, sarkī nè kumā ?
Kànde :   Hakà nē, yārònsà yā kāwō wani bàbban àkwàtì.
Maryamù :   Tô, mènē nè cikin àkwàtì ?
Kànde :   Bàn sanì ba.

Lesson 11

Quantifiers

1. The *quantifiers* are a subclass of nouns which include
the numbers and a few other words. Quantifiers typically
follow the noun they modify, but without employing the
-n/-r suffix.

gidā gōmà	ten houses
yârā nawà ?	how many boys ?
mutànē ɗukà	all the people
yārinyà biyu	two girls

With numbers it is not always necessary to use the plural
form of the noun.

2. The numbers 1–22 (see Lesson 32 for a complete
listing) :

1	ɗaya	10	gōmà
2	biyu	11	(gōmà) shâ ɗaya
3	ukù	12	(gōmà) shâ biyu
4	huɗu	18	àshìrin biyu bābù [1] *or* gōmà shâ takwàs
5	bìyar	19	àshìrin ɗaya bābù [1] *or* gōmà shâ tarà
6	shidà	20	àshìrin
7	bakwài	21	àshìrin dà ɗaya
8	takwàs	22	àshìrin dà biyu
9	tarà		*etc.*

Note that **shâ**, *and*, is only used with numbers 11–19.
The regular word for *and*, **dà**, is used with numbers above
20. For this reason the word **gōmà** is frequently omitted
from the numbers 11–19, since **shâ ɗaya** can only mean
11, **shâ biyu** 12, etc.

[1] Literally, ' 20, two/one there is not '.

3. The interrogative **nawà ?**, *how much/many ?*, is also a quantifier.

mùtûm nawà ?	how many persons ?
sàu nawà ?	how many times ?
sū nawà ?	how many of them (are there) ?
kuɗī nawà ?	how much (does it cost) ?

4. **Dukà/duk**, *all*, may also be employed as a quantifier.

yârā dukà	all the children	yârā ukù	three children
sū dukà	all of them	sū huɗu	the four of them

5. Quantifiers (except **nawà**) may sometimes suffix **-n** or be followed by **ɗin**.[2] In this case they precede the dependent possessive pronoun or, occasionally, an independent nominal. The meaning varies.

ɗayansù	one of them
biyunsù or biyu ɗinsù	twice their number
bìyar ɗinsù	five times their number
dukàn mutànē	all the people

6. *Ordinal numbers* are formed by employing the nominalizing particle **na** (feminine **ta**).

na/ta farkō/fārì	first (*lit.* of beginning)
na/ta biyu	second
na/ta gōmà	tenth
na/ta nawà ?	which (of a series) ? (*lit.* the how manyth)
kàrē na biyu	the second dog
rìgā ta takwàs	the eighth gown
littāfì na nawà ?	which (among several) book ?, which volume ?

Note that **farkō** or **fārì** is substituted for **ɗaya** in forming ordinals (except in the case of a numbered series, e.g. **littāfì na ɗaya,** *volume I*).

[2] Note that this high tone **ɗin** is a different word from **ɗîn** (Lesson 10, section 6).

7. The word **gùdā,** *a unit of,* is frequently used with numbers, as in the following examples. When **gùdā** occurs alone it means *one*.

yârā gùdā biyu	two boys
mutằnē gùdā huɗu	four persons
mōtằ gùdā	one car

VOCABULARY

Nominals
Numbers 1–22 :

àyàbằ	banana(s)
bàkī	mouth ; edge
daidai	correct, right
ɗukà, duk	all
fārì/farkō	beginning
gùdā	a unit of, one
gwēbằ	guava
kuskurề	mistake, error
lềmō/lềmū	citrus fruit, citrus tree
lìssāfì	arithmetic
mangwàrồ	mango
nawà ?	how many ?, how much ?
sàu	times
wùyā (*f.*)	difficulty
wuyằ	neck

Verbals

		Particles	
gānề	understand	fà ?	what about ?
mântā	forget	kâi !	Good Heavens ! wow !, oh boy !, gee ! (general exclamation)
zaunà	sit down	sai	only (see also Lesson 4)
		zuwằ	toward, to (see also Lesson 4)

Important Phrases
bâ kyâu   that's not good
bàkin hanyà   edge of the road

EXERCISES

Translate into English :

1. Gà mangwàrò biyu à kân tēbùr.
2. Lìssāfì dà wùyā nè. Àmmā nā gānè.
3. Yā sâ àyàbà à bàkinsà, yā ci.
4. Ìnā bàbban àkwàtì ? Bellò yā tàfi gidansù dà shī.
5. Kā kāwō gwēbà nawà ? Gùdā gōmà.
6. Kâi !, Audù yā mântà sūnāna. Wànnan bâ kyâu.

Translate into Hausa :

1. The girl sat down on the chair.
2. I made a mistake in my arithmetic.
3. He took the bicycle toward his home.
4. We followed a path at the edge of the river.
5. Good Heavens, there are eight people in that car !

Dialogue
Mālàmī : Biyu dà ukù nawà nē ?
Dàlìbī : Bìyar nè.
Mālàmī : Daidai nè. Shidà dà bakwài fà ?
Dàlìbī : Shâ ukù.
Mālàmī : Dà kyâu. Huɗu sàu biyu nawà ?
Dàlìbī : Tarà nē.
Mālàmī : Bābù ! Kā yi kuskurè.
Dàlìbī : Hakà nè. Sai takwàs.
Mālàmī : Tô. Nawà nē shidà sàu ukù ?
Dàlìbī : Àshìrin biyu bābù.
Mālàmī : Mādàllā. Wannàn lìssāfì dà wùyā nè ?
Dàlìbī : Ā'à, bâ wùyā.
Mālàmī : Tô dà kyâu.

Lesson 12

Subjunctive Aspect and Commands

1. The subjunctive aspect has a wide variety of uses, though only a few of them will be treated here (see also Lesson 27). Subjunctive constructions may usually be literally translated *let one do such-and-such*.

2. The subjunctive aspect person-aspect pronouns are characterized by low tone and a short vowel. Using the verb **zō**, *come*, as a model, the p-a pronouns in the subjunctive are :

let me come	**ìn zō**	**mù zō**	let us come
come ! (*m.*)	**kà zō**	**kù zō**	come ! (*pl.*)
come ! (*f.*)	**kì zō**		
let him come	**yà zō**	**sù zō**	let them come
let her come	**tà zō**		
let someone come	**à zō**		

3. The negative of the subjunctive aspect is formed by employing the negative particle **kadà** (this is often shortened to **kâr** in rapid speech) :

kadà kà zō	do not come
kadà yārð yà tàfi	don't let (*or, in context*, lest) the boy go away
kâr kà yi hakà	don't do that

4. The second person forms of the subjunctive aspect are commonly used to express both positive [1] and negative commands.

---

[1] A positive command may be strengthened by the use of **sai**, e.g. **sai kà shìga !** may mean *you must enter* (though it has a weaker meaning as well). See Lesson 29, section 2, for a fuller treatment.

kà shìga   enter ! (*m.*)
kù kāwō yārò   bring (*pl.*) the boy
kadà kì ci àbinci   don't (*f.*) eat (the) food

5. The *imperative* employs no p-a pronoun. There is, however, a special tone pattern for the verb in this type of construction : all syllables except the final syllable in words of two or more syllables must be low tone. The final syllable typically is high, occasionally is low. The imperative is not ordinarily used to address more than one person at a time.

(*a*) One-syllable verbs may be either high (unchanged) or low :

    zò/zō nân   come here !
    cì/ci àbinci   eat (your) food !

(*b*) Verbs with a basic low-high tone pattern will not change :

    tàfi gidā   go home !
    shìga   enter !

(*c*) Verbs with any other basic tone pattern will start with a low tone. A final long vowel on the verb will usually shorten in utterance final position :

    (**kāwō**) → **kàwō àbinci**   bring the food !
    (**barì**) → **bàri**   leave (it alone) !

6. Note the tonal contrast between the basic forms of the following verbs (as employed with the subjunctive p-a pronouns) and their imperative forms in the following examples. The meanings of the parallel constructions are the same.

    kà zaunà   sit down !   **zàuna**
    kà shigō   come in !   **shìgo**
    kà karàntā   read (it) !   **kàrànta**

7. In complex sentences it is often appropriate to translate a verb in a subjunctive aspect construction as a so-called English 'infinitive' (expressing purpose). Such a construction forms the predicate of the dependent clause, e.g. :

(a) The verb of the first clause may be in a completive or subjunctive aspect construction :

Nā zō ìn gaishē kà.	I've come *to greet* you.
Yā jē gidā yà kāwō ruwā.	He went home *to bring* water.
Kù zō kù yi aikìnkù.	Come *and/to do* your work.

(b) The verb of the first clause may be in the imperative :

Zō kù yi aikìnkù.	Come *and/to do* your work.
Zàuna kà shā ruwā.	Sit down *and/to drink* water.

VOCABULARY

Nominals

dājì	' bush ' country (*i.e.* uninhabited, uncultivated area)
ƙarfī	strength
ƙōfà (*f.*)	door (way)
rānā (*f.*)	sun, day
sā'ì	time (= **lōkàcī**)
saurī	quickness
shēkaranjiyà	day before yesterday
tāgà (*f.*)	window
zāfī	hotness

Verbals		*Particles*	
barì [2]	let, allow, leave (a thing)	**kadà, kâr** ...	do not ...
budè	open		

[2] The student should not attempt to use these verbs with objects until he has covered the material in Lesson 15.

gaishē   greet (before pronoun
objects only)
rufè   close
sāmù [3]   get, obtain
tāshì   get up, leave (from a
place)
tsayà   stand (up), stop

Important Phrases
dà saurī   quickly
rānā tā yi zāfī   the sun is hot

EXERCISES

Translate into English :

1. **Kadà kà yi aikìn nân.**
2. **Kadà yārinyà tà ci àbincin nàn.**
3. **Zō nân kì zaunà.**
4. **Kadà kù yi hakà.**
5. **Fìta kà rufè ƙōfà.**

Translate into Hausa :

1. Don't open the window.
2. Stop ! Enter ! Sit down !
3. Bring (*f.*) the food here.
4. Let him do his work.
5. Come (*pl.*) and eat your food in our home.

Dialogue
Hārūnà : **Yàƙubù, sàlāmù àlaikùn.**
Yàƙubù : **Yâuwā, àlaikà sàlāmù.**
Hārūnà : **Ìyālinkà lāfiyà ?**
Yàƙubù : **Lāfiyà ƙalau. Kā zō lāfiyà ?**
Hārūnà : **Lāfiyà. Bâ kōmē.**
Yàƙubù : **Mādàllā. Shìgō mù zaunà.**

[3] See footnote 2 on page 63.

Hārūnà : Tò dà kyâu. Kâi, rānā tā yi zāfī yâu.
Yàƙubù : Hakà nē. Yārò, kàwō ruwan shâ !
Hārūnà : Nā zō ìn gaishē kà nē.
Yàƙubù : Mādàllā. Nā gōdè. Kā zō dàgà kàsuwā nè ?
Hārūnà : Ā'à, nā zō dàgà gidā ɗàzu.
Yàƙubù : Tò bâ lâifī. Gà ruwā, kà shā.
Hārūnà : Tò nā gōdè. Nā tàfi yànzu.
Yàƙubù : Tò bâ lâifī. Sai wani sā'ì.
Hārūnà : Yâuwā, sai wani sā'ì.

Lesson 13

Non-aspect Verbals ; 'Yes' and 'No'

1. The non-aspect verbals are a small group of very useful words of frequent occurrence which may be followed by a noun, a noun phrase or a personal pronoun. The pronouns employed are the direct object pronouns. These verbals are not preceded by person-aspect markers.

2. **Àkwai,** *there is/are,* states the existence of something.

Àkwai yârā à gidā.	There are children at home.
Àkwai aikì dà yawà.	There is much work.
Àkwai kuɗī à wurinkà ?	Do you have any money ? (*lit.* is there money in your place ?)
Àkwai (sù).	There are some.

3. **Bābù** or **bâ,** *there is/are no/not,* means the opposite of **àkwai.** The pronouns employed after **bâ** are (as with **àkwai**) the object pronouns. **Bābù,** however, is followed by the independent pronouns (e.g. **bābù shī,** *there is none of it*).

Bābù yârā à gidā.	There are no children at home.
Bâ aikì cân.	There is no work there.
Àkwai kuɗī ? Bābù !	Is there any money ? No ! (*lit.* there is none)

4. **Gà,** *here/there is/are,* is used when pointing something out.

Gà gidammù cân.	There is our house over there.
Gà littāfìi à kân tēbùr.	There is the book on the table.

Gằ ni [1] nân.　　　　　　　Here I am.
Gằ rìgāta.　　　　　　　　Here is my gown.

5. *Yes* is ordinarily expressed by the use of the particle ī.
The expressions **hakà nē,** *thus it is,* **gàskiyā nḕ,** [2] *it is the
truth,* or **gàskiyarkà,** *your truth,* are frequently used as
well to indicate agreement.

Kā tàfi jiyà ? Ī.　　　　　　Did you go yesterday? Yes.
Kâi, rānā tā yi zāfī yâu !　　Goodness, the sun is hot
　Gàskiyarkà !　　　　　　　　today ! You're right !
Àkwai yârā dà yawà à nân.　There are many children
　Hakà nē.　　　　　　　　　here. You're right.

6. *No* is ordinarily expressed by the use of the particle
ā'à. For emphasis, the verbal **bābù** may be used.[3]

Kā kāwō àbinci ? Ā'à.　　　Did you bring any food ?
　　　　　　　　　　　　　　　No.
Kai àbōkinsà nē ? Bābù !　　Are you a friend of his ?
　　　　　　　　　　　　　　　(Emphatically) not !

7. In answering a negative question,[4] *hasn't he come ?,*
in Hausa, it is necessary to note the difference in the
choice of *yes* or *no.* The following example illustrates this
difference :

English : Hasn't he come ?
　　　　　No (he hasn't come).

---

[1] See Lesson 15, section 3, for the remaining forms of the direct
object pronoun.
[2] Although after the feminine noun **gàskiyā** one would expect **cḕ,**
nḕ is regularly employed in this stylized and frequently heard
expression. One explanation is that the original phrase was **àbin
gàskiyā nḕ,** *it is a true thing.*
[3] This usage, however, appears to be a recent development in
Hausa (probably due to the influence of European and/or other
non-native speakers of Hausa). **Kō kàɗan, . . .** (*not*) *even a little,*
or **fàufau,** lit. *utterly* (*not*), are much more commonly used by native
Hausa.
[4] For a fuller treatment of asking questions, see Lesson 21,
section 8.

Hausa :   **Bài zō ba ?** Hasn't he come ?
        Ī.   Yes (what you say is right : he has not
             come).
        Ā'à. No (what you say is wrong : he has
             come).

Mistakes can be avoided in interpreting the answer to a
negative question by mentally relating the *yes* or *no* to the
accuracy of the statement made in the question, not as a
direct reply to the question ; or by the use of the
American response ' right '.

Examples :

Kànde bà tà dāwō ba ?	Isn't Kande back ?
Ī (bà tà dāwō ba).	Yes (she has not come back).
Ā'à (tā dāwō).	No (she has come back).

VOCABULARY

Nominals

àràhā	inexpensiveness
dànkalì	sweet potato(es), ' European ' potato(es)
dōyà (*f.*)	(large) yam(s)
gàskiyā (*f.*)	truth
kuɗī	price, money (see Lesson 6)
kwabò	kobo
ƙwai	egg(s)
madarā (*f.*)	milk
mânyā	big ones (*pl.* of **bàbba**, Lesson 10)
nairà	1 naira
nāmà	meat, wild animal
sīsì	5 kobos
sulè	10 kobos
tarō	$2\frac{1}{2}$ kobos
tsàdā	expensiveness
wurī	place
yunwà	hunger

Verbals

dafà	cook
gudù	run away
kōmà	return (there), go to another place intending to stay there
shiryà	prepare
tsūfa	get old

Particles

kō ?	(question particle), or
nē ?	(question particle) (see Lesson 5)

Important Phrases

nā ji yunwà	I am hungry
yā yi tsàdā	it is expensive
yā yi àràhā	it is cheap, inexpensive

EXERCISES

Translate into English :

1. Nā ji yunwà. Àkwai àbinci ?
2. Kā kāwō mùtumìn nē ? Ī, gà shi.
3. Bābù cōkàlī nân ? Ī.
4. Yârā sun tàfi makarantā, kō ? Tùkùna.
5. Bà kù shiryà ba ? Ā'à.
6. Gà littāfìn Mālàm Garbà. Ìnā nàwa ?

Translate into Hausa :

1. Has my mother returned ? No, she has not returned.
2. Didn't Bello go to Kano yesterday ? Yes, he went.
3. Is there work ? Yes, there is much work but no money.
4. Are there eggs and milk here ? There is milk, but there are no eggs.
5. I am hungry. What about you ?

Dialogue

Mūsā : Àkwai dànkalì à kàsuwā yâu ?
Gàmbo : Ā'à, àmmā àkwai dōyà dà yawà.

Mūsā :   Tò dà kyâu. Nawà nē kuɗin dōyà ?
Gàmbo :   Sulè dà sīsì zuwà sulè biyu.
Mūsā :   Kâi, sun yi tsàdā !
Gàmbo :   Bābù ! Dukànsù mânyā nè.
Mūsā :   Tò bâ lâifī. Àkwai àyàbà kumā ?
Gàmbo :   Ī àkwai, àmmā bâ yawà.
Mūsā :   Tô, gwēbà fà ?
Gàmbo :   Dà yawà. Àkwai mangwàrò dà lèmō dà yawà
          kumā.
Mūsā :   Dà kyâu. Bàri mù jē mù sāmù.
Gàmbo :   Tò mù jē.

Lesson 14

Intransitive Verbs

1. Intransitive verbs are verbs which cannot take a direct object.[1]

Yā shìga.	He has gone in.
Kā tsayà.	You (have) stopped/stood up.
Yā fàru.	It (has) happened.

2. Intransitive verbs may be followed by expressions of place, time, manner and the like. These are not to be confused with objects of transitive verbs (see Lesson 15).

Yā tàfi gidā.	He went/has gone home.
Nā zō jiyà.	I came yesterday.
Yā tàfi dà wuri.	He went early.

3. Intransitive verbs of motion typically imply the concept of *to* or *toward* a place. Thus no special word is used for *to/toward* if the following word indicates a place.

Yā jē kàsuwā.	He has been to market.[2]
Sun tàfi Zāriyà.	They have gone to Zaria.[2]

4. If one wishes to express motion toward a person or other non-place noun, the words **wurin** or **wajen** are used.

---

[1] Many intransitives may, however, take indirect objects (e.g. **nā tsayà/tsayam masà,** *I went/stood surety for him*). See Lesson 15, section 2, for an introduction to indirect objects, section 8 and Lesson 37, section 4 (*c*), for further illustrations of intransitive verb forms before indirect objects. See Lessons 25 and 37 for an overall analysis of verbs.

[2] A general distinction may be made between **tàfi,** *go (away)*, *go to a place (and not have returned yet)*, and **jē,** *go to and return from.*

Yā tàfi wurin sarkī.   He has gone to the chief.
Yā zō wurin mutànemmù. He has come to our people.
Yā tàfi wajen itàcē.   He has gone to the vicinity
                                 of (towards) the tree.

VOCABULARY

Nominals

baƙī (*f*. **baƙā**)	black (thing)
dàbārà (*f*.)	scheme, plan, device
farī (*f*. **farā**)	white (thing)
hadarì	storm
inuwà (*f*.)	shade
irì (*pl*. **irì-irì**)	kind, sort ; seed
jā (*m*. or *f*.)	red (thing)
kāyā	load, implements
mài gidā	' man of the house ', house-owner, husband
tāyà (*f*.)	tyre
uwargidā	' woman of the house ', (senior) wife
wajē	place, region, environs
wutā (*f*.)	fire

Verbals   *Particles*

ɗaurè	tie (up), imprison	**ai**	well, why (a mild exclamation)
fàru	happen		
sàyā [3]	buy	**mài**	possessor of . . ., characterized by . . .
wucè	pass (by/on)		

Important Phrases

dà wuri	early, in good time
kāyan aikì	implements of work, tools
mài tēbùr	small market trader
nawà nawà ?	how much each ?

[3] The student should not attempt to use this verb with an object until he has covered the material in Lesson 15.

EXERCISES

Translate into English :

1. Mề ya fầru à gidan Yầƙubù ?
2. Hadarì yā wucề yànzu. Bàri mù yi wầsā.
3. Kà tsayầ kà ɗaurề kāyankà.
4. Dōkìnsà yā gudù dà saurī zuwầ gàrī.
5. Yā tầfi wurin àbōkinsà.

Translate into Hausa :

1. She passed by the door.
2. They went to sit in the shade of the tree.
3. It happened here yesterday.
4. Audu returned home the day before yesterday.
5. She went to market early.

Dialogue

Bellò :   Nawà nē kuɗin tayàr kềkē ?
Mài tēbùr : Ai irì ukù cē. Àkwai farā dà baƙā dà jā.
Bellò :   Tô, nawà nawà kuɗinsù ?
Mài tēbùr : Farā, nairà ɗaya dà sulề shidà cē.
Bellò :   Kâi, tā yi tsàdā !
Mài tēbùr : Àmmā ita cề mài kyâu.
Bellò :   Baƙā fà !
Mài tēbùr : Nairầ ɗaya dà sulề huɗu.
Bellò :   Jā fà !
Mài tēbùr : Jā cề mài àràhā à nairầ ɗaya dà sulề biyu.
Bellò :   Tô daidai nề.

(This Dialogue is continued in Lesson 15.)

Lesson 15

Transitive Verbs ; Object Pronouns

1. Transitive verbs may be followed by indirect and/or direct objects, or by no object at all.[1]

2. *Indirect objects* are introduced by the particle **ma-** before pronouns and, most frequently in Kano, **wà** [2] before nouns. With the exception of the first person singular form, it is the inseparable possessive pronouns treated in Lesson 9, section 4, to which the **ma-** is prefixed. The pronoun indirect objects are written as single words, and sometimes show one or more alternative forms. They are :

to/for me	**manì/minì, mîn**		
to/for you (*m.*)	**makà, mā**	**manà/mamù**	to/for us
to/for you (*f.*)	**makì/mikì, mā**	**makù/mukù**	to/for you (*pl.*)
to/for him	**masà, mâr**	**masù/musù**	to/for them
to/for her	**matà**		

Examples of indirect objects (see also section 8 below) :

(*a*) Pronoun indirect objects with transitive verbs :

Yā shiryà manà.	He prepared (it) for us.
Tā dafà minì.	She cooked (it) for me.

[1] As noted in Lesson 14 (section 1, footnote), intransitive verbs may also take an indirect object. Intransitives may not, however, take direct objects. See Lessons 25 and 37 for an overall analysis of verbs.

[2] With all verbs in some dialects, however (e.g. Sokoto), and with some verbs in all dialects, **mà** is used in preference to **wà**, e.g. **Nā yi mà sarkī aikì** (Sok.), *I did work for the chief* ; **Ya tāsam mà màtā tasà,** *He attacked his wife.*

(b) Noun indirect objects with transitive verbs :

> **Mun yi wà sarkī aikì.** We did work for the chief.
> **Nā kāwō wà mālàmī.** I brought (it) to the teacher.

3. A direct object may be a noun, a pronoun or a nominal phrase. The tone of a *direct object pronoun* is, in general, high following a low-tone syllable and low following a high-tone syllable, like **nē/cē** (see Lesson 6). The pronouns used as direct objects are as follows : [3]

me	**ni/nì**	**mu/mù**	us
you (*m.*)	**ka/kà**	**ku/kù**	you (*pl.*)
you (*f.*)	**ki/kì**		
him	**shi/shì**	**su/sù**	them
her	**ta/tà**		

4. When both indirect and direct objects are present, *the indirect object invariably precedes the direct object*,[4] and, if the *direct* object is a personal pronoun, it assumes the independent form (see Lesson 6, section 6, and example three below).

> **Yā kāwō manà àbinci.** He brought us food.
> **Nā yi wà sarkī aikì.** I did work for the chief.
> **Kà kai masà shī/ita.** Take it (*m./f.*) to him.

5. The verb **bā**, *give, give to,* is the commonest of a very limited number of verbs which require no indirect object indicator (**ma-/wà/mà**) before an indirect object. If the indirect object is a pronoun, the forms employed are the direct object pronouns.[5] If (as infrequently happens) the

---

[3] Note that there is no indefinite direct (or indirect) object pronoun corresponding to the **an/à** (etc.) p-a pronouns.

[4] Unless the less common (for expressing ' indirect objectivity ') **gà/gàrē** construction is employed. See Lesson 17, section 2.

[5] This fact leads some to suggest that **bā** actually governs two *direct* objects rather than one indirect and one direct (like other

direct object is a pronoun, the independent pronoun forms are employed, as in example three below.

> **Yā bā mù kuɗī.**   He gave us money.
> **Nā bā shì aikì.**   I gave him work.
> **Nā bā shì ita.**   I gave her/it to him.

If the indirect object is a noun, **bā** becomes **bâ**.

> **Yā bâ mùtûm kuɗī.**   He gave the man money.
> **Nā bâ Audù aikì.**   I gave Audu work.

Bā/bâ must take at least one object. When only one object occurs, it is most likely to be an indirect object. If only a direct object is employed, it must be preceded by **dà**.

> **Yā bā nì.**   He gave (it) to me.
> **Yā bā dà kuɗī.**   He gave money.

6. The verbs **sanì,** (*get to*) *know,* **barì,** *permit, leave,* and **ganì,** *perceive, see,* are abbreviated before an object. **Sanì** and **barì** never drop more than their final vowel.

> **Nā san shì.**   I know [6] him.
> **Yā bar gidā.**   He (has) left home.
> **Yā bar manà aikì.**   He (has) left us work.
> **Sun san Audù.**   They know Audu.

Ganī drops its final vowel before a pronoun object and its whole final syllable before a noun object. Before an indirect object it becomes **ganè.**

verbs). The analysis here presented seems preferable to the present authors, since it focuses on a syntactic similarity of function between the complements of **bā** and those of other verbs rather than on the (from this point of view) slight formal differences between complements filling the 'indirect object' position. If, however, the student finds it easier to think of **bā** as governing two direct objects, he should feel free to do so.

[6] See footnote 7, p. 77.

Nā gan shì.   I saw/see him.[7]
Nā ga Audù.   I saw/see Audu.
Kà ganè minì kèkēna !   Keep an eye on my bike (for
                                   me) !

7. One group of verbs (often termed *changing* or *variable
vowel verbs*) [8] change their terminal vowel (and their tones
if they have three or more syllables) before a direct object.
Transitive verbs with an initial low tone are of this type.
Before a noun direct object the terminal vowel becomes
-i. Before a pronoun it becomes **-ē**. All tones are low
except for a final high-tone syllable.

(sàyā)	**Nā sàyā.**	I (have) bought (it).
	Nā sàyi àbinci.	I (have) bought food.
	Nā sàyē shì.	I (have) bought it.
(tàmbayà)	**Na tàmbayà.**	I asked.
	Nā tàmbàyi Bellò.	I (have) asked Bello.
	Nā tàmbàyē shì.	I (have) asked him.

A very few verbs with initial high tones belong to this
group of verbs. Two common ones are **sāmù**, *get*, and
ɗaukà, *take, pick up*.

Mun sàmē shì.   We got it *or* we found him.
Yā ɗàuki kāyā.   He (has) picked up/carried the load.

Variable vowel verbs will be indicated in the vocabularies
by the presence of **(i/ē)** following the verb thus : **sāmù
(i/ē)**.

---

[7] Note that the English translation of the Hausa completive
aspect in contexts such as these is present (not past) tense. In the
case of **nā san shì** the literal gloss would be something like *I have
got to know him*, therefore *I (still) know him*. **Nā gan shì** literally
means *I have/had visually perceived him*, therefore meaning either
I saw him or (having visually perceived him) *I (still) see him*.

[8] This class of verb is Parsons' Grade II. The Parsons' classification
is introduced in Lesson 25.

8. Before a pronoun indirect object variable vowel verbs (and low-high intransitives) operate as follows :

(*a*) They may either become high-high(-high) and suffix **-r** (which assimilates to **-m**), e.g. :

(nèmā) → **Yā nēmam minì aikì.**	He sought work for me.
(sāmù) → **Nā sāmam masà kèkē.**	I got a bicycle for him.
(yàrda-intransitive) → **Mun yardam masà.**	We allowed him (to do it).
(tàmbayà) → **Yā tambayam minì.**	He asked me.

(*b*) Or they may become high-low(-high), e.g. :

(sàyā) → **Nā sayà masà àgōgō.**	I bought him a watch.
(fàɗā) → **Sun faɗà manà làbārì.**	They told us the news.
(yàrda-intransitive) → **Nā yardà makà.**	I allow you (to do it).
(tàmbayà) → **Sun tambàyā manà Audù.**	They asked Audu for us.
(kwàikwayà) → **Sun kwaikwàyā manà birì.**	They imitated a monkey for us.

9. Other transitive verbs, except those ending in **-ō,** also shorten their terminal vowel before a direct noun object (but not before a direct pronoun object, nor before an indirect object). These verbs likewise, if they consist of more than two syllables, drop the tone of the final syllable before a noun direct object.

Nā kāmà.	I (have) caught (it).
Nā kāmà shi/ta.	I (have) caught it.
Nā kāmà kīfī.	I (have) caught a fish.

Nā kāmà wà Mūsā kīfī	I have caught Musa a fish.
Nā karàntā.	I (have) read (it).
Nā karàntā shi.[9]	I (have) read it.
Nā karàntà littāfì.	I (have) read the book.
Sun karàntā manà shī.	They read it to us.
Nā kāwō.	I (have) brought (it).
Nā kāwō shì/tà.	I (have) brought it.
Nā kāwō kuɗī.	I (have) brought money.
An kirāwō shì.	He has been summoned.
An kirāwō Mūsā.	Musa has been summoned.

VOCABULARY

Nominals

àddā (f.)	matchet
dàlīlì	reason
fartanyà (f.)	hoe
gàrmā (f.)	large hoe, plough
gàtarī	axe, hatchet
kōmē	everything, whatever

Verbals

bā (bâ)	give
ɗaukà (i/ē)	pick up, carry
fàɗā (i/ē)	speak
ganī	see
ƙārà	increase, raise (price)
ragè	reduce (price)
sallàmā	agree to sell
tayà	make an offer (in buying)

Particles

àlbarkà	no sale ! (said by seller)
habà	come, come now !, nonsense !
ma-/wà/ mà	to, for

[9] Note that after a high-low-high verb a pronoun object does not follow the tonal polarity rule given in section 3 above, but, rather, is high toned.

Important Phrases

nā sàyā	I (agree to) buy (it)
ƙàrā minì	give me some more, increase your offer
ràgē minì	take some away, reduce the price for me

EXERCISES

Translate into English :

1. Bellò yā kāwō manà nāmà.
2. Kài masù littāfìn nân, kà dāwō dà wuri.
3. Wà ya bā kà ƙwai ? Mài tēbùr à bàkin hanyà.
4. Tā jē kàsuwā, tā sàyi dōyà mài tsàdā.
5. Kin ɗaukē sù. Kin kai sù gidan mài gidankù.

Translate into Hausa :

1. Did he see me ? Yes, but he doesn't know you.
2. He got meat. She cooked it. They ate it in a hurry.
3. We left three mangoes in his car. Go and get them.
4. She prepared food for us in the shade of the big tree.
5. He bought tools. I don't know the reason.

Dialogue

(Continuation of Dialogue in Lesson 14.)

Bellò :	Tô, nā sàyi ƙarâr nairà ɗaya dà sulè huɗu nè.
Mài tēbùr :	Àlbarkà. Shī nè kuɗin baƙâr.
Bellò :	Tô, nawà nē kuɗintà na gàskiyā ?
Mài tēbùr :	Nā ragè kwabò ukù.
Bellò :	Nā ƙārà sīsì.
Mài tēbùr :	Habà mālàm !
Bellò :	Fàɗi gàskiyā.
Mài tēbùr :	Kàwō nairà dà sulè bìyar dà sīsì.
Bellò :	Tô, nā tayà nairà dà sulè bìyar.
Mài tēbùr :	Nā sallàmā nairà dà sulè bìyar dà tarō.
Bellò :	Mādàllā, gà kuɗîn.

Lesson 16

The Future Aspects and Zâ

1. There are two future aspects in Hausa. The most used construction, here termed *future I*, employs the specialized verbal **zā** plus the subjunctive aspect person-aspect pronouns. Elision (including tonal) takes place in the first and third (masculine) persons singular (cf. Lesson 7, section 8 (*c*)).

I will come	**zân zō**	**zā mù zō**	we will come
you (*m.*) will come	**zā kà zō**	**zā kù zō**	you will come
you (*f.*) will come	**zā kì zō**		
he will come	**zâi zō**		
she will come	**zā tà zō**	**zā sù zō**	they will come
one will come	**zā à zō**		

2. The *future II aspect* is less used than the future I.[1] Use of this aspect sometimes tends to lend an air of indefiniteness to what is said. The use of the future I does not, though, necessarily imply more definiteness than does the use of the future II. The future II forms are :

I shall come	**nâ zō**	**mâ/mwâ zō**	we shall come
you (*m.*) will come	**kâ zō**	**kwâ zō**	you (*pl.*) will come
you (*f.*) will come	**kyâ zō**		
he will come	**yâ zō**	**sâ/swâ zō**	they will come
she will come	**tâ zō**		
one will come	**â zō**		

---

[1] Some Hausa dialects do not use it at all.

3. The negative of both future aspects employs the
bà . . . ba negative particles.

Bà zâi zō ba.	He will not come.
Bà mâ tàfi ba.	We will not go (away).
Bà zā sù ci àbinci ba.	They are not going to eat food.

4. In sentences of a narrative type, when a string of verbs
occurs all of which require the future aspect, the first verb
is preceded by a future I or II p-a pronoun and the rest
by the appropriate subjunctive aspect p-a pronoun.[2]

> **Gòbe Mālàm Audù zâi tàfi 'Yōlà, yà buɗè makarantā,
> yà dāwō, yà ci àbinci, yà hūtà.** Tomorrow M. Audu will
> go to Yola, open the school, return, eat and rest.

5. A widely used, specialized verbal related to **zā** is **zâ**,
will go to, am bound for. The special set of p-a pronouns
employed by this verbal *follow* rather than precede it.
They are the same forms (with the addition of **a**) as the
direct object pronouns given in Lesson 15, section 3.[3]

Zâ ni gidā.	I am going/will go home.
Ìnā zâ ka ?	Where are you (*m.*) going/will you go ?
Zâ ki Kanò.	You (*f.*) are going/will go to Kano.
Yāròn nan zâ shi makarantā.	This boy is going /will go to school.
Zâ ta gōnā.	She is going/will go to the farm.
Zâ a gàrī.	They (*impersonal*) are going/will go to town.
Zâ mu aikì.	We are going /will go to work.
Zâ ku kàntī.	You (*pl.*) are going/will go to the store.

---

[2] This use of the subjunctive may also be employed if the aspect
of the first clause is continuative or habitual (see Lesson 27, section
1 (*g*)).

[3] Note that in these examples the time of the action (present or
future) is more dependent than usual on the context.

Zâ su rawā.   They are going/will go to the dance/
                       games.

Zâ cannot be followed directly by a nominal.
Zâ constructions are negatived by the use of either the
bà . . . ba or the **bà . . . ba** negative sets :

Bà/bà zâ ni
  kàsuwā ba.   I am not going to the market.
Bà/bà zâ ku
  kàntī ba ?   Aren't you (*pl.*) going to the store ?

VOCABULARY

Nominals

gyàɗā (*f.*)	groundnuts, peanuts
jībi	day after tomorrow
kàntī	store
ƙwarai	very much
màganà (*f.*)	word, talk, matter
rawā (*m./f.*)	dance, game
sābō	new (thing)
sòsai	exactly, really, for sure, that's right !
tàfiyà (*f.*)	travelling, journey
tādì	conversation
tsōhō/tsōfō	old (thing or person)
yāwò	a walk, a stroll
zanè	woman's body cloth

Verbals

gàji	become tired
gayà	tell (requires an indirect object)
hūtà	rest, relax
nèmā (**i/ē**)	seek, look for
sâ	wear, put (clothing) on (see Lesson 9, Vocabulary)
sayar (**dà**)	sell
zâ	will go (to), am going (to)

Important Phrases

ìnā zâ ka ?   where are you going ?

EXERCISES

Translate into English :

1. Nā ji yunwà ƙwarai. Dòmin hakà zân ci àbinci yànzu.
2. Bà zā mù ci àbinci nân ba.
3. Mè zā kì yi ? Zân kōmà gàrī an jimà.
4. Zā kà gayà minì làbārìn tàfiyàrkà ?
5. Zâ ku kàsuwā yâu ? Ā'à, zâ mu gidan àbōkīna.

Translate into Hausa :

1. We will go to the dance in the market tomorrow.
2. You won't go to school.
3. They will ask you to give them money.
4. Where are you going ? I'm going for a walk.
5. Tomorrow Malam Bello will go to Kano. He will
   bring his father's horse.

Dialogue

Amìnā : Ìnā zâ ki, Kànde ?
Kànde : Zâ ni kàntī ìn sàyi sābon zanè.
Amìnā : Dom mè ?
Kànde : Dòmin ìn sâ, ìn tàfi rawā dà shī jībi.
Amìnā : Dà kyâu. Kâi, zanènkì na yànzu bâ kyâu !
Kànde : Gàskiyarkì. Yā tsūfa sòsai.
Amìnā : Mài gidankù yā bā kì kuɗîn ?
Kànde : Bābù ! Nā sayar dà gyàɗā nè.
Amìnā : Tò bâ lâifī.

Lesson 17

Relaters and Relational Nouns

1. Hausa employs several particles (here termed *relaters*) and nouns to introduce (or relate) phrases, clauses and sentences in much the way English does with prepositions and conjunctions. Some of the more important of these are listed below. (See Lesson 29 for further treatment of **sai** and **dà**.)

2. *Nominal phrase introducers* (relater-head nominal phrases).

à, *at, in, on* :

Nā gan shì à Kanò.	I saw him at/in Kano.
Yā yi aikìnsà à ɗākì.	He did his work in the hut.
Yā sâ tāsà à kân tēbùr.	He put the dish on the table.

dà, *with* :

Yā tàfi dà shī.	He has gone away with it/him *or* he has taken it/him away.
Yā gudù dà saurī.	He ran fast (*lit.* with speed).
Mun ci àbinci tàre dà shī.	We ate food with him.

dàgà, *from* :

Nā dāwō dàgà Kadunà.	I have returned from Kaduna.
Yā sāmù dàgà gidā.	He got (it) from home.
Yā zō dàgà wurin sarkī.	He has come from the chief.

gà/gàrē *to, for, in the presence of*, etc. (**gà** before nouns, **gàrē** before pronouns) [1] :

---

[1] In many contexts action performed for the benefit of someone may be expressed either by an indirect object construction or by the use of **gà/gàrē**, e.g. alternative ways of expressing examples one and three on page 86 would be : **Nā kai masà su,** and **Sun kāwō wà màlàmai ruwā.**

Nā kai sù gàrē shì.   I took/have taken them to him.
Yā nèmi aikì gà Àlī.   He sought work from Ali.
Sun kāwō ruwā gà   They brought water to the
  màlàmai.   teachers.
Sunà̀ gàrē shì.   They are with him/at his home.
Yā sāmù dàgà gàrē nì.   He got it from me.

sai, *until, except, only* (**sai** also has uses other than as a
phrase introducer—see below) :

Sai gòbe.   Until tomorrow.
Bàn ga wani àbù ba sai   I didn't see anything except
  tàkàlmī.   shoes.
Sai ɗayansù ya tàfi.[2]   Only one of them went.

3. *Connectors* (conjunctions). **Dà** is used (as a connector)
within serial nominal phrases only. **Kō** may connect
words, phrases, clauses or sentences.

dà, *and* ; **dà ... dà ...** *and, both ... and ...* :

Nā ga yārò̀ da ùbansà.   I saw the boy and his
                                   father.
Sarkī dà mutànensà sun tàfi. The chief and his men have
                                   gone away.
Dà nī dà shī zā mù yi.   He and I [3] will do (it).

kō, *or* ; **kō ... kō ...,** *or, either ... or ...,* *whether*
(*... or ...*) :

Bà zân ci dànkalì kō dōyà̀   I won't eat sweet-potatoes
  ba.   or yams.
Kō sarkī kō wàkilì̀ zâi jē. Either the chief or the
                                   deputy will go.

---

[2] The use of the short voweled p-a pronoun (**ya**) will be explained
in Lesson 20.

[3] Literally, ' I and he '. The Hausa custom in constructions like
this one is just the opposite of the English convention. In Hausa
one mentions oneself first.

Kō zâi yi, kō bà zâi yi ba, ôhō.

Whether he will do (it) or not, I don't know (or care).

4. *Clause introducers.*

àmmā, *but :*

Nā tàfi Kanō àmmā bàn dadè cân ba.

I went to Kano but I didn't stay there long.

Yā yi aikì àmmā bài sàmi kudī ba.

He worked but didn't get (any) money.

dà, *when, as soon as :*

Dà yā kōmà ya [4] ganī.

When he returned home he saw (it).

Dà yā kōmà zâi ganī.

As soon as he returns he will see (it).

in or **ìdan,** *if, when* (followed by completive aspect) :

In nā sāmù zân bā kà.

When/If I get (some) I will give (it to) you.

Ìdan nā gan shì zân gayà masà.

If I see him I will tell him.

sai, *then :*

Dà yā zō sai ìn tàfi.

As soon as he comes (then) I will go.

Kwabò yā fādì. Sai na [4] gan shì, na [4] daukà.

The kobo fell. Then I saw it and picked (it) up.

5. *Relational nouns* are not a special subcategory of nouns. They are, rather, typical nouns which are regularly used in contexts in which English-speakers expect a preposition or conjunction. Some are frequently used with relaters.

[4] The reason for the short vowel in the p-a pronouns is explained in Lesson 20.

G

bāyan (from **bāyā,** *back*), *behind, after :*

Ya fitō dàgà bāyan ɗākì.   He came out from behind the hut.

Bāyan wannàn lōkàcī ya [5]
  bar mù.   After this time he left us.

Bāyân dà ya [5] **tàfi bàn gan**   After he left I didn't see
  shì ba.   him.

cikin (from **cikī,** *inside* ; cf. **cikì,** *stomach*), *in* (*side*), *among :*

Yā shìga cikin ɗākì.   He went into the hut.

Mun gan shì cikin mutànē.   We saw him among the people.

gàban (from **gàbā,** *front*), *in front of, before :*

Yā fāɗì gàban sarkī.   He prostrated (himself) before the chief.

Yā gudù gàban mōtà.   He ran ahead of the car.

kàmar (from **kàmā,** *similarity*), *like, about, as if* ; **kàmar hakà** = *thus, like this :*

Audù kàmar Bellò nē.   Audu is like Bello.

Yā yi kàmar shèkarà gōmà.   He was about ten years (old).

Nà yi kàmar zân wucè.   I made as if I'd pass by.

kân (from **kâi,** *head*), *on, on top of :*

Yā sâ à kân tēbùr.   He put (it) on the table.

Yā zaunà à kân kujèrā.   He sat on the chair.

ƙarƙashin (from **ƙàrƙashī,** *underneath*), *under :*

Nā sâ ƙàrƙashin tēbùr.   I put (it) under the table.

[5] See footnote on page 87.

wajen (from **wajē**, *place, direction*), *about, to, from* (see also Lesson 14) :

Yā sàmi wajen bakwài.	He got about seven.
Nā jē wajen sarkī.	I went to the chief.
Mun ji wajen mutànen gàrī.	We heard (it) from the townspeople.

zuwà (from **zuwà**, *coming*), *to, toward* :

Zân gudù zuwà gidā	I will run to/toward home.
Yā kāmà hanyà zuwà Kanò.	He took the road to Kano.

6. Two relational words **don/dòmin**, *because of, in order to*, and **kàfìn/kàmìn**, *before*, must be treated separately. These words, though they look like nouns, have no extant forms without the **-n** suffix, and function entirely as relaters.

don/dòmin, *because of, in order to* :

Kà yī shì don Allà.	Do it please (*lit.* for God's sake).
Zân jē dòmin ìn gan sù.	I will go in order to see them.
Don hakà zâi tàfi.	For this reason he will go (away).
Dom mè bà kà jē ba ?	Why (*lit.* because of what) didn't you go ?

kàfìn/kàmìn/kàfin/kàmin, *before* (when introducing a clause **kàfìn**, *etc.*, is followed by the subjunctive aspect) :

Kà zō kàfìn ìn tāshì.	Come before I leave.
Kàmìn yà gan shì yā gudù.	Before he saw him he had run away.
Kàmìn gòbe zân zō.	By tomorrow I will come.

7. Chart of positional relaters.

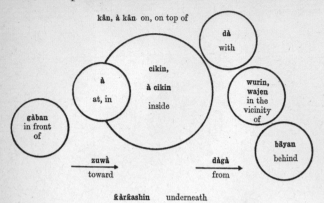

VOCABULARY

Nominals

barkà	greetings (= sànnu)
bāyā	back
cikì	stomach
dāwà (*f.*)	guinea corn
gàbā	front
kàmā (*f./m.*)	similarity
ƙàrƙashī	underneath, underside
rānā	sun, day, heat of sun
shèkarà (*f.*)	year
tàkàlmī (*pl.* tākalmà)	shoe, sandal (*or,* more frequently, a *pair* thereof)
tāsà (*f.*) (*pl.* tāsōshī)	(metal) bowl, (china) dish
wàkīlì	deputy, representative

Verbals   *Particles*

ɗaɗè   spend a long time   dà   when

Verbals   *Particles*
kāmà catch, seize   **in, ìdan**   if, when
                             kàfìn/kàmìn   before
                             kaɗai   only, alone
                             kawài   only, merely
                             òhō   what do I care ?
                                                I neither
                                                know nor care

Important Phrases
bāyan gidā   lavatory, toilet (*lit.* behind the
                         compound)
don Allà   ' please '
kāmà hanyà   take the path/road
watà mài zuwà,
  watàn gòbe   next month

EXERCISES

Translate into English :

1. **Yā fàdì cikin ruwā.**
2. **Bāyan wàsân zā mù jē wurin sarkī.**
3. **Ìdan yā dāwō, sai ìn tàfi.**
4. **Yā yi aikìnsà kàmar yārò.**
5. **Kàfìn ìn tàfi, zâi zō.**
6. **Bàƙō yā sâ tàkàlminsà ƙàrƙashin kujèrāta.**

Translate into Hausa :

1. I saw Yusufu and his father in their home.
2. Either she or I will come to the school tomorrow
   morning.
3. I looked for the goat under the table but didn't see it.
4. When I return next month, then I will buy it.
5. If you work for me you will get money from me.

Dialogue
Mammàn : Barkà dà aikì, Dōgo.
Dōgo :   Yâuwā, barkà dà zuwà.

Mammàn :   Ìnā wunì ?
Dōgo :   Lāfiyà, bâ kōmē.
Mammàn :   Mādàllā.
Dōgo :   Zâ ka gàrī nè ?
Mammàn :   Ā'à, zâ ni yāwò kawài.
Dōgo :   Tò bâ lâifī. Bàri mù zaunà, mù yi tāɗì.
Mammàn :   Tò dà kyâu. Gà inuwà mài kyâu à nân.
Dōgo :   Kâi, àkwai rānā yâu !
Mammàn :   Gàskiyarkà, lōkàcinsà nē.
Dōgo :   Hakà nē.
Mammàn :   Nā ji zā kà jē Kanò gòbe.
Dōgo :   Hakà ne. Zân tàfi cikin mōtà dà sāfē
Mammàn :   Tô, mè zā kà yi à wurîn ?
Dōgo :   Zân sayar dà dāwàtā à kàsuwā.
Mammàn :   Tò dà kyâu. Zā kà daɗè à Kanò ?
Dōgo :   Ī, zân nèmi aikì à wurîn.
Mammàn :   Tò bâ lâifī. Sai yàushè zā kà dāwō ?
Dōgo :   Sai watà mài zuwà.
Mammàn :   Tò dà kyâu. Zân tàfi yànzu.
Dōgo :   Tò bâ lâifī. Sai nā dāwō dàgà Kanò.
Mammàn :   Yâuwā, kà dāwō lāfiyà.
Dōgo :   Àmin.

Lesson 18

Continuative Aspect

1. The *continuative aspect* indicates action regarded as occurring as a process [1] rather than at a single point in time. This process may occur in present, past or future time as indicated by the context. In the absence of contextual evidence to the contrary, however, it is usually possible to assume that the reference is to a process involving present (rather than past or future) time.

2. This aspect employs the specialized verbal **nà,** *be in the process of, be at,* preceded by a high-tone, short-vowel set of person-aspect pronouns. These person-aspect pronouns are traditionally written as prefixes to **nà** rather than as separate words. A modifier (usually a noun) must follow **nà.**

I am working/ do work/ work	**inà aikì**	**munà aikì**	we are working
you (*m.*) are working	**kanà aikì**	**kunà aikì**	you (*pl.*) are working
you (*f.*) are working	**kinà aikì**		
he is working	**yanà aikì**	**sunà aikì**	they are working
she is working	**tanà aikì**		
one is working	**anà aikì**		

[1] Or, frequently, as a habit. See Lesson 26, footnote 1, and Lesson 27, section 2 (*a*).

3. The *negative* of this aspect employs a specialized verbal
bā plus a special set of low-tone, long-vowel p-a pronouns
which follow the verb.

I don't work (*etc.*)	**bā nằ aikì** [2]	**bā mừ aikì** [2]	we don't work
you (*m.*) don't work	**bā kằ aikì**	**bā kừ aikì** [2]	you (*pl.*) don't work
you (*f.*) don't work	**bā kì aikì** [2]		
he doesn't work	**bā yằ aikì** [2]	**bā sừ aikì** [2]	they don't work
she doesn't work	**bā tằ aikì**		
no one works	**bā ằ aikì**		

4. A large number of nouns indicating an action,
activity, state, place, etc., may occur with **nằ** in the
continuative.

yanằ màganằ	he is talking
yanằ gidā	he is at home
yanằ lāfiyằ	he is well
yanằ Kanò	he is at Kano
yanằ nan	he is here
yanằ zàune	he is sitting down/seated [3]

5. *Have* indicating possession is expressed by the use of
the continuative aspect construction plus **dà** plus the
possessed object.

---

[2] Other forms not infrequently heard are: **bā nì** . . ., *I* . . .; **bā
kyằ** . . ., *you* (*f.*) . . .; **bā shì** . . ., *he* . . .; **bā mằ/mwằ** . . ., *we* . . .;
bā kwằ . . ., *you* (*pl.*) . . .; and **bā sằ/swằ** . . ., *they* . . .
[3] See Lesson 19, section 7.

inà dà shī [4]   I have it
munà dà aikì   we have work
yanà dà kuɗī dà yawà   he has a lot of money

6. *Have not* is expressed in either of two ways :

(*a*) Employing the specialized verbal **bā** plus the set of person-aspect pronouns listed in section 3 above.

bā nà dà kuɗī   I haven't any money
bā yà dà mōtà   he doesn't have a car

(*b*) Employing the specialized verbal **bâ** plus the set of p-a pronouns listed with **zâ** in Lesson 16.

bâ ni dà shī [4]   I don't have it
bâ shi dà kyâu   it's no good (*lit.* has no goodness)
bâ ku dà hankàlī   you (*pl.*) don't have (any) sense

7. The forms **anà dà** and **bā à dà/bâ a dà** are rarely, if ever, used.

VOCABULARY

Nominals

barcī, baccī	sleep(ing)
bùkātà (*f.*)	need(ing)
dōgō	tall, long, high (thing)
ɗan'uwā [5]	brother (*lit.* son-of-mother), *pl.*
(*pl.* **'yan'uwā**)	means siblings (*i.e.* without reference to sex)
fushī	anger
gàjērē	short

[4] Note that it is the independent pronouns (see Lesson 6, section 6) which are employed after **dà** in these constructions. This is true whenever the direct object of the verb(al) is introduced by **dà** (see Lesson 25, sections 4–6).

[5] Note that the glottal catch which occurs (but is not written) before every word beginning with a vowel must be written when **ɗan'uwā** is written as a single word.

hankàlī   consciousness, sense, savoir-faire,
                                   circumspection, caution, slowness,
                                   care
itàcē   tree, wood
jirgī   canoe, boat
ƙasā (*f.*)   earth, ground, land, country
samà   sky
sô   wanting, desire, liking, love

Verbals		*Particles*	
dākàtā	wait (for)	kō ?	maybe ?
fi	surpass, be more/		perhaps ?
	better than	wàtàkīlà,	probably,
mutù	die	watakīlà	perhaps [6]
shâidā	inform, testify		
yàrda	agree, consent, accept		
yìwu	be possible		

Important Phrases

jirgin ƙasā   railway train
jirgin samà   aeroplane
kā yàrda, (kō) ?   do you agree ?
mun jimà dà yawà   (another reply to sai an jimà)
yā yìwu, yâ yìwu,
   yanà yìwuwā   it is possible [6]
yi fushī   get/become angry

EXERCISES

Translate into English :

1. Bâ ni dà kāyan nōmā.
2. Ùbansà yanà zuwà yànzu.

----

[6] The time reference of these expressions is determined by which aspect is employed in the following clause, e.g. **yā yìwu zâi zō** = *it is possible he will come* ; **yanà yìwuwā ya rigā ya zō** = *it is possible (that) he has already arrived.*

3. Màtātā tanằ aikì dà kyâu à gōnā.
4. Sarkī yanằ sô yà zō yà yi màganằ dà mū gòbe.
5. Uwargidā tanằ dà àbincimmù cikin ɗākìntà.
6. Mutằnen gàrîn bā sừ rawā.

Translate into Hausa :

1. They are talking together.
2. It is possible he is now at Lagos.
3. He has a big tree in front of his home.
4. He has three brothers and sisters (*i.e.* siblings) at home.
5. I don't have it. Please don't get angry !
6. If he is here I won't go by train.

Dialogue

Jàtau : Inằ sô ìn yi màganằ dà mài gidā.
Gàjēre : Mài gidā bā yằ nân yâu.
Jàtau : Tô, yàushè zâi dāwō nè ?
Gàjēre : Ai, bàn sanì ba. Yā tàfi Ìkko.
Jàtau : Yā tàfi cikin jirgin samằ nē ?
Gàjēre : Ā'à, cikin jirgin ƙasā.
Jàtau : Kwānā nawà zâi yi à wurîn ?
Gàjēre : Ai bà zâi fi sātī gùdā ba.
Jàtau : Tô, zâi sàyi kāyā cân nē ?
Gàjēre : Wàtàkīlằ. Àmmā yā tàfi dòmin ɗan'uwansà yā mutù.
Jàtau : Tô, kō zâi dāwō sātī mài zuwằ ?
Gàjēre : Hakà nē.
Jàtau : Ìdan yā dāwō kà gayằ masà inằ bùkātàr tàimakonsà.
Gàjēre : Tô, zân shâidā masà.
Jàtau : Dà kyâu. Sai an jimằ.
Gàjēre : Tô, mun jimằ dà yawằ.

Lesson 19

Verbal Nouns [1]

1. Frequently, the noun employed after the continuative
nà is a nominalized form of a verb, commonly termed a
verbal noun. Most verbs have one or more verbal nouns
corresponding to them.

2. Verbal nouns of transitive one-syllable verbs almost
always [2] have a falling tone.

(**sō,** *want*)	**inà sôn kuɗī**	I want (some) money.
(**yi,** *do*)	**yanà yî/yînsà**	he is doing/making (it)
(**ji,** *sense*)	**munà jîn zāfī**	we are warm (*lit.* we feel heat)
(**ci,** *eat*)	**bā yà cîn nāmà**	he doesn't eat meat

3. A large number of transitive verbs [3] employ a verbal
noun ending in **-wā** in the continuative. If, however,
there is an object (direct or indirect) the basic verb is
employed followed by the regular indirect and/or direct
object constructions.

(**sâ,** *put*)	**yanà sẫwā**	he is putting (it) on (*i.e.* article of clothing)

---

[1] The formation of verbal nouns and their functioning is one of
the most complex aspects of Hausa grammar. The following
should, therefore, be regarded as ' helpful hints ' rather than as a
complete treatment.

[2] The only exception is **ban,** *giving, causing (of)*, whose use is
confined to set phrases.

[3] Those of Parsons' Grades I, IV, V, VI and VII. See Lessons
25 and 37.

	yanà sâwā à tēbùr	he is putting (it) on the table
	yanà sâ shi à tēbùr	he is putting it on the table
(**kāmà**, *catch*)	**yanà kāmàwā**	he is catching (it/them)
	yanà kāmàwā à dājì	he catches (them) in the bush
	yanà kāmà su	he is catching them
(**kāwō**, *bring*)	**yanà kāwôwā** [4]	he is bringing (it)
	yanà kāwō manà kāyā	he is bringing us loads
(**sayar**, *sell*)	**yanà sayârwā** [4]	he is selling (things)
	yanà sayar dà kāyā	he is selling things

4. Many intransitive verbs [5] employ this same **-wā** suffix.

(**fitō**, *come out*)	**sunà fitôwā** [4]	they are coming out
(**dāwō**, *return here*)	**yanà dāwôwā** [4]	he is returning here

5. Some common intransitives employ a slightly different suffix or no suffix at all.

(**zō**, *come*)	**yanà zuwà**	he is coming
(**tàfi**, *go away*)	**yanà tàfiyà**	he is travelling
(**tsūfa**, *get old*)	**yanà tsūfā**	he is getting old

6. The usual form of the verbal noun of a *variable vowel transitive verb* [6] is the same shape as that of the verb when no object follows.

[4] Note that before the suffixed **-wā** a high-tone syllable becomes falling.

[5] Especially of Parsons' Grade VI.

[6] Parsons' Grade II verbs.

(**kàrɓā,** *receive*)   **yanà kàrɓā**   he is (regularly)
                                           receiving (it/them)

(**sāmù,** *get*)   **yanà sāmù**   he is getting (it)

(**tàmbayà,** *ask*)   **yanà tàmbayà**   he is asking (about it)

(*a*) Many variable vowel verbs (including many of the
commonest of them), however, have irregular verbal
nouns of various types, e.g. :

Verb		*Verbal Noun*	
borrow (other than money)	**àrā**	**arō**	borrowing, a loan
marry	**àurā**	**aurē**	marrying, marriage
beat, thrash	**bùgā**	**bugù**	beating, thrashing
beat, thrash	**dòkā**	**dūkà**	beating, thrashing
shoot at	**hàrbā**	**harbì**	shooting at, hunting
throw at	**jèfā**	**jīfà**	throwing at
seek	**nèmā**	**nēmā**	seeking, looking for
till a farm	**nòmā**	**nōmā**	farming, tilling
request, beseech	**ròƙā**	**ròƙō**	requesting, a request
steal	**sàtā**	**sātà**	stealing, theft
buy	**sàyā**	**sàyē**	buying
cut off a piece of	**yànkā**	**yankā**	butchering

(*b*) What might (because of its English translation) be
regarded as a direct object construction with variable
vowel verbal nouns is actually a noun plus noun/
pronoun possessive construction, e.g. :

sāmù → **yanà sāmùn**   he is getting money (*lit.*
  kuɗī   he is in the process of *the
                              getting of money*)

tàmbayà → **sunà**
  tàmbayàta [7]   they are asking me

[7] Note that **tàmbayà** (the verbal noun) is feminine and, therefore,
requires the feminine possessive pronoun suffix.

harbì → munà harbìn   we are hunting wild
   nāmà   animals
sàyē → inà sàyen àbinci I am buying food

(c) If an indirect object (± a direct object) is expressed
the verb form rather than the verbal noun is employed (as in section 3 above).[8] Some speakers prefer
the verb construction to the verbal noun construction
(described in (b) above) with direct objects as well.

Examples :
   I.O. ± D.O. :

yanà sayà manà
   àbinci   he is buying us food
sunà nēmam minì   they are seeking (it) for me

   D.O. only :

yanà tàmbàyē shì   he is asking him (= yanà
                       tàmbayàrsà)
anà bùgi yārò   the boy was/is being beaten
                       (= anà bugùn yārò)

7. There is in Hausa, in addition to the verbal nouns, a
group of nominalized verbs sometimes termed *nouns of
state* which regularly occur with nà. These indicate a state
resulting from the action of the verb.

(zaunà, *sit down*)   yanà zàune   he is seated
(tsayà, *stand*)   yanà tsàye   he is standing
(ɗaurà, *tie up*)   yanà ɗàure   it is tied up; he is in
                                   prison
(būɗè, *open*)   yanà bùɗe   it is open
(tàfi, *proceed*)   gà shi nan   here he comes (*lit.*
               tàfe   there he is
                      proceeding)

---

[8] See Lesson 15, section 8, for a discussion of indirect objects of
variable vowel verbs.

VOCABULARY

Nominals

dādī	pleasantness
kàràtū	reading (see **karàntā**, Lesson 8)
kōwànè (*f.* kōwàcè)	every, any
ƙòƙarī	worthy effort (usually successful), good try, hard work
ƙwaryā (*f.*)	calabash (gourd bowl)
mōtōcī	automobiles (*pl.* of **mōtà**, see Lesson 10)
nauyī	heaviness
rùbùtū	writing (see **rubùtā**, Lesson 8)
sauƙī	easiness
tàtsūnìyā (*f.*)	fable
wàhalà (*f.*)	trouble, difficulty

Verbals   *Particles*

cigàba	continue, make progress (**ci** + **gàba**)	**màna**	indeed
hūrà/fūrà	light (a fire), blow		
iyà	be able to . . .		
shārè	sweep		
wankè	wash		

Important Phrases

ī màna	yes indeed !
inà sôn . . .	I want . . .
kōwànè lōkàcī	all the time, every time
sai + sub-junctive	one ought to . . ., one must . . . [9]
yā fī makà . . .	it is the most . . . for you

---

[9] See Lesson 29, section 2, for a fuller treatment of this construction.

EXERCISES

Translate into English :

1. Tanà shân ruwā.
2. Yanà būɗè ƙōfà ? Ī, yanà būɗèwā.
3. Sunà sayar dà mōtōcī ? Ī, sunà sayârwā.
4. Àkwàtìn nân yanà dà nauyī.
5. Aikìn nân bâ shi dà wùyā.

Translate into Hausa :

1. The door is open. Close it.
2. She is bringing a calabash.
3. Is he buying food ? Yes, he is.
4. Didn't she light a fire ? Yes, she did.
5. He is standing with a heavy load on his head.

Dialogue

Mālàmī : Cikin aikìn makarantā mè ya fī makà wùyā ?
Dàlìbī : Ai lìssāfì kawài yanà bā nì wàhalà.
Mālàmī : Àshē ? Tūrancī fà ?
Dàlìbī : Tô, Tūrancī yanà dà wùyā sòsai, àmmā lìssāfì yā fī shì.
Mālàmī : Kàràtū bā yà dà wùyā ?
Dàlìbī : Ī. Yanà dà sauƙī. Kàràtū yanà dà dāɗī kumā.
Mālàmī : Tò dà kyâu. Kanà kàràtū dà yawà nē ?
Dàlìbī : Ī mànà ! Kōwànè lōkàcī.
Mālàmī : Àmmā bà kà iyà lìssāfì ba ?
Dàlìbī : Ā'à, nā iyà mànà. Àmmā yanà dà wùyā.
Mālàmī : Tò bâ lâifī. Sai kà cigàba dà ƙòƙarinkà.

Lesson 20

The ' Relative ' Aspects ; Relative Constructions

1. One completive and one continuative aspect in Hausa are known as *relative* aspects because of the fact that these aspects, not their counterparts, are employed in *relative* constructions (see sections 4–7 below for illustrations of the contexts in which these aspects are employed). The meanings of the relative aspects are essentially the same as their non-relative counterparts (see Lessons 7 and 18) and they share the negative constructions described for their counterparts (Lessons 7 and 18).

2. The *relative completive aspect* person-aspect pronouns are characterized by a high-tone, short-vowel syllable with, in some cases, a **-kà** suffix.[1] With, for example, the verb **kāwō** the forms are :

... I brought [2]	... na kāwō [2]	... mukà kāwō	... we brought
... you (*m.*) brought	... ka kāwō	... kukà kāwō	... you (*pl.*) brought
... you (*f.*) brought	... kikà kāwō		
... he brought	... ya kāwō	... sukà kāwō	... they brought
... she brought	... ta kāwō		
... one brought	... akà kāwō		

[1] Note that the **-kà** suffix is employed with the same persons as have the **-n** suffix in the non-relative completive aspect (see Lesson 7).

[2] See footnote 3 on page 105.

The negative of the relative completive aspect is indistinguishable from the negative of the completive aspect. See Lesson 7, sections 6 and 7, for the forms.

3. The *relative continuative aspect* employs the same high-tone, short-vowel person-aspect pronoun (minus the -**kà** suffix) plus the specialized verbal **kè**, *be in the process of, be at.*

... I want [3]	... na kè sồ [3]	... mu kè sồ	... we want
... you (*m.*) want	... ka kè sồ	... ku kè sồ	you (*pl.*) want
... you (*f.*) want	... ki kè sồ		
... he wants	... ya kè sồ	... su kè sồ	... they want
... she wants	... ta kè sồ		
... one wants	... a kè sồ		

The negative of the relative continuative aspect is indistinguishable from the negative of the continuative aspect. See Lesson 18, section 3, for the forms.

4. *Relative constructions* are usually modificational constructions which typically consist of an entire clause but are employed within nominal phrases as modifiers.

Such constructions are common in English. Each of the following English nominal phrases is divisible into a head nominal (labelled *Head*) and a modificational construction (labelled *Modifier*). Note that each of the

[3] Since these forms occur in contexts too long to conveniently list here, the student is asked to supply in place of the three dots some such context as **àbìn dà** ... = *the thing that* ..., or **mutằnên dà** ... = *the people that* ...

modifiers introduced by *relative* words such as *that*,
which, *who*, *when*, etc., includes a whole clause. These
clauses are the relative constructions.

Non-relative Constructions :

Head	Modifier
the home	of the chief
the boy	of Malam Yahaya

Relative Constructions :

Head	Modifier
the home	that the chief built
the boy	that Malam Yahaya gave the money to
the knife	that I dropped by the road
the man	who comes to see us
the time	when we had no work

5. Relative constructions in Hausa are usually introduced by **dà** or **wandà/wândà** (*f.* **waddà, wâddà** ; *pl.*
waɗàndà) meaning *that, which, who, the one which/who*,
etc. The final syllable of the nominal preceding **dà** takes
the **-n/-r** referential suffix (see Lesson 8).[4] If the final
syllable of this nominal is on a high tone, it becomes
falling before **dà**. Neither the referential nor the tone
change is necessary before **wandà**.

Non-relative constructions :

Head	Modifier
gidan	**sarkī**
the home of the chief	
yāròn	**Audù**
Audu's boy	

---

[4] Consideration is here confined to the commonest type of relative
clause, often termed ' restrictive relative clauses ', i.e. those in which
the clause serves to define or particularize one of a class of objects.
Actually there are in Hausa, as in English, a number of other types
of relative clauses as well.

Relative constructions :

Head	*Modifier*
gidân	**dà sarkī ya ginà** (= **gidā wandà . . .**)

the home that the chief built

yāròn **dà Audù ya aikà** (= **yārồ wandà . . .**)
the boy that Audu sent

wuƙâr **dà ta fāɗì à bàkin hanyà** (**wuƙā waddà . . .**)
the knife that fell by the side of the road

mùtumìn **dà ya kè** [5] **zuwà yà gan mù** (= **mùtûm wandà . . .**)
the man who comes to see us

lōkàcîn **dà mukà tàfi Kanồ**
(the time) when we went to Kano

dōkì **wandà na kè hawā** (= **dōkìn dà . . .**)
the horse which I ride

mutằnē **waɗàndà bà mù sanì ba** (= **mutằnên dà . . .**)
people whom we don't know

wurîn **dà sukà tàfi**
the place where they went

àbîn **dà ya bā nì**
the thing that (= what) he gave me

6. **Wan-** occasionally serves by itself as the head of a nominal phrase containing a relative construction. In each example the **wan-, waɗàn-, wad-** part of the first word is the head, the relative construction introduced by **-dà** is the modifier :

wandà ya sāmù	the one which he obtained
waɗàndà mukà ganī	those that we saw
waddà ki kè sồ	the one (*f.*) that you (*f.*) want

7. The relative aspects are employed in the following contexts :

[5] In the third person the person-indicator (**ya, ta, sukà**) is frequently omitted : **mùtumìn dà kè zuwà . . .**

(a) In *relative constructions*. See above (sections 5 and 6) for illustrations.

(b) When a construction that characteristically occurs after the predicate in a clause is shifted to pre-predicate position for *emphasis*. Common instances of inversion for emphasis are :

    (i) *Adverbial nominals* indicating time, place, manner, etc. :

jiyà mukà tàfi	we went away *yesterday*
à gidā mu kè aikì	we work *at home*
cikin mōtà sukà zō	they came *in a car*
ran Tàlātà yârā sukà jē	the children went *on Tuesday*
lāfiyà su kè	they are *well*

    (ii) *Interrogatives*, whether adverbial or not, whenever they precede the verb :

mè sukà yi ?	what did they do ?
mè ka kè sô ?	what do you want ?
yàushè sarkī ya dāwō ?	when did the chief return ?
wà ya sanì ?	who knows ?
ìnā ka kè ?	where are you ?

    (iii) *Objects* (usually a direct object, occasionally an indirect object) :

sarkī mukà bi	it is the *chief* (that) we followed
aikì mu kè yî	we are doing *work* (not something else)
shī na gayà wà [6]	*he is* the one I told (it to)

---

[6] Note that when an indirect object is moved into the emphasis position the indirect object marker (always **wà**) is left behind.

(iv) Emphasis constructions involving **nē** which have been moved back into the emphasis position from either the post or the pre-predicate position. Virtually all the examples under (i) and (iii) above may alternatively involve a **nē**.

sarkī nè̄ ya tàfi	it is the *chief* (who) went away
jiyà nē sukà dāwō	it was *yesterday* they came
aikì nē mu kè̄ yî	it is *work* (that we are doing
cikin mōtà̄ nē mukà zō	it is *by car* (that) we came

(c) In *narrative*. The relative completive aspect is used in preference to the completive aspect throughout a narrative or extended ' chronological ' account. See the fable at the end of this lesson for an illustration. Typical introducers of narrative or ' chronological ' accounts (and, therefore, of these aspects) are **rân nan**, *one day* ; **sai**, *(just) then, so . . .* ; and **sā'àn nan**, *then*.

(d) The relative aspects are always used after **dà**, *when* (referring to a single act in the past) : **bāyân dà**, *after* ; **kō dà**, *when, though* ; **sai dà**, *only when, (not) until* ; and **tun dà**, *since*.

VOCABULARY

Nominals

dâ	(in) the past, formerly
dūniyà̄ (*f.*)	world
kūrā (*f.*)	hyena
ƙàdangarè̄	lizard
màmākì	surprise, amazement

nēmā	seeking, looking for
ràbō	one's lot, destiny, luck (in life)
rāmì	hole
sātà	stealing
tsòrō	fearfulness, fearing
wākē	beans
yĩ	doing, making
zāmànī	period of time

Days of the week (are all feminine)

Lahàdì/Lâdì	Sunday
Lìttìnîn	Monday
Tàlātà	Tuesday
Làràbā	Wednesday
Àlhàmîs	Thursday
Jumma'à	Friday
Àsabàr, Sātī	Saturday

Verbals		*Particles*	
aikà (i/ē)	send (on errand)	àshē	well!, why!, is
cê, cè	say		that so ?
ginà	build		

Important Phrases

rân nan	a certain day, one day
ran Tàlātà	Tuesday
zāmànin dâ	long ago, in ancient times

EXERCISES

Translate into English :

1. Mutànên dà su kè zuwà zā sù daɗè nân.
2. Wandà ya zō yâu yā tāshì dà wuri.
3. Bã wândà su kè tsòrō.
4. Mè akà yi à Kanò shēkaranjiyà ?
5. Bàn ga waɗàndà ka kè sô à wurîn ba.

Translate into Hausa :

1. It was the *teacher* we saw.
2. That woman works here.
3. When did you (*f.*) come ?
4. There are the children who will go in the car.
5. We will meet them at the place where we saw them yesterday.

Fable

Kūrā dà Kàdangarè dà Kàrē [7]

Zāmànin dâ àkwai wata kūrā. Rân nan ta ji yunwà ƙwarai. Sai [8] ta tāshì, ta fìta. Tanà nēman àbinci sai gà [9] ƙàdangarè, yanà sātàr wākē. Dà ta ga ƙàdangarè ta kāmà shi. Zā tà cī shì sai ta ga kàrē.

Sai ta cè, ' Bàri ìn kai ƙàdangarè gidā kàmìn ìn dāwō ìn kāmà kàrē.'

Sai ta tàfi gidantà dà ƙàdangarè.

Dà ta dāwō bà tà ga kàrē ba. Lōkàcîn dà ta kè tàfiyà dà ƙàdangarè kàrē yā gudù zuwà dājì.

Dà kūrā ta kōmà gidā bà tà ga ƙàdangarè ba. Lōkàcîn dà ta kè nēman kàrē ƙàdangarè yā bar rāmìn kūrā yā shìga dājì.

Kūrā ta yi màmākì, ta cè, ' Àshē, kōmē ka nèmā à dūniyà, in bà ràbonkà ba nè, bà zā kà sāmù ba ! '

---

[7] See *Ka Kara Karatu*, page 1, and Abraham, R. C., *Hausa Literature*, page 35, for another version of this story.

[8] **Sai** commonly means *then* or *so* . . . in narrative contexts.

[9] **Sai gà** is an idiomatic phrase used to introduce the appearance of a new character in a story.

Lesson 21

Interrogative and Indefinite Nominals

1. The various Hausa interrogatives (and the indefinite nominals formed from them) belong to several of the subclasses of nominals. The majority of them are adverbial nominals, three are independent nominals, one is a quantifier and one is a specifier.

2. The indefinite nominals are formed by prefixing **kō** to any of the interrogative nominals. In Hausa printed literature, some of the indefinite nominals are written as single words (e.g. **kōmē,** *whatever, anything,* **kōwā,** *whoever, everyone*). Others are officially [1] written as two words (e.g. **kō inā,** *wherever, everywhere,* **kō yàushè,** *whenever*). It seems preferable to be consistent and to write them all as single words. This will be the practice throughout this book. Indefinite nominals, when (as frequently) used to introduce relative clauses, are followed by the ' relative ' aspects. Note that they do not (as do regular nouns) require a following **dà** to introduce the relative clause, e.g. **kōmē ka sāmù,** *whatever you get,* as opposed to **àbîn dà ka sāmù,** *what(ever) you get.*

3. *Adverbial* interrogative and indefinite nominals.

inā, *where?, how?* (see also Lesson 4) :

Ìnā ya kè ?	Where is he ?
Ìnā mutànemmù ?	Where are our people ?

---

[1] By decision of the Hausa Language Board. But this convention is subject to change from time to time.

Înā na sanì ?   How should I know ?

Yā tàfi ìnā nè ? [2]   Where did he go ?

kō'ìnā,[3] *wherever, everywhere :*

Kō'ìnā ka tàfi cùtā zā tà   Wherever you go illness will
sâmē kà.   befall you.

Yârā sunà cân kō'ìnā.   Children are there every-
                                     where.

ƙàƙà, *how ?* (not as widely used as **yàyà** below) : [4]

Kàƙà zā kà yi ?   How will you do (it) ? What
                                     will you do ?

Kàƙà sukà sanì ?   How do they know ?

kōƙàƙà, *however, any way possible :*

Anà sāmùn kuɗī kōƙàƙà.   People get (their) money
                                     any way possible.

À yī shì kōƙàƙà.   Do it any way possible.

yàushè, yàushe, *when ? :*

Yàushè nē ya zō ?   When was it he came ?

Sai yàushè zā sù ɗāwō ?   (By) when will they return ?

kōyàushè, kōyàushe, *whenever, all the time :*

Sunà nan kōyàushè.   They're here all the time.

Kōyàushè mu kè Kanò sai   Whenever we're in Kano we
mù zìyàrcē shì.[5]   visit him.

---

[2] Note that the regular (not the relative) completive aspect p-a
pronoun is used here since the regular (i.e. non-emphatic) word
order is employed which places the interrogative word in the
regular object position after the verb.

[3] Note that the glottal catch which occurs (but is not written)
before any word beginning with a vowel must be written when
kō'ìnā is written as a single word (see also **ɗan'uwā**, Lesson 18).

[4] Indeed in some dialects (e.g. Zaria) its use is considered
impolite !

[5] See Lesson 29, section 2, for a discussion of this usage of **sai** plus
subjunctive.

yàyà, *how?, what?* (referring, for example, to actions) :

Yàyà mu kè ?	How are you ? (*lit.* how are we ?)
Yàyà zā à yi dà shī ?	What should be done with it ?

kōyàyà, *however, any way possible* :

Kōyàyà zā à gyārà shi bà zâi yi aikì ba.	However it is fixed it (still) won't work.
Kōyàyà akà sāmù zân sàyā.	No matter how it was obtained I'll buy it.

4. *Independent interrogative and indefinite nominals.*

mè, *what?* (introduced in Lesson 5, Vocabulary) :

Mè ya fàru ?	What happened ?
Mè ka kè sô ?	What do you want ?
Mè ya yi ? *or* **Yā yi mè ?** [6]	What did he do ? *or* He did what ?
Mènē nè ? *or* **Mècē cè ?**	What is it (*m.* or *f.*) ?

komènē nè, *whatever it is* :

Zân sàyā kōmènē nè màganàrkà.	I'll buy (it) whatever you say (*lit.* whatever your word is).
Kōmènē nè ya kè yî bâ shi dà kyâu.	Whatever he does is not good.

kōmē[7] *anything, everything, whatever* :

Bài kāwō kōmē ba.	He didn't bring anything.
Allà yā san kōmē.	God knows everything.

[6] See footnote 2 on page 113.

[7] Note that in these compounds, which are always written as single words, the interrogatives (**mè** and **wà**) change to high tone.

Tā shiryà kōmē dà kōmē.   She (has) prepared every-
                                 thing (necessary).
Kōmē ka sāmù ràbonkà nē.   Whatever you get is your lot.

wà (*pl.* **su wà**), *who?* (introduced in Lesson 6, Vocabulary) :

Wà ya yi ?   Who did it ?
Wànē nè ? *or* **Wàcē cè ?** Who is it (*m.* or *f.*) ?
Su wànē nè sukà zō ?   Who (*pl.*) came ?

kōwànē nè, *whoever it is :*

Kōwànē nè ya zō kà   Whoever comes accept him.
kàrɓē shì.

kōwā,[8] *anyone, everyone, whoever :*

Kōwā yā tàfi gidā.   Everyone has gone home.
Bài ga kōwā ba.   He didn't see anyone.
Kōwā dà kōwā sukà zō.   Everyone came.

wànnē (*f.* **wàccē** ; *pl.* **wàɗànnē**), *which one? :*

Wànnē akà kāwō ?   Which one was brought ?
Wàccē ta dafà wannàn   Which one (*f.*) cooked this
nāmà ?   meat ?

kōwànnē (*f.* **kōwàccē** ; *pl.* **kōwàɗànnē**), *whichever, everyone, anyone :*

Kōwànnē ya bā kà kà   Whichever he gives you
ɗaukà.   take (it).
Kōwàɗànnensù sukà bar mù.   Everyone of them left us.

5. Interrogative and indefinite *quantifiers* (see also
Lesson 11).

nawà, *how much?, how many? :*

Kuɗinsà nawà nē ?   How much does it cost ?
Kā sàyi gōrò nawà ?   How many kolanuts did
                                 you buy ?

[8] See footnote 7 on page 114.

kōnawà, *however much, however many* :

Kōnawà ya bā nì, yanà dà kyâu.	However much/many he gives me it's okay (with me).
Kà sàyā kōnawà kuɗinsà.	Buy it whatever its price.

6. Interrogative and indefinite *specifiers*.

wànè (*f.* wàcè ; *pl.* wàɗànnè), *what (one)?, which (one)?* :

Wànè aikì zâi yi ?	What work will he (*or* is he to) do ?
Wàcè hanyà zā mù bi ?	Which path shall we follow?
Wàɗànnè mutànē sukà zō ?	Which people came ?

kōwànè (*f.* kōwàcè ; *pl.* kōwàɗànnè), *every (one), any (one), whatever* :

Kōwànè mùtûm yanà dà mōtà à ƙasarmù.	Everyone has a car in our country.
Àkwai maròƙā à kōwàcè kàsuwā.	There are beggars in every market.

7. The interrogative and indefinite specifiers are often followed by irì, *kind, sort*. In this context the gender and number of the specifier is determined not by irì but by the nominal following irì. Irì retains its masculine singular form.

Wànè irìn aikì zā mù yi ?	What kind of work will we do ?
Wàcè irìn fìtilà ka sàyā ?	What kind of lantern did you buy ?
Wàɗànnè irìn mutànē nè waɗànnân ?	What kind of people are these ?
Zâi kāwō kōwàcè irìn rìgā.	He will bring every kind of gown.
Àkwai kōwànè irìn àbinci à wurìn.	There is every kind of food in that place.

Note : This rule applies also with the specifiers **wani,** **wannàn** and **wancàn** introduced in Lesson 10.

Wani irìn tsuntsū nḕ.	It's a certain kind of bird.
Nā ga wata irìn rìgā à cân.	I saw a (different) kind of gown there.
Irìn waɗànnân [9] **mutånē bâ kyâu.**	These kinds of people are no good.

8. There are several ways of *asking a question* in Hausa :

(*a*) By using an interrogative nominal (plus interrogative intonation) :

Ìnā gàrī ?	Where is the town ?
Mḕnē nḕ wannàn ?	What is this ?

(*b*) By using the particles **kō** [10] or **nē,** or the expression **kō bâ hakà ba ?,** *or isn't it so ?*, at the end of a sentence (plus interrogative intonation) :

Kanà dà kuɗī kō ? [10]	Have you any money ?
Yārò yā zaunà nē ?	Has the boy sat down ?
Yārò yā tàfi kàsuwā nḕ ?	Has the boy gone to market ?
Gàskiyā nḕ, kō (bà hakà ba) ? [10]	It is true, isn't it ?

(*c*) The particle **shin/shîn,** *could it be* ? (plus interrogative intonation) is also common in interrogative contexts such as the following : [11]

---

[9] Hausa prefers to reverse the normal order of *specifier* + **irì** with **wannàn** and **wancàn,** although **waɗànnân irìn mutånē** would also be understood.

[10] **Kō** used as a question word is actually an abbreviated form of **kō bâ hakà ba.** Note the parallel expression in English, *Are you coming or . . . ?* for *. . . or aren't you ?*

[11] The use of this particle is similar to that of *say* or *look* (*here*) as question introducers in English, e.g. *Say, are you coming ?*, *Look, can you prove that ?*

Shin kā san shì ?   Do you (by any chance)
                               know him ?

Shîn dà aikì à wurinkà ?   Say, do you have a job
                               (for me) ?

(*d*) A change of the intonation pattern of the utterance
as described in Lesson 3, section 6, is frequently
employed by itself to change an utterance from a
statement to a question and, in addition, is regularly
employed with each of the above question words by
most speakers. A partial exception to this rule is
that some speakers will not employ interrogative
intonation at all times with interrogative nominals
(category (*a*) above).

VOCABULARY

Nominals

àllūrà (*f.*)	needle, inoculation
bàɗi (*f.*)	next year
bana (*f.*)	this year
bàra (*f.*)	last year
cīwò	illness, injury
fātā	hope, hoping that
kō'ìnā	everywhere, anywhere
kōwā	everyone, anyone
kōwànnē	whichever, everyone, anyone
kōyàushè, kōyàushe	whenever
kōyàyà	however, in whatever way
likità	doctor
māgànī	medicine
maròƙī (*pl.* maròƙā)	beggar
muryà (*f.*)	voice

wànnē (*f.*
  wàccē ; *pl.*
  wàɗànnē)   which one ?
yàyà   how ?
zàzzàɓī   fever, malaria

Verbals		*Particles*	
bā dà	give (when no indirect object follows)	shin/shîn	could it be ?
dūbà	look at, look around		
gwadà	measure, test, try to do		
kashè	kill		

Important Phrases

cīwòn kâi	headache
cīwò yā kāmà ka	you have become ill (*lit.* sickness (has) caught you)
shā māgànī	take medicine
(yanà) dà saukī *or* yā yi saukī	it (illness) is (a bit) better
zàzzàɓī yā kāmà ni	I have a fever (*lit.* a fever has caught me)

EXERCISES

Translate into English :

1. Ìnā kuɗîn dà na bā kà jiyà ?
2. Wàcè mōtà zā kà tàfi à cikī ?
3. Nā ga wani irìn wàsân dà bàn ganī ba dâ.
4. Kōyàushè zâi zō bā nà sô in gan shì.
5. Yâu bà zân sàyi kōmē à kàsuwā ba.

Translate into Hausa :

1. Do you know him ? He's got malaria.
2. Where did you go with our car ?

3. What kind of gown did you bring from the store ?
4. I have a lot of work everywhere in this town.
5. There I saw the chief who came to town yesterday.

Dialogue

Sulè :   Uwargidā tā gayà minì bâ ka dà lāfiyà.
Būbà :   Hakà nē.
Sulè :   Mề ya dằmē [12] kà ?
Būbà :   Cīwòn kâi nē.
Sulè :   Kâi, sànnu ! Kā shā māgànī nề ?
Būbà :   Ī. Likitầ yā yi minì àllūrầ.
Sulè :   Tồ dà kyâu. Àkwai zàzzàɓī kumā ?
Būbà :   Àkwai dâ, àmmā yànzu yā yi sauƙī.
Sulè :   Mādàllā. Yàushè ya kāmầ ka ?
Būbà :   Ai, jiyà nē, lōkàcîn dà na kề nōmā.
Sulè :   Tồ, inà fātā Allầ zâi bā dà sauƙī.
Būbà :   Ầmin.

---

[12] From dằmā (i/ē), *bother*.

Lesson 22

Noun Plurals

1. Noun pluralization is a highly complex feature of Hausa grammar. It is usually advisable simply to memorize the most common plural form of a given noun. It is, however, possible to classify Hausa noun plurals, and to arrange them in four major and several minor classes. Some nouns employ more than one plural, but usually a single plural form will be more prominent in a given area than any of the other forms. See Lesson 38 for further treatment of noun plurals.

2. *Class I* plurals are characterized by all high tones and an -ō . . . ī ending. The -ō . . . ī replaces the final vowel of the singular form, with the final consonant of the singular form reappearing between the ō and the ī.[1] Class I is the largest class of plurals and includes most of the recent

---

[1] Here, as a rule (note two exceptions below—both recent borrowings from English), as throughout the language, the following consonants occurring before **a, o** or **u** change before a final **i** or **e** as follows:

t	becomes **c,**	e.g. :	**mōtā̀**	car, lorry	**mōtōcī** (Class I)
d, z	become **j,**	e.g. :	**gidā**	home	**gidàjē** (Class III)
			ōdā̀	order	**ōdōjī** *or* **ōdōdī** (Class I)
s	becomes **sh**	e.g. :	**tāsā̀**	bowl	**tāsōshī** (Class I)
w	*often* becomes **y**	e.g. :	**kà̀suwā**	market	**kàsuwōyī** (sometimes **kàsuwōwī**) (Class I)

Illustrations of these changes in verbs are :

yā sà̀tā	he stole (it)	**yā sà̀ci rìgāta**	he stole my gown
yā cìzā	it (*i.e.* snake) bit (it)	**yā cìjē nì**	it bit me
yā fànsā	he redeemed (it)	**yā fànshē shì**	he paid the ransom for him
canjì	(a noun) change	**yā canzà̀/ canjà̀ (shi)**	he changed (it)

loanwords from English. The singular forms of most (but
by no means all) of Class I nouns end in **-ā**.

hanyà (*f.*)	path, road	hanyōyī
tēbùr	table	tēburōrī
tàmbayà (*f.*)	question	tambayōyī
fartanyà (*f.*)	hoe	fartanyōyī

3. *Class II* plurals are characterized by a **-u ... à**
ending with all tones high except the final **-à**.[2] The
-u ... à replaces the final vowel of the singular, the
consonants **n, w** or **k** being the most common ones
appearing between the **u** and the **à**. Class II is the second
largest class of plurals and includes many recent loan-
words. Most of the disyllabic nouns with a low-high tone
pattern in the singular and many with a high-low pattern
(ending in a vowel other than **a**) belong to this class.
Some nouns reduplicate their final syllable before the
plural suffix, like the third and fourth examples below.

kèkē	bicycle	kēkunà
ɗākì	hut, room	ɗākunà
àbù	thing	abūbuwà
sulè	shilling	sulūlukà [3]

4. *Class III* plurals are characterized by a **-à ... ē**
ending with a high-low-high tone pattern. The consonant
appearing between the **à** and the **ē** is typically either **y** or,
where the first syllable of the root consists simply of a
consonant plus a short vowel, the consonant introducing
the final syllable of the singular form. Many of the oldest

---

[2] Note that these Class II plurals are virtually the only plurals in
the language with a low final tone.

[3] Several shilling (10k) coins ; in computing money the singular
form is used with a number, e.g. seven shillings (70k) is **sulè** (*not*
sulūlukà) **bakwài**.

and commonest nouns in the language—especially those with a high-high tone pattern—belong to Class III.

sūnā	name	sūnàyē
tsuntsū	bird	tsuntsàyē
birnī	(walled) city	birànē
wuƙā (f.)	knife	wuƙàƙē
wurī	place	wuràrē
gidā	home	gidàjē

5. *Class IV* plurals are characterized by a **-ai** (infrequently **-au**), **-ī** or **-ū** suffix with all tones but that of the suffix low. Many nouns whose singulars consist of more than two syllables belong to Class IV. Some nouns reduplicate their final syllable before this plural suffix. Note that derived nouns of place and implement introduced in Lesson 30, sections 4 (*b*) and (*c*), belong in this class.

àbōkī	friend	àbòkai
làbārì	news	làbàrai *or* làbàrū
mālàm(ī)	teacher	màlàmai
kwabò	penny	kwàbbai (see note 3 on page 122)
tsōhō/tsōfō	old (thing)	tsòfàffī
bàƙō	guest	bàƙī
gōnā	farm	gònàkī
kujèrā (f.)	chair	kùjèrū
màganà (f.)	word	màgàngànū
makarantā (f.)	school	màkàràntū

6. Among the minor classes of noun plurals are :
Class V—those with terminal **-à** . . . **ā/ū** :

sirdì	saddle	siràdā
ƙarfè	metal	ƙaràfā
dūtsè	rock, stone	duwàtsū
idò	eye	idànū
ƙafà (f.)	leg	ƙafàfū

Class VI—those with terminal -ā or -à in the plural from singulars with terminal -ī or -ē :

(*a*) Plurals of **mā . . . ī** derived nouns signifying *agent*, etc. (see Lesson 30, section 4 (*a*)) :

maɗìnkī	tailor	**maɗìnkā**
maƙèrī	blacksmith	**maƙèrā**
maròƙī	beggar	**maròƙā**

(*b*) Plurals ending in -à with high-high-low tones (with, on occasion, a change of penultimate vowel) :

cōkàlī	spoon	**cōkulà**
ƙànƙanè	small (thing)	**ƙanānà**
tàkàlmī	shoe(s)	**tākalmà**

(*c*) Plurals ending in -ā with high-high tones :

màcè	woman, wife	**mātā**
mijì	male, husband	**mazā**

Class VII—other plurals ending in ā :

(*a*) Those with falling-high plurals :

bàbba	big (thing)	**mânyā**
yārò	boy	**yârā**
zōbè	ring	**zôbbā**

(*b*) **āwā** plurals (usually pluralizing ethnic designations whose singulars involve a **bà-** prefix—see Lesson 30, section 2) :

Bàtūrè	European	**Tùràwā**
talàkà	peasant	**talakāwā**
Bàkanè	Kano person	**kanāwā**
bàdūkù	leather worker	**dùkàwā**

Class VIII—**akī/ākī** plurals :

àkwiyà	goat	**awākī**
dōkì	horse	**dawākī**
kāyā	loads	**kāyàyyakī**
tunkìyā	sheep	**tumākī**

Class IX—those with terminal **-ū** and all high tones :

māshì	spear	māsū
nāmǎ	animal (wild)	nāmū
sâ, sānìyā	bull, cow	shānū
yātsǎ	finger	yātsū

Class X—*reduplicative* plurals : [4]

| irì | kind | irì-irì |
| en'è | Native Admini-stration | en'è-en'è |

7. Among the common plurals not classifiable as 'regular' in terms of the above classes are the following :

(*a*) The specifiers (see Lessons 10 and 21, section 6) e.g. :

wannàn	this	waɗànnân
wani	a (certain)	waɗansu
kōwànè	every(one)	kōwàɗànnè

(*b*) Kinship terms (see also Lesson 35) :

ɗā	'yā (màcè)	'yā'yā
son	daughter	children, offspring
		'yā'yā mazā
		sons
		'yā'yā mātā
		daughters
ùbā	uwā	iyàyē
father	mother	parents
ɗan'uwā	'yar'uwā	'yan'uwā
brother	sister	brothers and sisters, siblings
ɗan'ùbā	'yar'ùbā	'yan'ùbā
half-brother	half-sister	half-brothers and half-sisters

[4] See Lesson 28, section 9, for another reduplicative construction sometimes regarded as pluralization.

wâ	yâ	yâyyē
elder brother	elder sister	elder siblings
ƙanè	ƙanwà	ƙânnē
younger brother	younger sister	younger siblings

'yam mātā (employed
as a plural of
yārinyà, *girl*, or of
bùdurwā, *unmar-
ried, young woman*)

Plurals of previous vocabulary words not listed as
examples above.

Class I

kàsuwā (*f.*)	market	kāsuwōyī/kāsuwōwī
ƙōfà (*f.*)	door(way)	ƙōfōfī
lâifī	fault	laifōfī (*or* Class II laifuffukà)
likità	doctor	likitōcī
muryà (*f.*)	voice	muryōyī
nāmà	animal (wild)	nāmōmī (*or* Class VII nāmū)
tāgà (*f.*)	window	tāgōgī
tàtsūnìyā (*f.*)	fable	tātsūniyōyī
tāyà (*f.*)	tyre	tāyōyī

Class II

àddā (*f.*)	matchet	addunà
aikì	work	ayyukà
gàrī	town	garūruwà *or* garurrukà
itàcē	wood, tree	itātuwà
jàkī	donkey	jākunà
kàntī	store	kantunà
kàrē	dog	karnukà
kògī	river	kōgunà
māgànī	medicine	māgungunà

rāmì	hole	rāmunà *or* rāmummukà
rìgā (*f.*)	gown	rīgunà
sarƙī	chief	sarākunà
zanè	body cloth	zannuwà

Class III

baƙī	black (thing)	baƙàƙē
ɓērā	mouse, rat	ɓēràyē
dōgō	long (thing)	dōgàyē/dōgwàyē
farī	white (thing)	faràrē
jirgī	boat	jiràgē
ƙasā	country	ƙasàshē
mùtûm	man	mutànē
uwā (*f.*)	mother	uwàyē, iyàyē

Class IV

àkwàtì	box	àkwàtai (*or* Class II akwātunà)
àllūrà (*f.*)	needle	àllùrai
bùkātà (*f.*)	need	bùkàtai *or* bùkàtū
dàlīlì	reason	dàlìlai
fìtilà (*f.*)	lamp	fìtilū (*or* Class I fitilōlī)
gàjērē	short (thing)	gàjèrū *or* gàjèjjèrū
kuskurè	mistake	kùskùrai *or* kùràkùrai
littāfì	book	littàttàfai *or* littàfai
sābō	new (thing)	sàbàbbī
shèkarà (*f.*)	year	shèkàrū
wàkīlì	representative	wàkìlai

EXERCISES

Translate into English :

1. Mōtōcī sun kashè mutànē dà yawà bàra.
2. Anà sô likitōcī sù yi aikìnsù dà kyâu.
3. Mazā sun fi mātā ƙarfī.
4. Ìnā gidàjên dà mukà bar kāyammù à cikī jiyà ?

5. Yā àikē nì wurin mânyan mutànen gàrī dòmin sunà sô
   ìn yi musù màganà.

Translate into Hausa :

1. There are many schools in African countries.
2. Hausa have many chairs in their homes.
3. Certain books have fables in them.
4. There are not many cars in some countries.
5. The beggars that were here yesterday are not here
   today.

Dialogue

Sùlèmānù :   Mè a kè yî à gàrîn ?
Ishàƙù :   Ai sunà wàsā — wàsan ran kàsuwā.
Sùlèmānù :   Tò dà kyâu. Wànè irìn wàsā su kè yî ?
Ishàƙù :   Kōwànè irì. Bâ irìn dà bà zā sù yi ba.
Sùlèmānù :   Mutànē dà yawà sunà wurìn nē ?
Ishàƙù :   Sòsai ! Àkwai mazā dà mātā, yârā dà
             tsòfàffī.
Sùlèmānù :   Zā sù yàrda ìn jē ìn ganī ?
Ishàƙù :   Ai zā sù yàrɗa mànà ! Bàri mù jē tàre.
Sùlèmānù :   Tò dà kyâu. Zā kà yi rawā nè ?
Ishàƙù :   Kâi ! Nī, bā nà rawā yànzu. Nā tsūfa
             ƙwarai !
Sùlèmānù :   Tò bâ lâifī.
Ishàƙù :   Kai fà ? Zā kà gwadà wàsân ?
Sùlèmānù :   Ā'à. Nī, bàn iyà irìn nākù rawân ba.
Ishàƙù :   Tô, bàri mù tsayà mù dūbà kawài.
Sùlèmānù :   Tò dà kyâu.

Lesson 23

Adjectival Nominals ; Comparison

1. *Adjectival* nominals are distinguishable as a subclass of nominals primarily by the fact that, when they are employed as modifiers, they ordinarily precede rather than follow what they modify. Adjectival nominals (with the exception of the quantifiers—see Lesson 11) also typically have both masculine and feminine as well as plural forms.

2. It is important to recognize that adjectival nominals are true nominals, not simply adjectives called by a more technical name. There is no separate category of words in Hausa corresponding to what are termed ' adjectives ' in European languages. An adjectival nominal in Hausa is a noun which designates basically *a person or thing characterized by the particular quality indicated*—not merely the quality itself.

Adjectives in European languages cannot stand alone (with an article) as sentence subjects or objects. Sentences like the following are not correct in English :

> The big went home.
> He hit the red.

In Hausa, however, since the words which translate English adjectives are nouns and can stand alone as sentence subjects or objects, it is perfectly proper to say :

Bàbba yā tàfi gidā.	The big (one) went home.
Yā bùgi jân.	He hit the red (one).
Tsōhuwā tā dāwō.	The old (woman) has returned.
Mânyā sun zō gàrimmù.	Important (people) have come to our town.

3. The referential **-n/-r,** when employed to join two nominals, is always suffixed to the first. When the first nominal is an adjectival nominal, this means that the referential is suffixed to the modifier (the adjectival nominal) rather than to the head nominal of the phrase, e.g. :

Modifier	Head	
bàbban	gidā	the large home
dōguwar	hanyà	the long road

Note that this is a slightly different usage of the referential in Hausa ; ordinarily the **-n/-r** is suffixed to the head nominal rather than to the modifier, e.g. :

Head	Modifier	
gidan	sarkī	the home of the chief
màtar	Bellò	Bello's wife

The reason for this is that ordinary nouns (technically known as *independent nominals*) when employed as modifiers follow the noun (the head of the phrase) that they modify. Adjectival nominals ordinarily precede the noun that they modify. The referential is in either case suffixed to the first nominal.

4. The most common adjectival nominals are :

Masculine	Feminine	Plural	Meaning
bàbba	bàbba	mânyā	a big thing
ƙàramī	ƙàramā	ƙanānà	a small thing
ƙànƙanè	ƙànƙanùwā	ƙanānà	a small thing
gàjērē	gàjerìyā	gàjèrū	a short thing
dōgō	dōguwā	dōgwàyē	a tall/long thing
sābō	sābuwā	sàbàbbī	a new thing
tsōhō/tsōfō	tsōhuwā/		
	tsōfuwā	tsòfàffī	an old thing
mūgù	mūgùwā/	miyàgū/	
	mugunyà	mûggā	an evil thing

Masculine	Feminine	Plural	Meaning
jā	jā	jājàyē	a red thing
baƙī	baƙā	baƙàƙē	a black thing
farī	farā	faràrē	a white thing
kōrè	kōrìyā	kwârrā	a (light) green thing
shūdì	shūdìyā	shûdɗā	a (light) blue thing
ràwayà	ràwayà	ràwàyū	a yellow thing

5. Adjectival nominals may also be employed appositionally as modifiers. The referential -n/-r is not used in appositional constructions.

gidā bàbba   a large house (*lit.* a house, a big one)

This type of construction is, however, less common than that described in section 3 above for nearly all the adjectival nominals except the quantifiers and **ƙànƙanè :**

Yārò ƙànƙanè yā zō.   A small boy has come.
Sarkī biyu sunà nân.   Two chiefs are here.

6. A more common type of appositional modification involves the particle **mài** (*pl.* **màsu**), *possessor of...*, *characterized by...* (see Lesson 14). Many independent nominals, and even nominal and verbal phrases, may be converted into modifiers by adding **mài** as a prefix or introducer.

Yā bā mù àbinci mài dādī.   He gave us (very) good food.

Yanà dà kuɗī mài yawà (*or* **dà yawà**).   He has a lot of money.
Yā yi manà aikì mài kyâu.   He did good work for us.
Àkwai dawākī màsu girmā [1] **à wurîn.**   There are (very) large horses there.

The word **maràs** (*pl.* **maràsā**), *lacking*, is employed to introduce appositional constructions as the negative of **mài :**

[1] Only **girmā** (never **bàbba**) can be used with **mài, maràs,** or in comparison, to mean *big/large*.

Wani yārò maràs [2] **hankàlī yā zō.**	A certain senseless boy has come.
An bā mù abūbuwà maràsā àmfànī.	They have given us useless things.

Constructions introduced by **mài** and **maràs** are frequently employed independently (not as modifiers) as well :

Mài gidā bài dāwō ba tùkùn.	The head of the house has not returned yet.
Ìnā mài mōtà ?	Where is the owner/driver of the lorry ?
Bā à sôn maràs [2] **kyâu.**	No one wants a poor (quality) one.
Màsu dawākī sun dāwō.	The horsemen have returned.

7. Doubling of the colour terms indicates less intensity than the original forms. The final vowel of the colour term shortens in both occurrences.

Hannūnā yā kōmà baƙi-baƙi.	My hand has become blackish.
Wàndonsà shūɗì-shūɗì nē.	His trousers are bluish.
Fātàrsà tā zama ràwayà-ràwayà.	His skin was yellowish.

8. *Comparison* in Hausa involves the use of the verbs **fi**, *surpass*, and **kai**, *reach, arrive at*, e.g. :

A surpasses B in . . .

Bellò yā fi Mūsā girmā. [3]	Bello is bigger than Musa.

---

[2] It is common for the first consonant of the following word to replace the -s of **maràs** in pronunciation (though the -s is ordinarily written). Thus the pronunciations here would be **maràh hankàlī, maràk kyâu.**

[3] See footnote 1 on page 131.

Yārò yā fi ùbansà wàyō.	The boy is cleverer than his father.
Rìgā tā fi wàndō tsàdā.	A gown is more expensive than trousers.
Sulè yā fī sù dukà ƙarfī.	Sule is stronger than all of them.

A does not reach B in . . .

Bellò bài kai Mūsā girmā [4] ba.	Bello is not as big as Musa.
Talàkà bài kai sarkī arzìkī ba.	A peasant is not as rich as a chief.

A is the same as B in . . .

Audù yā kai ùbansà tsawō.	Audu is as tall as his father.
Wutā tā kai rānā zāfī.	Fire is as hot as sunshine.

A surpasses all in . . .

'Yarsà tā fi dukà kyâu.	His daughter is the most beautiful of all.
Jirgin samà yā fi dukà gudù.	An aeroplane is the fastest of all.
Aikìn lēbùrà yā fi dukà wùyā.	Working as a labourer is the most difficult (work) of all.

VOCABULARY

Nominals

àmfànī	usefulness
arzìkī	wealth
fātà (*f.*) (*pl.* fātōcī *or* fātū)	skin, hide
girmā	bigness
gudù	running, speed
hàƙurī	patience

[4] See footnote 1 on page 131.

jìkī	body
kàɗan	a small amount
kibiyà (f.) (pl. kibiyōyī or kìbau)	arrow
kōrè̀ (f. kōrìyā ; pl. kwârrā)	a (light) green thing
kūkā	a cry
ƙànƙanè̀ (f. ƙànƙanùwā ; pl. ƙanānà̀)	a small thing
lēbùrà̀ (pl. lēburōrī)	labourer
mahàrbī (pl. mahàrbā)	hunter
mūgù (f. mūgùwā ; pl. miyàgū)	an evil thing
ràwayà̀ (pl. ràwàyū)	a yellow thing
shāhò̀ (pl. shāhunà̀)	hawk
shūɗì (f. shūɗìyā ; pl. shûɗɗā)	a (light) blue thing
talàkà̀ (pl. talakāwā)	peasant, commoner
tsawō	length, height
tsūtsà̀ (f.) (pl. tsūtsōtsī)	worm, grub
wàyō	cleverness
'yā	daughter

Verbals

gàmu (dà)	meet (with)
ƙi	refuse, hate
sàkā (i/ē)	release
sākè̀	change, repeat
sàuka	get off, descend, land, arrive, lodge
zama	become

Particles

maràs (pl. maràsā)	lacking, without
màsu	possessors of . . ., doers of . . . (plural of mài)

Important Phrases

an jimà̀ kàɗan (or jìm kàɗan)	a little while later

EXERCISES

Translate into English :

1. Waɗansu mânyan jiràgen samà sun sàuka à Kanò.
2. Màsu nēman àbinci sun sàmi kàɗan.
3. Wannàn ƙàramin littāfì yā fi wancàn bàbba dāɗin kàràtū.
4. Kanānàn yârā sunà wàsā à gidan tsōhō.
5. Yā sâ bàbbar rìgā àmmā bài yi rawā ba.

Translate into Hausa :

1. Kano is not as big as Lagos.
2. His gown is reddish.
3. His horse is as fast as mine.
4. Many short people are seated in the hut.
5. The white ones are prettier than the black ones.

Fable

Kōwā Yanà Dà Wandà Ya Fì Shì Karfì [5]

Wata rānā wani ƙaramin tsuntsū ya kāmà tsūtsà. Zâi cî tà, sai tsūtsà ta yi kūkā, ta cè, ' sàkē nì mànà ! '

Tsuntsûn ya cè, ' Ã'à, ai zân cî kì, don nā fì kì ƙarfì.' Sai ya ɗauki ƙàramar tsūtsà, ya cî tà.

Dà ya gamà cîntà sai wani shāhò ya gan shì. Sai shāhòn ya kāmà ƙàramin tsuntsū. Zâi cî shì, sai tsuntsûn ya yi kūkā, ya cè, ' Kà yi minì hàƙurī, kà sàkē nì ! '

Shāhòn ya ƙi, ya cè, ' Ai kai nè àbincīnā yâu, don nā fì kì girmā.'

Sai shāhòn ya ci tsuntsûn dà ya ci ƙàramar tsūtsà.

Kàfìn shāhòn yà gamà cîn tsuntsûn sai gà wata mīkìyā [6] ta fāɗì à kânsà. Sai shāhòn ya fàrà kūkā, àmmā mīkìyâr bà tà sàkē shì ba dòmin tā fì shì ƙarfì.

---

[5] See *Ka Kara Karatu*, page 18, and Abraham, R. C., *Hausa Literature*, page 43, for another version of this story.

[6] A large bird of prey whose ornithological name is Ruppell's griffon.

K

An jimà kàɗan mīkìyâr ta tāshì samà. Bà tà daɗè ba
sai ta ji kibiyà à jìkintà. Àshē wani mahàrbī yā gan tà, ya
kashè ta.

Mīkìyâr tā gàmu dà wandà ya fī sù dukà ƙarfī kè nan.

Lesson 24

Adverbial Nominals and Ideophones

1. Adverbial nominals, though they regularly occur in positions occupied by nominals (and, therefore, must be classified as nominals), differ from other subclasses of nominals in several ways :

(*a*) They do not have plural forms.
(*b*) They rarely occur as subjects or objects.[1]
(*c*) They rarely end in a long vowel.
(*d*) Many adverbial nominals are derived from independent nominals (see section 2 (*b*) below).
(*e*) They cannot be preceded by **mài/màsu**.
(*f*) They do not ordinarily take the referential (**-n/-r**) suffix.[2] Modifiers of these nominals are, therefore, typically introduced by a relater (usually **dà**).

2. Adverbial nominals are divisible into two major subclasses :

(*a*) Those which are not derivable from independent nominals. Some of the more important of these words are :

bàɗi	next year	**dàban**	different
bana	this year	**daidai**	exactly
banzā	worthlessly	**dōlè**	of necessity
bàra	last year	**ɗàzu**	just now
dâ	previously	**gabàs**	east

---

[1] When they do occur as subjects they usually take *feminine* concords (see the next to last example under 2 (*a*) below).
[2] Except when followed by **nàn/nân,** e.g. **banan nàn** = *this (very) year*.

gòbe	tomorrow	ƙwarai	very much
hakà	thus	lallē	certainly
jībi	day after	nēsà	far away
	tomorrow	sànnu	slowly
jiyà	yesterday	sòsai	really
kàɗan	a small amount	tīlàs	of necessity,
kawài	only		perforce
kullum	always	yànzu	now
kusa	close	yâu	today

Bā yà sô yà yi aikì à banzā. — He doesn't want to do work that is not worthwhile *or* work for nothing

Nā kāwō wani àbù dàban. — I have brought something different.

Lìssāfìnsà bà daidai ba nè. — His arithmetic is not correct.

Zâi yàrda nè ? Ai, tīlàs nē. — Will he agree ? Why, of necessity (=he'll have to).

Yanà zuwà wurimmù kullum. — He regularly comes to (see) us.

Dà ya zō kusa mukà gan shì. — When he came close we saw him.

Lallē zâi zō. — He will come for sure/he is sure to come.

Sànnu bā tà̀ hanà zuwà. — (Going) slowly doesn't prevent (one's) arriving.

Tīlàs nē à yī shì. — It must be done.

(b) Those which are derivable from independent nominals. The majority of the nominal relaters listed and illustrated in Lesson 17, section 5, are suffixed forms of many of the same independent nominals. The adverbial nominal form is typically the same as the independent nominal form except that the final vowel is short. Sometimes there is a change of tone as well. Some of the more important of this type of adverbial nominal are :

arèwa	northwards	**kudù**	southwards
bāya	backwards	**ƙasà**	downward
cikī	inside	**nīsa**	far away
dāma	to the right	**samà**	upward
gàba	in front (of)	**wàje**	outside
hagu/hagun	to the left	**yâmma**	westward

Yā tàfi arèwa dà Kanò.	He has gone north of Kano.
Mun bi hanyàr dāma.	We followed the road to the right.
Yā fāɗì ƙasà.	He fell down to the ground.
Tsuntsū yā tāshì samà.	The bird took wing.
Sun fìta wàje.	They have gone outside.

3. Certain adverbial nominals may be intensified or made more definite by doubling, e.g. :

Dâ dâ akà ginà wannàn bangō.	A long long time ago this wall was built.
Anà yayyafī kàɗan kàɗan.	It's drizzling a (very) little bit.
Mun yi kusa kusa (*or* kurkusa) dà shī.	We got very close to him.
Kùnkurū yanà tàfiyà sànnu sànnu.	The tortoise is walking very slowly.
Zâi yī shì yànzu yànzu.	He will do it right now.
Zâi yī shì yâu yâu.	He will do it today (for sure).
Jirgin samà yā yi ƙasà ƙasà.	The aeroplane began to descend.
Yā yi samà samà.	It went right up.

4. A large number of relater phrases and stylized phrases

of other types function adverbially in Hausa. Most, but
by no means all, of these are introduced by the relater **dà**.
A few of the more common expressions of this type are :

(à hankàlī)	**Sai kà riƙè shi à hankàlī.**
	You must hold it carefully.
(an jimà)	**Zâi zō an jimà.**
	He will come after a while.
(bâ làbārì)	**Bâ làbārì ya kāmà shi.**
	Without warning he caught it.
(bâ shakkà)	**Bâ shakkà zā kà san shì.**
	Without a doubt you will know him.
(dà dàmunā)	**Anà ruwā dà yawà dà dàmunā.**
	It rains a lot in the rainy season.
(dà kyar)	**Dà kyar na fid dà shī.**
	With difficulty I got (= I hardly got) it out.
(dà ƙarfī)	**Yā yi kūkā da ƙarfī.**
	He cried loudly (*lit.* strongly).
(dà fārì)	**Dà fārì zā mù nèmi tashà.**
	First of all we will look for the station.
(dà rānī)	**Dà rānī bā à ruwā.**
	It doesn't rain during the dry season.
(dà saurī)	**Yā iyà gudù dà saurī.**
	He can run fast.
(dà wuri)	**Zō nân dà wuri.**
	Come here in good time !
(gàba ɗaya)	**Sun tāshì gàba ɗaya.**
	They left all together (and at one time).
(har yànzu)	**Bài zō ba har yànzu.**
	He still hasn't come.
(nan dà nan)	**Nan dà nan sukà gudù.**
	At once they ran (away).
(tun dà daɗèwā)	**Yanà nan tun dà daɗèwā.**
	He has been here for a long time.

(tun dà wuri)   **Nā zō tun dà wuri.**
                       I came early/in good time.
(tun dâ)   **Anà yînsà hakà tun dâ.**
                       It has been done this way from olden
                             times.

5. *Ideophones* are a large group of very specialized
particles varying widely from each other and, very
often, from all other words in the language. A given
ideophone is, typically, restricted in its usage to occurrence in quite a limited number of contexts (often as a
modifier of but a single word) :

(*a*) Ideophones modifying nominals.
    Each colour term (and many other nominals) has
    one or more ideophones which occur with the term to
    intensify what it indicates :

jà ³ wur ; jà ³ jir ; jà ³ zur	red as red can be, scarlet, blood-red
bak̃ī k̃irin ; bak̃ī sidik̃ ; bak̃ī sil	jet-black, black as pitch
farī fat ; farī kal	snow-white
kōrè shar	bright green
arèwa sak	due north
kudù sak	due south
mutànē tìnjim	people beyond number, people galore
lāfiyà lau	completely well
sābō ful	brand new
daya tak	one and only one
k̃arfè gōmà cif	exactly ten o'clock

(*b*) Ideophones modifying verbals.
    A number of ideophones are employed as verb
    modifiers. Some of these are onomatopoeic. :

³ Note that with **wur/jir/zur** the tone of **jà** drops to low.

tā sàuka jirif	it (*e.g.* a vulture) landed 'kerplunk'
yā cìka fal	it's chock full
yā ƙōnè ƙùrmus	it's completely burnt up, burnt to ashes
yi maza !	be quick !
yā yi tsit	he kept silence, kept mum
yā yi but	he suddenly 'popped out' (from hiding)
yā fitō ɓutuk	he emerged stark naked
an kullè kam	it was locked securely
sun yi jùrum	they stood despondently
kà yi farat	do (it) at once
yanà zàune sùkùkù	he's sitting despondently
sun bī sù wōhò wōhò	they followed them, booing
kà yi shirū	be quiet !, shut up !

6. Three particles of frequent occurrence which are usually labelled 'adverbs' are **wàtàkīlà/watakīlà/kīlà**, *probably, perhaps*, **tùkùn(a)**, *not yet, first*, and **ainù(n)**, *very much*.

Wàtàkīlà zâi zō gòbe.	Probably he will come tomorrow.
Bài dāwō ba tùkùn.	He hasn't returned yet.
Bàri ìn shiryà kāyānā tùkùna.	Let me prepare my loads first.
Yanà gudù dà saurī ainù.	He is running very fast.

VOCABULARY

Nominals

arèwa	northward
bangō (*pl.* **bang(w)àyē**)	wall, book cover
banzā	worthlessly, useless thing, *etc.*
dàban	different

dāma	to the right
dàmunā (f.)	rainy season
dōlè	of necessity, perforce
gabàs	east
hagu/hagun	to the left
kudù	southwards
kullum/kullun	always
kusa	close
lallē	certainly
nēsà	far away
rānī	dry season
shakkà (f.)	doubt
tashà (f.)	(railway) station
tīlàs	of necessity, perforce
wàje	outside

Verbals

cìka	become full
cikà	fill, complete, fulfil
fitar (dà)/	
fìd dà	put out, take out
hayè	cross over (*e.g.* a river)
rìkè	hold (on to), keep

Particles

ainù(n)	very much
dà kyar	with difficulty
har	to the extent that, until
maza	quickly
tun	since

EXERCISES

Translate into English :

1. Dà dàmunā wannàn kògī ya cìka fal dà ruwā.
2. Dukàmmù mukà tāshì gàba ɗaya, mukà fitar dà shī wàje.
3. Dà na gan shì sai bà làbārì ya hau dōkì, ya gudù.
4. Dâ dâ àkwai wani tsōhō wandà ya shiryà gōnarsà à bàkin wannàn hanyà.
5. Tīlàs nē sù sàmi aikì dà wuri. Zā kà bā sù ?

Translate into Hausa :

1. The tyre that I saw was brand new.
2. Run quickly and bring water.
3. She will prepare the food today for sure.
4. I want to go to my home first.
5. After a little while we will return to our homes.

Dialogue

Lawàl : Kâi, dằmunā tā yi sòsai !

Hasàn : Gàskiyarkà. Nā jē kồgī dà sāfē. Bàn iyà in hayề ba.

Lawàl : Tô, yā cìka nề ?

Hasàn : Yā cìka fal ! Har ƙarfin gudùnsà yā bā nì tsồrō.

Lawàl : Lallē àbin tsồrō nề. Yanà gudừ dà saurī ainùn.

Hasàn : Sòsai ! Har wani sā'ì zâi tàfi dà mùtûm.

Lawàl : Hakà nề. Ìdan wani yā fādì à cikī sai yà mutù.[4]

Hasàn : Sòsai ! Irìn wannàn kồgī mūgùn àbù nē.

Lawàl : Tô, yầyà zā mù yi ?

Hasàn : Ai, sai mù bi wata hanyầ dàban.[4]

Lawàl : Àmmā wata hanyầ zā tà yi nīsā. Kō bầ hakà ba ?

Hasàn : Hakà nề. Àmmā bầ wata dàbārà.

Lawàl : Gàskiyarkà. Ai dōlề nē mù bi dōguwar hanyầ kề nan.

Hasàn : Tô, mù tàfi.

---

[4] See Lesson 29, section 2, for usages of **sai** plus subjunctive.

Lesson 25

Verb Forms

1. The intricacy of the Hausa verb system is one of the more fascinating aspects of Hausa grammar. The most adequate overall classification of verbs to date is that of F. W. Parsons.[1] The major features of this system and the vast majority of Hausa verbs are organizable into seven categories (called 'Grades' by F. W. Parsons) on the basis of their terminal vowels and tone patterns.

Of these seven grades, the first three may be termed 'basic', while the remaining four may be termed 'derived'. That is, though there are several verbs which have derivative forms in more than one of the first three grades, the basic form of the majority of Hausa verbs will be either a Grade I, a Grade II or a Grade III form. From this basic form, however, may be derived up to four additional forms distinctive in both shape and meaning from the basic form. These derived forms are labelled Grades IV–VII, e.g. :

Basic Grades

	I		II		III	
	gamà [2]	tārà	sàyā	kàrɓā	shìga	sàuka

Derived Grades

IV	gamè	tārè	sayè	karɓè	shigè	saukè
V	gamar	tārar	sayar	—	shigar	saukar
VI	gamō	tārō	sayō	karɓō	shigō	saukō
VII	gàmu	tàru	sàyu	kàrɓu	shìgu	sàuku

---

[1] See his *The Verbal System in Hausa* listed in the Bibliography of which the following is a summary. We are deeply grateful to Mr. Parsons both for the privilege of incorporating his analysis here and in Lesson 37, and for his detailed amplifications and corrections of this summary.

[2] See section 2 below for the meanings of these forms.

With many verbs certain of the forms do not occur.
This is usually either because such forms would be
meaningless or because the meaning that would be
conveyed is already covered by some other word, making
such a form unnecessary.

2. The characteristic patterns of the grades are as
follows. Irregular forms and patterns of low frequency
are not dealt with :

Grade	Terminal Vowel	Tone Pattern	General Meaning
I	-ā	high-low(-high/low)	Basic : most Grade I verbs transitive, a few intransitive (**gamà**, *join together, finish* ; **tārà**, *gather together*)
II	-ā	low-high(-low)/(low-)low-high	Basic : *always* transitive (**sàyā**, *buy* ; **kàrɓā**, *receive*)
III	-a ³	low-high(-low) ³	Basic : intransitive (**shìga**, *enter (there)* ; **sàuka**, *descend*)
IV	-ē	high-low(-high/low)	Derived : most transitive, some intransitive. Signifying more complete or thorough action than basic (**tārè**, *gather all* ; **sayè**, *buy all* ; **karɓè**, *take away* ; **shigè**, *go through* ; **saukè**, *put down a load*)

³ A few Grade III verbs end in **-i** (e.g. **tàfi, gàji**) and a few have a
high-low tone pattern (e.g. **tāshì, fādì**).

Grade	Terminal Vowel	Tone Pattern	General Meaning
V	-ar	high-high(-high)	Derived : transitive (requiring **dà** before direct object). Often a causative meaning, sometimes more specialized (**gamar,** *cause to become complete* ; **sayar,** *sell* (lit. *cause to buy*) ; **shigar,** *put inside* ; **saukar,** *lower*)
VI	-ō	high-high(-high)	Derived : most transitive, some intransitive. Typically signifying action completed in vicinity of speaker (**gamō,** *finish and come*; **tārō,** *gather here* ; **sayō,** *buy and bring* ; **karɓō,** *receive and bring* ; **shigō,** *enter here* ; **saukō,** *come down*)
VII	-u	(low-)low-high	Derived : intransitive. Usually passive meaning (**gàmu,** *have met* ; **tàru,** *have gathered together* ; **sàyu,** *has been (well), bought* ; **kàrɓu,** *has been collected in full* ; **shìgu,** *be crowded* ; **sàuku,** *be comfortably settled in*)

Note that, in general, monosyllabic verbs (e.g. **ci, bi,** etc.), high-high toned verbs ending in **-ā** (e.g. **kirā, jirā, biyā**) and certain other verbs (e.g. **gudù, mutù, sanì, ganì**), including some of the commonest in the language, do not fall within this system and may, therefore, be termed irregular, though even most of these have several derived grade forms.

3. The *Grade IV* or **-ē** form has, in addition to its **-ē** termination, a high-low or falling-high tone pattern for two-syllable verbs and a high-low-high pattern for three-syllable verbs.[4] If (rarely) the verb has more than three syllables, the final two syllables are low-high and all preceding syllables high. The **-ē** forms frequently indicate more complete, extensive or thorough action than the basic form of the verb.[5] With many verbs, however, the **-ē** form has virtually replaced the basic form in common usage so that very little, if any, difference in meaning remains between the **-ē** form and the basic form of those verbs. With a great many verbs, further, the **-ā** form is transitive and the **-ē** form intransitive.

open	**būɗà**	**būɗè**	open (and leave open)
beat	**bugà/**		
	bùgā	**bugè**	knock over/out
blow	**būsà**	**būshè**	get dry
eat	**ci**	**cînyē**	eat all of
fill	**cikà**	**cikè**	fill completely
increase	**daɗà**	**daɗè**	spend a long time
pick up	**ɗaukà**	**ɗaukè**	remove (completely)
tie up,			
tie on	**ɗaurà**	**ɗaurè**	tie up, imprison
sew, make			
by sewing	**ɗinkà**	**ɗinkè**	sew up (completely)

[4] Subject to the changes noted in Lesson 15, section 9.
[5] Also often connoting excessive or destructive action.

go out	ƙita	wucè/	
		ficè [6]	pass by
chat (con-			
fidentially)	gànà	gànè	understand (completely)
rub (on)	gōgà	gōgè	rub (completely), rub off
go around	kèwàyā	kèwàyē	go around, surround
dip out	kwāsà	kwāshè	collect and remove all
increase	ƙārà	ƙārè	finish
step over	ƙētàrā	ƙētàrē	cross (*e.g.* river, road)
reduce			
(price)	ragà	ragè	reduce (anything)
cover	rufà	rufè	cover, close
buy	sàyā	sayè	buy all of
enter	shìga	shigè	pass by, (event) come and go
(basic form		warkè	recover completely
apparently lost)			(from illness)
cut up	yankà	yankè	cut off, sever
pour	zubà	zubè	spill

4. The *Grade V* or **-ar** form (often termed *causative*) also has, in addition to its **-ar** termination, all high tones. The meaning of the **-ar** form of a given verb typically indicates that the performer of the action caused the action of the verb to come about.[7] The relater **dà** is required to introduce a direct object following an **-ar** verb. When a direct object follows, therefore, the final **-r** of the verb often becomes **-d**, e.g. **ƙitad dà**. Some dialects and individual speakers regularly employ **-s** in place of the final **-r**, especially in sentence-final position, e.g. **yā sayas.**

---

[6] Note the change from **-t-** (before **-a**) to **-c-** (before **-è**). See footnote 1, Lesson 22.

[7] But there are other meanings as well, and these cannot always be readily deduced from that of the basic form of the verb (e.g. **gayar**).

eat	ci	ciyar (dà)	feed (animal)
go out	fìta	fìtar (dà)	take out, remove
tell	gayà	gayar (dà)	greet
return	kōmà	kōmar (dà)	take back (something)
lie down	kwântā	kwantar (dà)	put down, lay down
take the place of	màyā	mayar (dà)	put back, restore
dismount, descend	sàuka	saukar (dà)	set down, lower
buy	sàyā	sayar (dà)	sell
drink	shā	shāyar (dà)	water (an animal)
be sure	tabbàtā	tabbatar (dà)	confirm (a fact)
stand, stop	tsayà	tsayar (dà)	cause to stand, stop, detain
get well	warkè	warkar (dà)	heal
sit down, live	zaunà	zaunar (dà)	seat (someone), settle (people in a place)
pour, throw (away) [8]	zubà	zubar (dà)	throw away,[8] pour/ spill out

5. If an indirect object is employed, it follows the **-ar** form immediately, e.g. :

Yā fìtar minì.   He removed (it) for me.
Nā sayar masà.   I sold (it) to (or for) him.

If a direct object follows an **-ar** form (whether or not there is an indirect object), it is introduced by **dà**. If a pronoun object is employed, it takes the independent form (just as it would elsewhere after a relater).

Sun mayar dà kēkunànsù.   They returned their bicycles.

[8] I.e. a number of things simultaneously.

An zaunar dà mū.   We were (caused to) sit down/settle.

Tā kwantar dà yārò.   She laid the boy down.

If both indirect and direct objects occur, the order is verb + indirect object + **dà** + direct object,[9] e.g. :

Yā sayar minì dà mōtā.   He sold me a car.

Nā saukar masà dà kāyansà.   I set his loads down for him.

Sun shāyar manà dà shānū.   They watered the cattle for us.

Kà gayar minì dà shī.   Greet him for me.

6. Several **-ar** forms have a shortened form which is commonly employed when a direct object, but no indirect object, follows. A **-she** form may also be employed before a pronominal direct object with no following **dà**. The direct object pronouns are used with this form.

(ciyar)	Yā cī dà shī.	He fed it.
	Yā cīshē shì.	He fed it.
(fitar)	Nā fid dà yārò.	I expelled/extricated the boy.
	Nā fisshē shì.	I expelled/extricated him.
(gayar)	Mun gai dà sarkī.	We greeted the chief.
	Mun gaishē shì.	We greeted him.
(mayar)	Yā mai dà shānū.	He returned the cattle.
	Yā maishē sù.	He returned them.
(sayar)	Yā sai dà jàkinsà.	He has sold his donkey.
	Yā saishē shì.	He has sold it.
(shāyar)	Yā shā dà dōkì.	He watered the horse.
	Yā shāshē shì.	He watered it.

[9] Where the indirect object is a noun, Kano speakers frequently omit the **dà**, e.g. **yā sayar wà Audù mōtā** (rather than ... **dà mōtā**), *he sold Audu a car.*

(tsayar) **Mun tsai dà mōtà.**   We stopped the car.
          Kadà kà tsaishē nì.   Do not detain me.
(zubar)   **Sun zub dà tàkàrdū.**   They threw the papers
                                     away.

7. The longer **-ar** forms may occur with no object at all.
In this case the **dà** does not occur.[10]

Wancàn mùtûm yā kōmar.   That man returned (it).
Wancàn mùtûm yā fitar.   That man took (it) out.
Ìnā mōtàrkà ? Ai, nā sayar.   Where's your car ? Oh,
                                     I've sold (it).

8. The *Grade VI* or **-ō** form has, in addition to its **-ō**
termination (whatever the tonal pattern of the basic form
of the verb), all high tones. The meaning of the **-ō** form
of a given verb typically indicates that the action
performed had reference to, or was completed in, the
vicinity of the scene of the conversation or (in a story) the
centre of interest at the time.

send (out)	**aikà**	**aikō**	send here
pick up, take	**ɗaukà**	**ɗaukō**	pick up and bring here, fetch
(basic form apparently lost)		**dāwō**	return (here)
go out	**fita**	**fitō**	come out
go (and return)	**jē**	**zō** [11]	come
carry, convey, reach (there)	**kai**	**kāwō**	bring, reach here
catch	**kāmà**	**kāmō**	catch and bring here
return (there)	**kōmà**	**kōmō**	return (here)
seek	**nèmā**	**nēmō**	seek and bring

[10] Nor does the **dà** occur when, as in a relative clause, the object
precedes the verb, e.g. **jàkìn dà na sayar,** *the donkey that I sold.*

[11] Note the change from **j-** (before **-e**) to **z-** (before **-o**). See
Lesson 22, footnote 1.

get	sāmù	sāmō	get and bring
arrive (there), get down	sàuka	saukō	arrive (here), come down
enter (there)	shìga	shigō	enter (here)
go (away)	tàfi	tafō/ tahō	arrive, come
leave (on journey hence)	tāshì	tāsō	leave (and arrive from journey hither)

9. The *Grade VII* or **-u** form has, in addition to its **-u** termination, a low-high tone pattern (all tones low except the final syllable which is high). The meaning of the **-u** form of a verb is typically passive, often with the added connotation of thoroughness or potentiality.

fall in, collapse	aukà	àuku	happen, befall
cook	dafà	dàfu	be cooked (thoroughly)
bother	dàmā	dàmu	be worried
begin	fārà	fàru	happen
join, finish	gamà	gàmu	(people) meet
rub	gōgà	gògu	be experienced
repair (thing)	gyārà	gyàru	be repaired (completely)
put on, wear	jità	jìtu	(people) get along well
establish	kafà	kàfu	be established
increase (thing)	ƙārà	ƙàru	be increased
squeeze	matsà	màtsu	be under pressure
wind, appoint	naɗà	nàɗu	be wound, appointed,
cause to meet	sādà	sàdu	(people) meet
get, obtain	sàmā/ sāmù	sàmu	be obtainable/ available, occur
gather (*trans.*)	tārà	tàru	(group) gather (*intr.*), assemble
do, make	yi	yìwu	be possible

VOCABULARY

Nominals

àsīrī (*pl.* àsìrai)	secret
bàtun	concerning (from the noun bàtū = *conversation, matter, affair*)
hàsārà/àsārà	loss due to some unlucky incident, misfortune
kwānò (*pl.* kwānōnī)	basin, bowl, headpan, corrugated iron sheeting
ƙarfè	iron
tsàmmānì	thinking, thought
wāƙà (*f.*) (*pl.* wāƙōƙī)	song, poem, hymn
zūcìyā (*f.*) (*pl.* zūciyōyī *or* zūkàtā)	heart

Verbals

àuku	happen
bugà	beat
būshè	get dry
dàmu	be worried
gōgà	rub
gyārà	repair, fix
jìta	(people) get along well
kafà	set up, establish, erect
kēwàyē	go around, go roundabout
kwântā	lie down
kwāshè	collect and remove
ƙārè	finish
ƙētàrē	cross over
matsà	squeeze, press
naɗà	appoint (*e.g.* a chief), wind (*e.g.* a turban), fold (a cloth)
shigè	pass by (= **wucè**)

tabbàtā	be sure
tārà	gather together (*trans.*)
warkè	get well (from illness)
zubà	pour, throw (a number of things)
zubar/zub (dà)	pour (out), throw away
zubè	(something) spilled

Important Phrases

bà sù jìtu ba	they don't get along with each other/ 'hit it off'
(kà) gai dà shī!	greet him!
(kà) gayar minì dà shī	give him my greetings, remember me to him
kadà kà dàmē ni!	don't bother me!
kâr kà dàmu!	don't worry (about it)!
mè ya fàru?	what has happened?
mun sàdu dà shī	I (*lit.* we) met him
sàukad dà shī!	let it down! lay it down!
sun tàru	they (a group) have gathered
kà zub dà shi!	throw it away!

EXERCISES

Translate into English :

1. An fisshē tà dàgà aikìn.
2. Kà sayar minì dà shī don Allà.
3. Kadà kù dàmu, bâ àbîn dà ya àuku tùkùna.
4. Zùbà shi cikin kwānò. Bāyan hakà kù shāyar dà dōkì.
5. Dom mè bà zā kà fid dà àsīrinkà dàgà cikin zūcìyarkà ba?

Translate into Hausa :

1. Don't throw it away! Catch it and go inside.
2. They bought some wood and brought it back.
3. Are you sure she drank it all up? Yes, she did.

4. Put it down here. Now lay it down (flat).
5. We took it out and stood it up.

Dialogue

Ùmarù : Kā dāwō dàgà birnī ?

Bàlā :   Ĭ. Nā dāwō shēkaranjiyà dà sāfē.

Ùmarù : Tô. Àmmā nā ji wàhalà tā àuku à wurîn.

Bàlā :   Sòsai ! Kâi ! Wutā tā kāmà waɗansu gidàjē, tā
          ƙōnè su ƙùrmus !

Ùmarù : Kâi ! Mutằnē sun yi hàsārằ ƙwarai ! Kai fà ?

Bàlā :   Ai, lāfiyằ na kề. Àbîn bài zō kusa dà wurîn dà
          na kề zama ba.

Ùmarù : Mādàllā ! Dằ nā yi tsàmmānì kō wàtàkīlà tā zō
          wurinkù nē.

Bàlā :   Ā'à. Bà tà dằmē mù ba kō kàɗan. Àmmā
          waɗansu sun shā wàhalằ dà yawằ.

Ùmarù : Lallē.

Bàlā :   Ai, rân nan na gàmu dà àbōkīnā, na tàmbàyē
          shì bàtun wutâr. Ya cê, gidansù duk yā ƙōnè.

Ùmarù : Tabɗì ! Mề ka yi ?

Bàlā :   Ai, dōlè nē ìn shiryằ masà wurī à ɗākìna.

Ùmarù : Tô, àmmā mề ya fằru gà ìyālìnsà ?

Bàlā :   Ai sun sàuka à gidan wani.

Ùmarù : Mādàllā ! Sai yàushè kằmìn sù kafà sābon
          gidā ?

Bàlā :   Bà zā sù daɗè ba. Zā sù tārà kāyā sù fārà dà
          wuri.

Ùmarù : Tô dà kyâu. Allằ yà tàimàkē sù.

Bàlā :   Ằmin !

Lesson 26

The Habitual Aspect ; ' Auxiliary ' Verbs ; Exclamations

1. The habitual aspect is employed to indicate action that occurs intermittently, customarily or habitually.[1] The habitual aspect person-aspect pronouns are formed from a high-tone, short-vowel set of p-a pronouns prefixed to the particle **-kàn**. Since, however, these forms are traditionally written as two words (e.g. **na kàn,** etc.) they will be so represented here. With the verb **zō** the forms are :

I regularly come	**na kàn zō**	**mu kàn zō**	we regularly come
you (*m.*) regularly come	**ka kàn zō**	**ku kàn zō**	you (*pl.*) regularly come
you (*f.*) regularly come	**ki kàn zō**		
he regularly comes	**ya kàn zō**	**su kàn zō**	they regularly come
she regularly comes	**ta kàn zō**		
one regularly comes	**a kàn zō**		

---

[1] It must, however, be pointed out that customary or habitual activity in Hausa is more frequently expressed by employing the continuative aspects than by the use of the habitual (see also Lesson 27, section 2 (*a*)). For example, if a Hausa person wanted to say *he comes every day,* he would be more likely to say **yanà zuwà kōwàcè rānā** than to say **ya kàn zō kōwàcè rānā,** though either would be correct. Sometimes, however, a distinction is indicated by the contrast between continuative and habitual aspects, e.g. **yanà shâ** = *he is a (habitual) drinker ;* **ya kàn shâ** = *he takes a drink from time to time.*

2. This aspect, even more than the others, must often be
reinforced by the use of an adverbial nominal to indicate
the time of the action.

Dâ su kàn zō kōwànè mākò.   They used to come every
                                         week.

Su kàn zìyàrci Kanò lōtò-   They visit Kano from time
   lōtò.   to time.

3. The negative of the habitual aspect employs **bà . . . ba.**

Bà na kàn zō ba.   I don't regularly come.
Bà su kàn ci àbincimmù ba.   They don't eat our (kind
                              of) food (very often).

4. There are in Hausa a number of verbs which are often
termed *auxiliary* verbs because the meaning of the
utterance in which such verbs occur is determined not so
much by the verb itself as by that which immediately
follows the verb. Several of these are treated below.

5. The verb **rigā/rìgāyà** = *have already done* . . . (generally in the regular completive aspect) : [2]

Yā rigā yā tàfi.   He has already gone.
Nā rìgāyà nā tàmbàyē shì.   I have already asked him.
Sun rigā sun fārà.   They had already begun.

6. The verbs **rìkà** and **dingà** followed by a noun or verbal
noun = *regularly do . . ., keep on doing . .* : [3]

---

[2] Unlike the other verbs here illustrated, **rigā** is followed not by a
verbal or other noun, but by another *verb construction* in the same
aspect as itself. These two verbs are closely co-ordinated—even
to the extent that in the negative the final **ba** always comes after
the *second* verb construction which ordinarily takes a positive, *not* a
negative, p-a pronoun, e.g. **bài rigā yā tàfi ba,** *he had not yet gone*
(though **bài rigā bài tàfi ba** is also possible).

[3] They differ slightly in meaning in that **dingà** usually implies
that the thing being continued is already being done, whereas **rìkà**
may be applied to something not yet started.

Sai kà riƙà shân wannàn mãgànī.	You must regularly drink this medicine.
Yā dingà zuwà gidammù.	He kept on coming to our home.
Kadà kà riƙà cîn bāshì.	Don't always borrow (ci bāshì = incur a debt).

7. The verb taɓà, touch, followed by certain types of nouns or verbal nouns = have ever . . . :

Kā taɓà zuwà Kanò ?	Have you ever been to Kano ?
Bàn taɓà ganinsà ba.	I have never seen him.
Nā taɓà cî.	I have eaten it (at some time in the past/once or twice).

8. The verbs ƙārà, daɗà and sākè = repeat . . ., do . . . again :

Bàn sākè ganinsà ba.	I didn't see him again.
Yā ƙārà zuwà.	He came again.

9. The verbs ƙārà and daɗà = increase . . ., add . . . to :

Nā ƙārà masà kuɗī.	I increased his pay.
Yā daɗà ƙòƙarī.	He tried harder.

10. The verbs cikà and fayè = be full of . . ., be characterized by . . . :

Yā cikà kàràmbànī.	He's extremely meddlesome, a big nuisance.
Àbîn yā fayè minì wùyā.	The thing was too difficult for me.
Bàn cikà sô ba.	I don't really like (it).

11. The verb iyà = be able to do . . . :

Yā iyà Hausā.	He can speak Hausa well.
Yanà iyà aikìn.	He can do the work.
Bà zân iyà zuwà ba.	I won't be able to come.

12. The verb **yi,** *do,* may be translated in a variety of ways according to what follows (or precedes) it, e.g. :

Yā yi aikì mài kyâu.	He did good work.
An yi ruwā.	It (has) rained.
Yā yi girmā.	He's big. *Or* He grew up.
Mun yi yāwò.	We wandered about.
Àbinci yā yi.	The food is ready.
Yā yi ƙaryā.	He lied.
Yā yi barcī.	He slept.
Nā yi masà màganà.[4]	I talked to him (about a specific topic).

13. Hausa, like other languages, has its share of exclamatory utterances. These expressions are usually specialized particles, though certain nominals, verbals and stylized phrases may also be employed as exclamations. The following exclamations have already been introduced :

Particles :

ā'à	no	Lesson 13
ai	why!, well!	Lesson 18
àlbarkà	no sale !	Lesson 15
àmin	may it be so, amen	Lesson 4
àshē	well !, is that so ?	Lesson 20
habà	nonsense, come now !	Lesson 15
ī	yes	Lesson 13
mādàllā	fine, praise God !	Lesson 4
mànà	indeed	Lesson 19
tabɗì	(utter amazement)	Lesson 25 (Dialogue)
tô/tò	well, okay	Lesson 4
yâuwā/yâuwa	fine, okay	Lesson 4

Nominals :

kâi	wow ! Good Heavens !	Lesson 11
sànnu	greetings !	Lesson 4

[4] Note that the **-i** of **yi** does not lengthen before an indirect object.

Verbal :

bābù	no ! (emphatically)	Lessons 4, 13

Phrases :

don Allà	please	Lesson 25
shī kè nan	that's that !	Lesson 6

14. Several additional exclamations to listen for and learn to use are listed below. There are many more. Though it is very difficult adequately to illustrate in writing the usage of exclamations, it is hoped that the examples below will be found helpful.

a'a	exclamation of (real or feigned) amazement
a'àhā	expression of concern at hearing of misfortune
af/ap	expression of surprised recognition
allà ?	really ?
allà	it is true (reply to **allà ?**)
m'm̀	expression of sympathetic concern
na'àm	expression of interest or agreement (*e.g.* in a story or account which is being narrated)
nà'am	yes ? (in reply to one's name being called)
wâyyô	(exclamation of despair), alas !
wâyyô Allà	alas !
wâyyô nī	woe is me !

Examples :

(**a'a**) After the tortoise has made the statement to the hare that he can outrun him in a race, the hare might reply :

> **A'a ! Kai, zā kà cī nì dà gudù ? Habà !** The thought of it ! You, you will beat me in a race ? Nonsense !

(a'àhà)   In the dialogue in Lesson 25 where **Ùmarù**
           used the comparatively neutral **tabdì** to
           express his amazement he might alternatively
           have used **a'àhā,** since the subject of the
           discussion was a misfortune.

(af/ap)   When two visitors come to the home of some-
           one who knows one of the visitors well and
           the second of them less well, the householder
           and the visitor he knows well will commonly
           exchange greetings between themselves only,
           at first. Then the householder will typically
           turn to the second visitor (whom we will call
           Bello) with feigned surprise (as if he had not
           seen him standing there until this moment)
           saying :

           Af Bellò ! Kā zō nè ? Barkà dà zuwà. Why,
           Bello ! Have you come (too) ? Greetings
           at (your) coming.

(allà)   If a person relates a remarkable incident, it is
           very common for either of the two following
           exchanges to take place :

           Person A : **Allà ?**   Did that really
                                        happen ?
           Person B : **Allà (kùwā)** Every word of it is
                                        true.
           Or

           Person A : **Hakà nē ?** *Or* **Gàskiyā nè ?** Is
                        it a fact ?
           Person B : **Allà.** It certainly is.

(m'ṁ)   If a story is being related in which someone
           gets into difficulty (usually, though not
           necessarily, minor), it would be common for
           a listener to express his concern by the use of
           this particle.

(na'àm) As a longish story (such as a fable) is being narrated by one person, it is appropriate for the listener(s) fairly frequently to interject a casual **na'àm** (*or* **tô**) to signal to the narrator continued interest in and/or agreement with what he is saying.

(nà'am) If a person is called by name, he will commonly answer by using this particle, e.g. :

Audù :	**Mammàn !**	Mamman !
Mammàn :	**Nà'am ?**	What ?, Yes ?
Audù :	**Zō nân !**	Come here !

(wâyyô) This cry of utter despair is reserved for real emergencies. One Hausa fable relates the story of a careless fisherman casting his hook too near to other people and before long hooking the ear of one of the others. This situation seemed appropriate for the story-teller to put the exclamation **wâyyô Allà** in the mouth of the unfortunate person who had been hooked. See the fable at the end of this lesson for another illustration.

VOCABULARY

Nominals

allà	it is true, is it true ?
bāshì	debt, loan
ganī	seeing (verbal noun of **ganī**, *see*)
jàkā (*f.*)	
(*pl.* **jakunkunà**)	(small) bag, ₦200
kàràmbànī	nuisance/putting one's nose in some-one else's business
ƙaryā (*f.*)	a lie
lōtò	time (= **lōkàcī**)
mafàshī	
(*pl.* **mafàsā**)	highway robber

mākò   week (= sātī)
sā'à (pl. sā'ō'ī)   luck, good fortune ; time, hour
sabò dà/sabòdà   because of
sātī   week (= mākò)
zìyārà   visiting, a visit

Verbals   *Particles*

daɗà	repeat ..., do ... again	a'a	(exclamation of amazement)
dingà	keep on doing ...	a'àhā	(exclamation of concern over misfortune)
fāɗà	fall upon, fall into (*cf.* fāɗì)	af/ap	(exclamation of surprised recognition)
fayè	be characterized by ...		
rigā/rìgāyà	have already done ...	dai	(emphasis particle), on the other hand, for my part
rìƙà	keep on doing ..., do regularly and repeatedly		
		m'ṁ	(exclamation of sympathetic concern)
taɓà	touch ; have ever ...	na'àm	(exclamation of interest or agreement)
zìyartà (i/ē)	visit		
		nà'am	(reply to a call), yes ?, what ?
		wâyyô̂	(exclamation of despair), alas !

Important Phrases

Allà yà bā mù ...   may God give us ...
Allà yà sâ   may God bring (it) about
baƙin dājì   forest (*lit.* dark bushland)
ci bāshì   incur a debt
ɗuk dà hakà   in spite of this, nevertheless, yet

| lōtò-lōtò | from time to time |
| zūrà dà gudù | break into a run |

EXERCISES

Translate into English :

1. Allà yà sã mù yi sā'à cikin cìnikimmù. In bà hakà ba dōlè nè mù ci bāshì.
2. Bàri ìn daɗà ƙòƙarīnā cikin aikìn nân. Af, bà kà gàji ba ? Bà zā kà barì ba tùkùna ?
3. Bàn taɓà ganin irìn wannàn rawâr ba. Bàri ìn gwadà yîntà. A'a ! Kâi, bà zā kà iyà ba !
4. Nā yi màganà dà shī mākòn dà ya wucè àmmā bài ƙārà zuwà sātin nàn ba.
5. Dã a kàn hau dōkì àmmā yànzu an fi sôn mōtà. Allà ? Allà kùwā.

Translate into Hausa :

1. I visited the chief's home but he had already gone away.
2. Gosh !, that man is a terrible liar (*translate*, is full of lying) ! Because of this I don't like him.
3. It rains a lot during the rainy season. That's so.
4. He hasn't been in Nigeria long but he speaks Hausa fluently (*translate*, like a Kano donkey).
5. I want to take out a loan in order to buy a new car.

Fable

Audù dà Àlī [5]

Audù dà Àlī sunà cikin tàfiyà. Zâ su kàsuwā dà kāyā. Sai gà wani àbù à bàkin hanyà. Àlī ya ɗaukà, ya dūbà. Àshē jàkar kuɗī cè.

Sai Audù ya cê, ' Kâi, yâu mun yi sā'à.'

---

[5] See *Ka Kara Karatu*, page 12, and Abraham, R. C., *Hausa Literature*, page 41, for another version of this story.

Àlī ya cê, ' A'a ! Mū mukà yi sā'à nē ? Kō dai nī, na
yi sā'à ? '

Audù ya cê, ' Tò shī kè nan, Allà yà bā mù lāfiyà.'

Sukà cigàba dà tàfiyàrsù har sukà shìga wani bàkin
dājì. Sai waɗansu mafàsā sukà fāɗà musù. Audù dà Àlī
sukà zūrà dà gudù. Su mafàsā sukà bī sù.

An jimà sai Àlī ya gàji sabòdà nauyin kāyansà. Ya cê,
' Wâyyô. Yâu mun yi hàsārà.'

Audù ya cê, ' A'a ! Mū mukà yi hàsārà nē ? Kō dai
kai, ka yi hàsārà ? '

Lesson 27

Uses of Aspects

1. The *subjunctive aspect* has a wider variety of uses than
any other aspect in Hausa. In addition to its use to
express commands (see Lesson 12), the subjunctive is
commonly employed :

(a) In a large number of contexts that may in English be
translated by the infinitive, notably in subordinate
clauses (see also Lesson 12, section 7) :

Nā tàfi ìn gan shì.	I went to see him.
Zā sù jē sù hàrbi nāmà.	They will go to/and shoot (some) meat.
Inà sô kà zō nân.	I want you to come here.
An cê masù sù zō.	They were told to come.
Yā yàrda yà yī shì.	He agreed to do it.
Yā fi kyâu à dākàtā kàɗan.	It would be better to wait a little.
Yā yìwu à biyā kà gòbe ?	Is it possible to pay you tomorrow ?
Inà jirànsà yà dāwō.	I'm waiting for him to return.

(b) In many contexts that may be translated by ' in
order to ' (see also some of the examples above) or,
negatively (with kadà), ' lest ' :

Yā zō (don) yà tàimàkē mù.	He came (in order) to help us.
Sun gudù (don) kadà à kāmà su.	They ran so that they would not be caught.

M

(c) In some contexts that may be translated by *that* (which does not in Hausa always require a special word) :

Munà fātā kà dāwō lāfiyà.	We hope (that) you will come back safely.
An cè manà (wai) mù dākàtā.	We were told (that) we should wait.

(d) In contexts relating to seeking, denying or assuming permission :

Tô mù jē !	Well, let's go !
În shìga kō ?	May/shall I (am I to) enter ?
Kadà kōwā yà shā wannàn.	Nobody is to drink this.

(e) Following certain relaters :

kàmìn/kàfìn, *before :*

Kàmìn ìn tāshì sun rigā sun zō.	Before I left they had already come.
Zā mù hūtà kàɗan kàmìn mù ci àbinci.	We will rest a little before we eat.

dòmin/don (see also above, section (b)), *in order to/ that :*

Yā kāwō shì dòmin ìn ganī.	He brought it so I could see it.

har, *until* (future) :

Bàri mù dākàtā nan har sù isō.	Let's wait here until they come.

Note : **har,** in contexts indicating action in the past, requires the relative completive or the regular completive p-a pronouns :

Mun dākàtā har sukà isō.	We waited till they came.

gāra/gwàmmà, *it is better that* :

Gāra mù yi hakà.   It is better that we do thus.

Dà tàfiyà̀ banzā gwàmmà à zaunà à gidā.   It is better to stay home than to travel without purpose.

saurā, *there remain (only), all but* :

Saurā mintì gōmà sù isō.   They will be here in ten minutes.

Saurā kàɗan yà fāɗì.   He nearly fell.

(*f*) Ìn ji ... (lit. *let me hear*) is a stylized expression employing the subjunctive which means ... *says* or *according to* ... : [1]

Zâi zō gòbe, ìn ji Audù.   He will come tomorrow, according to Audu.

Ìn ji wà ?   Who says so ?

Kadà kà sākè zuwà̀, ìn ji sarkī.   The chief says don't come again.

(*g*) In an utterance describing future (or habitual) action and involving several predicate constructions, only the first verb need be preceded by the future (or habitual) p-a pronouns—the remaining predicates are typically subjunctive (see also Lesson 16, section 4) :

Gòbe Mālàm Ūsmân dà Mìnistà̀ na Ilmì zā sù tàfi Sakkwato, sù būɗè makarantar 'yam mātā, sù zìyàrci asìbitì, sù dāwō Gùsau, sù bā dà laccà̀ dà yâmmā.

---

[1] Ìn ji is also used whenever the verb *says/said* comes at the end of, or in the middle of, a quotation. Cề, *say*, cannot be used in such positions. See paragraph 4, line 1, of the fable at the end of this Lesson for an example.

Tomorrow Mr. Usman and the Minister of Education
will go to Sokoto, (will) open a girls' school, (will)
visit a hospital, (will) return to Gusau, (and will) give
a (political) speech in the evening.

2. The *continuative aspect*, in addition to expressing
simple continuative action (see Lesson 18), has the
following more specialized uses :

(*a*) The continuative is employed to express customary
or habitual action, natural abilities or disabilities,
and the like :

Yanà zuwà kōwàcè rānā.	He comes every day.
Bā yà aikì sòsai.	(It is characteristic of him that) he doesn't work hard.
Àladè bā yà tāshì.	Pigs can't fly.

(*b*) The continuative is often employed in a subordinate
clause after a main clause employing a completive or
continuative aspect to indicate an action occurring
simultaneously with the action of the main clause :

Nā gan shì yanà aikì.	I saw him working.
Yā tāshì inà barcī.	He got up (while) I was (still) asleep.
Munà zuwà yanà ganimmù.	(As) we were coming he watched us.
Inà aikì yanà ta sùrūtù.	(As) I worked he chattered foolishly.
Yā dadè yanà aikì.	He has been working for a long time.

3. The *future aspects* and the specialized verbal **zâ,** in
addition to expressing simple future action (Lesson 16),
are frequently employed to express :

(a) Intent :

Dà zuwànsà zâi yi màganà sai . . .	When he arrived he intended to say something but . . .
Mwâ zō.	We intend to come.
Dâ zâ ni gidā . . .	I had originally planned to go home . . ., I *was* going home (but . . .).
Dâ mā zân kōmà, . . .	I was planning all along to return . . .

(b) To be about to :

Zâ shi Ingìlà sai ùbansà ya mutù.	He was about to leave for England when his father died.
Dà na shiryà, zân hau kèkēnā, gà shi bābù iskà.	When I was ready, (and) was about to climb on to my bicycle, why! there was no air (in the tyre).

(c) Conditional action :

Bàn sàmi wandà zâi yī shì ba.	I didn't find anyone who would do it/to do it.[2]
Dà yā nūnà minì dà zân sàyā.	Had he showed (it) to me I would have bought (it).

4. The *completive aspect* may be employed within a sequence of relative completive clauses to express a more remote past (the English pluperfect) than that indicated by the relative completive predicates :

Dà sukà shiryà sukà tàfi. Màkānīkì yā gyārà masù mōtàrsù.

---

² Another meaning could be ' I didn't find the (particular) man who was going to do it '.

When they had got ready they left. The mechanic had (previously) repaired their lorry for them.

Sā'àn dà mātā sukà dāwō dàgà kàsuwā, ya tàmbàyē tà, ya cê, ' Yàyà cìnikī ? Yā yi kyâu ? ' Sai ta amsà, ' Yā yi kyâu.'

When the women returned from market, he asked her, he said ' How was the trading ? Did (completive) it go well ? ' Then she answered, ' It went (completive) well.'

Nominals

asìbitì (*pl.* asibitōcī)	hospital
cêwā	saying (verbal noun of cê)
dabbà (*f.*) (*pl.* dabbōbī)	animal
dàriyā (*f.*)	laughter
fādà	chief's residence
fiffìkè (*pl.* fìkàfìkai)	wing
hakōrī (*pl.* hakòrā)	tooth
hannū (*pl.* hannàyē)	arm (including hand), hand
hàrājì	tax
ilmì, ilìmī	knowledge, book-learning
iskà (*f.* or *m.*) [3]	wind, air
jēmāgè (*pl.* jèmàgū)	fruitbat
kàshègàrī	on the following day
laccà	political speech, lecture
màkānīkì (*pl.* màkànìkai)	mechanic
màmā	breast, mother, mother's milk
mìnistà (*pl.* ministōcī)	minister (of government)
ōfìs/ōfishī (*pl.* ōfisōshī)	office
râi (*pl.* rāyukà)	life
saurā	remainder
sùrūtù	(senseless) chatter

---

[3] The plural **iskōkī** means (*evil*) *spirits*.

tùnằnī	reflecting, thinking
tsakằ/tsakiyằ (*f.*)	centre
tsàkānī	between
wàkīlì	representative

Verbals

amsằ	answer
haifù (i/ē)	give birth to
hàrɓā (i/ē)	shoot
isō	arrive (here)
kàrɓā (i/ē)	receive, accept
kirā	call, summon
ƙyālề	not bother with, ignore
saurā	be left over, remain

Particles

gāra	it is better that
gwằmmà	it is better that
mā	(emphasis particle), even, too, actually
wai	quote, they say

Important Phrases

dâ mā	it has been planned that, it is well known that, already
ìn ji . . .	. . . says, according to . . .
kuɗin ƙasā	taxes (*lit.* money for the land)
nan dà nan	immediately
rânkà yà daɗề [4]	may you live long ! (said to a chief or other social superior)
tsakàr-tsàkānī	betwixt and between
yā fi kyâu (plus subjunctive)	it is better/best (that . . .)
yanằ ta . . .	he continuously . . .

---

[4] Often heard as **rânkài daɗề**.

EXERCISES

Translate into English :

1. Dâ mā zâ ni gidansà ìn gaishē shì, sai na ji làbārì, na cê, yā fi kyâu ìn gayà masà.
2. Kàmìn yà fārà zuwà nā daɗè inà aikì à nân.
3. Dà na sàmē shì, nan dà nan sai ya zūrà dà gudù.
4. Àbincimmù yā ƙārè nē ? Ā'à, dà ⁵ saurā kàɗan. Kanà sô ìn dafà wani ? ⁶
5. Mìnistàn Màkàràntū zâi yi laccà à Gùsau ? Ī, bàri mù shiryà, mù jē.

Translate into Hausa :

1. Certain highway robbers wanted me to tell them the news of the town.
2. I came upon him while he was working. He is a mechanic. He has been repairing automobiles for a long time.
3. Originally he had agreed to wait here until I came, but now I don't know what ⁷ he will do.
4. The chief says don't ever come to his home again. It is better that you meet him at his office.
5. He can speak Hausa, but it is very difficult for him.

Fable

Jēmāgè Bā Yà Biyàn Hàrājì ⁸

Wata rānā sarkin dabbōbī ya kirā wàkīlìnsà, ya cê masà, ' kà kēwàyē cikin ƙasātā kà jē gidàjen dabbōbī dukà kà kàrɓi kuɗin ƙasà à hannun kōwànnensù.'

Wàkīlì ya cê, ' Rânkà yà daɗè, nâ yi nan dà nan.'

----

⁵ In this context **dà** = **àkwai** (see Lesson 37, section 3).
⁶ In contexts such as this **wani** means *some more*.
⁷ Translate *what* as *the thing which* (**àbîn dà . . .**).
⁸ See *Littafi Na Karantawa*, page 8, for another version of this story.

Sai wàkīlì ya kēwàyē cikin ƙasâr, ya kàrɓi hàrājì à kōwànè gidā. Àmmā dà ya isō gidan jēmāgè, jēmāgè ya ƙi biyàn kuɗîn.

'Ai, nī bà dabbà ba cè,' ìn ji jēmāgè. 'Kō cikin talakāwan sarkin dabbōbī àkwai mài fìkàfìkai kàmar nī? Àkwai wandà ya iyà tāshì samà kàmar nī? Ai, bā nà biyàn hàrājì gà sarkin dabbōbī!'

Shī kè nan. Wàkīlìn sarkin dabbōbī ya bar shì, ya kōmà fādà, ya shâidā wà sarkinsù. Sarkī dai, ya yi tùnànī, ya cè, 'Lallē, gàskiyarsà. Jēmāgè bà irìmmù ba nè, à ƙyālè shi.'

Kàshēgàrī sarkin tsuntsàyē ya kirā nāsà wàkīlì, ya àikē shì yà kàrɓi kuɗin ƙasā à hannun kōwànè tsuntsū. Dà wàkīlìn ya isō gidan jēmāgè, ya tàmbàyē shì kuɗin ƙasā, sai jēmāgè ya yi masà dàriyā, yanà cêwā, 'Nī, bā nà biyànsà hàrājì.'

Wai, 'Kō kā taɓà ganin tsuntsū mài haƙòrā?' 'Kō wandà ya kàn hàifi 'yā'yansà dà râi, yà bā sù màmā? Kâi! Nī bà talàkàn sarkin tsuntsàyē ba nè!'

Dà wàkīlìn ya kōmà fādà ya shâidā wà sarkin tsuntsàyē, sai sukà yàrda cêwā jēmāgè bà tsuntsū ba nè.

Sabòdà hakà jēmāgè yanà tsakàr-tsàkānī, bā yà cikin dabbōbī, bā yà, kùwā, cikin tsuntsàyē.

Lesson 28

Reduplication

1. Hausa employs various types of reduplication for various purposes. Sometimes only a syllable is reduplicated, sometimes the whole word. Examples of the most frequent types of reduplication follow.

2. Reduplication of the first syllable of a *verb* gives it an *intensive meaning* (e.g. *keep on . . ., do . . . time after time, do . . . in succession*). Typically, the first syllable is reduplicated with accompanying duplication of the initial consonant of the original verb (which has now become the first consonant of the second syllable). If the original first syllable has a final consonant, it may remain or may be assimilated as a doubled consonant.[1] The great majority of reduplicated verbs have at least three syllables and their tones follow the regular patterns for three- and four-syllable verbs. Thus :

(*a*) High-low verbs become high-low-high :

beat	**bugà**	**bubbùgā**	keep on beating
cook	**dafà**	**daddàfā**	keep on cooking
look	**dūbà**	**duddūbā**	look everywhere

(*b*) Low-high verbs [2] become low-high-low :

go out	**fìta**	**fìffìtà**	keep going out

[1] When, for example, the first syllable ends in a nasal, assimilation does not take place, e.g. **tàntàmbayà** (not **tàttàmbayà**), and it is optional where the first syllable ends in some other consonants, e.g. **fìffìtà** or **fìrfìtà**, **sàssayà** or **sàisayà**, **kakkāwō** or **kankāwō**.

[2] If the base verb is a variable vowel (Grade II) verb, the derived intensive verb will also be a *v.v.* verb. Thus the rules for final vowel and tone change before direct objects (as well as all other *v.v.* verb rules) apply, e.g. **sun nànnĕmi shānunsù, sun nànnĕmē sù,** *they looked all over for their cattle/them.*

look for	nēmā	nànnēmà [3]	look all over for
buy	sàyā	sàssayà	buy a variety of things

(c) Verbs with all tones high remain all high :

bring	kāwō	kakkāwō	keep on bringing
call	kirā	kikkirā	call various people
sell	sayar	sassayar	keep on selling

(d) Three-syllable verbs [4] merely reduplicate the first syllable (tone and all) [5] while retaining the original tone pattern on the original three syllables :

read	karàntā	kakkaràntā	read in succession
ask	tàmbayà	tàntàmbayà	keep on asking

3. An *adjectival nominal* may be formed from most transitive and certain intransitive verbs by reduplicating and doubling the final consonant of the original word, while replacing the final vowel with an -aCCē suffix (CC = doubled final consonant of the original word). The meaning of such a form is typically *something which has been . . ., something characterized by. . . .* These, like other adjectival nominals, have feminine as well as plural forms (the examples below list the forms in the order : masculine, feminine, plural).

(a) These forms *derived from two-syllable words* have the initial syllable low toned, with all following syllables

---

[3] When the original verb has an -ē- or an -ō- in the root, this becomes -a- in the reduplicate syllable, if this -ē- or -ō- is preceded by a *velar* consonant (**k, g, k̃**), it becomes -ya- and -wa- respectively, e.g. **kḕtà**, *tear*, **kyakkḕtā**, *tear to shreds* ; **gōgā**, *rub (against)*, **gwàggōgà**, *rub vigorously (against)*.

[4] See footnote 2 on page 176.

[5] Some verbs, in addition to a form which shows first syllable reduplication, have an alternative form (with the same meaning) in which it is the second syllable that is reduplicated, e.g. **ajìyē**, *put down/aside→* **ar'ajìyē/a''ajìyē** or **ajìjìyē**, *put down/aside a number of things*.

high except for the plural form, in which all syllables
are low except the final one, e.g. :

(cìkà, *fill*)	cìkakkē cìkkakkiyā,[6] cìkàkkū (something) filled, complete
(dàfà, *cook*)	dàfaffē, dàfaffiyā, dàfàffū (something) cooked
(fàrà, *start*)	fàrarrē, fàrarriyā, fàràrrū · (something) started
(ganī, *see*)	gànannē, gànanniyā, gànànnū (something) seen
(màntā, *forget*)	màntaccē, màntacciyā, màntàttū (something) forgotten
(nèmā, *look for*)	nèmammē, nèmammiyā, nèmàmmū (something sought)
(sanī, *know*)	sànannē, sànanniyā, sànànnū (something) known

(b) These forms *derived from three-syllable words* have the
first two syllables low, with all following syllables
high except for the plural form, in which all syllables
are low except the final one, e.g. :

(ajìyē, *set aside*)	àjìyayyē, àjìyayyiyā,[6] àjìyàyyū (something) set aside
(fàhimtà, *understand*)	fàhìmtaccē, fàhìmtacciyā, fàhìmtàttū (something) understood
(làfiyà,[7] *health*)	làfìyayyē, làfìyayyiyā, làfìyàyyū healthy (person or thing)
(tabbàtā, *be sure*)	tàbbàtaccē, tàbbàtacciyā, tàbbàtàttū (something) certain
(tàfasà, *boil*)	tàfàsasshē, tàfàsasshiyā, tàfàsàssū (something) boiled

---

[6] There is an alternative feminine form in **-aCCà**, which is not
uncommon, especially with the longer words, e.g. **tàfàsassā**.

[7] This form is derived from a noun rather than a verb. It is
apparently the only such exception in the whole language.

Examples :

Mūjìyā sànanniyā cè à ƙasarmù.	The owl is well-known in our country.
Dàfaffen àbinci nè mu kè sô.	We want *cooked* food.
Zīnārìyā nèmammiyar àbā cè.[8]	Gold is a sought after (*i.e.* valuable thing).
Mu kàn shā tàfàssasshen ruwā kawài.	We drink only boiled water.
Tàbbàtaccē nè.	It is certain.

4. Certain *nouns indicating a quality* have a derivative adjectival nominal which is formed by reduplicating the first syllable and changing the final vowel to **-ā**. The tone pattern of the new form is low-high-high in the singular. The plural form (which duplicates the final consonant in an **-àCā** suffix) has a high-low-high pattern. The meaning is usually intensive.[9]

(ƙarfī, *strength*)	ƙàƙƙarfā, ƙarfàfā (*pl.*)	very strong thing/ person
(kyâu, *goodness*)	kyàkkyāwā, kyāwàwā (*pl.*)	excellent (looking) thing/person

Examples :

Màcè kyàkkyāwā cè.	The woman is beautiful.
Sū ƙarfàfā nè.	They are very strong.
Kyāwàwā na sàyā.	I bought very good looking ones.

5. *Adverbial nominals and ideophones* may be intensified by reduplicating the whole word (see also Lesson 24, section 3).

---

[8] Where the noun to which it refers is feminine **àbù**, *thing*, has a feminine form **àbā**. Many Hausa, however, would say **Zīnārìyā nèmammen àbù nē**.

[9] I.e. more so than a simple **mài** compound, e.g. **mài zurfī**, *deep* ; **zùzzurfā**, *very deep*.

(maza,
  quickly)   **Kù zō maza-maza !**   Come very quickly !
(shirū,   **Audù shiru-shirū**   Audu is very soft
  silence)   **nè.**   spoken.
(sànnu,   **Yanà tàfiyà sànnu-**
  slowness)   **sànnu.**   He is walking slowly.

6. Complete reduplication of *adjectival nominals* of *colour* and some others lessens their intensity (see also Lesson 23, section 7). Note that the final vowel becomes short in both the second and (with few exceptions, like **jā-ja** below) the first occurrence of the reduplicated word.[10]

(farī, *white*)   **Nā sàyi fari-fari.**   I bought the whitish one.
(bakī, *black*)   **Baki-baki yā fi kyâu.**   The blackish one is best.
(jā, *red*)   **Wannàn, jā-ja nè.**   This is reddish/pink.
     Wadànnân jājàye-   These are reddish/
     jājàye nè.   pink.
(tsōfō, *old*)   **Tsōfuwa-tsōfuwa cè.**   She is rather elderly.

7. Complete reduplication of quantifiers and monetary terms is employed to give the sense of, for example, ' two each '.[11]

Sīsì sīsì nē.   They are 5 kobos each.
Bà su gōmà gōmà.   Give them each ten.
Nawà nawà nē wadànnân ?   How much apiece are these ?
Màsu kafà hudu hudu.   Quadrupeds.

---

[10] In a few cases the vowel remains *long* and the meaning is *intensive*, e.g. **Sū mânyā-mânyā nè,** *They are very large/important (of people).*

[11] If the quantifier is a compound only the last word is repeated, e.g. **yā bā sù nairà shâ daya dà sī-sìsì,** *he gave them ₦11·6 each* ; **kudinsù sulè bâ kwabò kwabò,** *they cost nine pence apiece.*

8. The plurals of certain nouns are formed by reduplication (see also Lesson 22, section 6).

en'è, *pl.* en'è-en'è   Native Administration
àkàwū, *pl.* àkàwū-àkàwū   clerk (other plurals also occur)

9. Complete reduplication plus final -e and a low-high tone pattern is employed with many *nouns denoting an activity* to indicate (frequently) something like *varieties of . . ., various kinds of . . .* or simply *a number of instances of this kind of activity*, e.g. :

gudū̃, running → gùje-gùje, running (various types of) races
tsallē, jumping → tsàlle-tsàlle, (various kings of) jumping [11]
tādī̀, chatting → tàɗe-tàɗe, (various) chattings
shāwarà, advising → shàwàrce-shàwàrce, advisings (of various kinds).

10. Complete reduplication of *certain nouns* may be employed to indicate . . . *like.* Note that the final vowels are short.

ruwa-ruwa   watery, liquid (*i.e.* water-like)
gàri-gàri   powdery (*i.e.* flour-like)
gishiri-gishiri   salty (in taste)

VOCABULARY

Nominals
àkàwū (*pl.* akāwunà *or*
   àkàwū-àkàwū)   clerk
ɗanyē (*f.* ɗanyā, *pl.* ɗànyū)   raw, uncooked, unripe
firāmàrē   primary school

---

[12] Thus the term for *track and field competition* is gùje-gùje dà tsàlle-tsàlle.

giyà (f.)   beer (local brew)
gwangwan (pl. gwangwàyē)   tin can
jarràbâwā (f.)   test, examination
kwalabā/kwalbā (f.) (pl.
  kwalàbē)   glass bottle
kyàkkyāwā (pl. kyawàwā)   excellent (looking), hand-
                                       some, beautiful
ƙārā (f.)   .   a complaint (e.g. in court),
                                       cry, noise
ragì   reduction (as in trading)
sakandàrè   secondary school
simintì/sumuntì   cement
tàbbàtaccē   (something) certain
takàrdā (f.) (pl. tàkàrdū)   paper, letter
Tūrai   Europe
yādì   European cloth, a yard
                                       (measurement)
zīnārìyā (f.)   gold

Verbals
ajìyē   put (thing) down, set
                                       (aside), give (thing to
                                       someone else to keep for
                                       you)
fàhimtà (i/ē)   understand
tàfasà   boil (intransitive)

Particles
câ   thinking (from cêwā; see
                                       Important Phrases below)
shirū   silence (ideophone)

Important Phrases
àbin màmākì   an amazing thing
àbin shâ   something to drink, a drink
àbin shâ na kwalabā   bottled drink

bâ ragì	no reduction (of price—in trading)
bàbban àkàwū	head clerk
bā dà màmākì	cause amazement, wonder
câ na kè	I thought (*lit.* thinking I was)
ci jarràbâwā	pass an examination
nan ƙasā	(in) this country
yi jarràbâwā	take an examination

EXERCISES

Translate into English :

1. Ai, nā mântā ìn kāwō àbinci dàfaffē. Nā kāwō shì ɗanyē.
2. Gwàmmà kà dākàtā nân tùkùn. Kàfìn kà sākè dāwôwā lōkàcin àbinci yā yi.
3. Mun tàntàmbayà kō'ìnā cikin gàrī àmmā bà mù sàmi làbārìnsà ba.
4. Kâi ! Wani àbin màmākì yā faru jiyà—ƙārar jirgin samà tā bā nì tsòrō har saurā kàɗan ìn gudù !
5. Zâ ni kàntī ìn sàyi àbincin gwangwan dà giyà ta kwalabā dà sauran abūbuwàn dà na kè bùkātà.

Translate into Hausa :

1. How much apiece are guavas ? A penny apiece, no reduction.
2. I thought you would come tomorrow but you came yesterday.
3. There are many wonderful things in the world today.
4. You should eat cooked food and boiled water lest you get ill.
5. If I don't take the examination I won't pass it.

Dialogue
Talle :   Daudà !
Daudà :   Nà'am.

Talle :   Ìnā zâ ka ?
Daudà :   Zâ ni gidā. Yànzu nè na tāsō dàgà aikì.
Talle :   Tồ bâ lâifī. À inā nè ka kề aikì ?
Daudà :   Ai, nī àkàwū nè à kàntī.
Talle :   Àshē ? Câ na kề kanà makarantā.
Daudà :   Â'à. Bàra nè na fìta firāmàrề. Bàn sàmi shìgar
           sakandàrề ba.
Talle :   Bà kà ci jarràbâwā ba nè ?
Daudà :   Ī, tā yi minì wùyā ainùn. Àmmā bâ kōmē, tun
           dà na sàmi aikì.
Talle :   Tồ dà kyâu. Wànề irìn aikì nē ka kề yî ?
Daudà :   Ai, inà dà ayyukà irì-irì : wani sā'ì na kàn
           shisshìryà kāyā, wani sā'ì na kàn sayad dà kāyā,
           wani sā'ì mā, bàbban àkàwū yanà bā nì aikìn
           takàrdā ìn yi.
Talle :   Tồ. Yawancin kāyankù dàgà ƙasàshen Tūrai nè
           a kề kāwō sù ?
Daudà :   Ī. Àmmā yànzu an fārà yîn waɗansu abūbuwà
           nan ƙasā—kàmar su tākalmà, dà yādì, dà
           simintì, dà àbin shâ na kwalabā.
Talle :   Mādàllā ! Gàskiyā nề sai dà tàfàsasshen ruwā
           a kề yîn àbin shâ na kwalabā ?
Daudà :   Sồsai ! Bà kàmar irìn tāmù giyàr ba !
Talle :   Àbincin gwangwan fà—dukànsà dàfaffē nè ?
Daudà :   Hakà nē. Wai, sā'àn dà a kề shirìnsà anà
           daddàfâwā.[13]
Talle :   Tabdì. Àbin màmākì nē yaddà ya yìwu à dafà
           àbinci dà yawà à rufề shi cikin gwangwan à
           ajìyē shi har shềkarà bìyar !
Daudà :   Gàskiyarkà. Ai, hakà nē dūniyà yànzu—cìke
           ta kề dà abūbuwà màsu ban [14] màmākì.
Talle :   Lallē, hakà nē.

---

[13] Verbal noun from **daddàfā**.
[14] See Lesson 19, footnote 2.

Lesson 29

The Relaters Sai and Dà

1. The relaters **sai** and **dà** (the spelling of which actually represents several different words) are among the most frequently occurring words in the Hausa language. They each have a wide variety of usages, the more important of which, not already noted in Lesson 17, section 2, are treated below.

2. **Sai** as a clause introducer is often followed by the subjunctive aspect. There are two kinds of meaning indicated by this construction :

(*a*) The weaker (and more common) meaning is to indicate a regular contingent habit or an inevitable contingent consequence, e.g. : [1]

In nā tāshì dà sāfē sai ìn shā tî	When I get up in the morning I (always) have a cup of tea.
In bà kà bâ ganyên nan ruwā ba, sai yà mutù	If you don't water that plant, it will surely die.
Ìdan yā zō, sai mù gaishē shì.	When(ever) he comes we will (certainly) greet him.

(*b*) The stronger meaning, often limited to shorter contexts, is as a strong command, typically meaning *must*, *ought to* or the like, e.g. :

Sai kà tàfi.	You ought to go, *or* Get away !

[1] See Lesson 24, dialogue (footnoted phrases), for two additional examples.

Bài zō ba tùkùna. Sai mù   He hasn't come yet. We'll
  kirā shì.   have to call him.

3. Stylized utterances such as **sai kà cê,** *as if,* and (less
frequently) **sai kà ganī,** *you ought to see it,* are frequently
interjected for emphasis.

Yanà tàfiyà, sai kà cê sarkī.   He goes around as if he
                                                              were a chief.

Aikìnsà, sai kà cê bài iyà ba.   His work (is) as if he
                                                              doesn't know how.

Wannàn àbù, sai kà ganī,   This thing—you'll have to
  àbin màmākì nē.   see it (to believe it)—is
                                                              really amazing.

4. **Sai** often introduces a nominal phrase which indicates
an exception to the preceding statement. (See also
Lesson 17, section 2.)

Bâ mài iyàwā sai kai.   There is none able to do it
                                                              except you.

Bā à sāmùn ilmì sai dà   One doesn't get knowledge
  ƙòƙarī.   without (a lot of) effort.

Nī kàm, sai àbîn dà ka cê.   As for me (I'll do) only
                                                              what you say.

5. **Sai** meaning *until* often introduces clauses in the completive, sometimes in the continuative.[2]

Bà zân tàfi ba sai nā gamà.   I won't go until I finish.

Bà zân tàfi ba sai inà sôn   I won't go until I want to
  tàfiyà.   go.

Sai kā dāwō.   See you when (*lit.* until) you
                                                              return.

[2] Quite often, though not invariably, the **sai**-introduced clause is
a dependent clause following an independent clause in the negative
(see the first two examples).

Sai nā shiryà tùkùna.   (Don't bother me.) Let me
                              get ready first.

Sai yā zō zā mù ci.   We won't eat until he
                              comes (*lit.* Only when he
                              has come will we eat).

6. **Sai** and **har** each often mean *until*. When, as often, a contrast is intended, **har** focuses on the completion or fulfilment of the action at the end of the prescribed time, whereas **sai** may simply refer to the action in general or focus on the start of it, e.g. :

Bà zân tàfi ba sai gòbe.   I won't go until tomorrow.

Bà zân tàfi ba har gòbe.   I won't go (at least) until
                                tomorrow (has come).

**Bàn yi barcī ba sai dà gàrī   I didn't get to sleep until
ya wāyè.**   dawn.

**Bàn yi barcī ba har gàrī ya   I didn't get a wink of sleep
wāyè.**   all night.

7. **Sai** is frequent in narrative as a clause (sentence) introducer indicating sequence and translatable as *then* or *so*. (See also Lesson 17, section 4.)

Mun gan shì nan dà nan. Sai mukà gaishē shì.
We saw him immediately. Then/so we greeted him.

Sun zō. Sai sukà zaunà. Sai sukà hūtà sòsai.
They came. (Then) they sat down. (Then) they rested well.

8. **Dà . . . sai** is commonly used for *when . . . then*, with reference to events in the past.

**Dà na gan shì (sai) nā jē   When I saw him (then) I
wurinsà.**   went to him.

Dà zuwànsà [3] **sai aikì.**   When he comes (then)
                                (there's a lot of) work.

[3] **Dà zuwànsà**, lit. *on his coming.* A verbal noun may usually be substituted for a finite verb in this construction.

Dà ya shìga (sai) mukà   When he entered (then) we
    tsayà.   stopped.

9. **Dà** meaning *with* or *and* is amply illustrated in Lesson
17, sections 2 and 3. The use of **dà** as introducer of the
direct object after the **-ar** form of a verb is treated in
Lesson 25, section 4 and following. **Dà** meaning *when* is
illustrated above. **Dà** as introducer of the thing possessed
after the continuative is illustrated in Lesson 18,
sections 5 and 6.

10. **Dà** (or **wandà**) is employed to introduce relative
clauses. It may mean *that, whom,* etc. (See also Lesson 20,
sections 5 and 6.)

àbîn dà na ganī   the thing that I see
lōkàcîn dà zâi tàfi   when (= the time that) he
                                                 will go
an kòri mùtumìn dà akà   they chased away the man
    aikō   that was sent
yārò wandà bâ shi dà
    hankàlī   a boy who has no sense

11. **Dà** is employed as an auxiliary with certain other
relaters.

Tun dà bài bā mù ba bâ   Since he didn't give it to us
    kōmē.   it doesn't matter.
Kō dà bài gan mù ba munà   (Even) though he didn't see
    wurîn.   us, we were there.

VOCABULARY

Nominals
àgōgō (*pl.* **agōgunà**)   watch, clock
àlāmà/hàlāmà (*f.*) (*pl.*
    àlàmū, alāmōmī)   indication, sign
àlkalàmī (*pl.* **alkalumà**)   pen

àlmakàshī (*pl.* àlmàkàsai)	(pair of) scissors
awà (*f.*)	hour
bukkà (*f.*) (*pl.* bukkōkī)	grass hut ; market stall
cìyāwà (*f.*) (*pl.* cìyàyī)	grass
dinkì	sewing
hūtū	vacation, rest
kàkī	khaki cloth
kirkì	excellence of character or quality
madìnkī (*pl.* madìnkā)	tailor
sàna'à (*f.*) (*pl.* sana'ō'ī)	trade, occupation, profession
tufāfì (*sing.* tufà)	garments, clothes
wàhalà (*f.*)	trouble, difficulty
wàndō (*pl.* wandunà)	trousers

Verbals

dinkà	sew, make by sewing
hanà [4]	prevent, hinder, keep from, refuse, forbid
jirā	wait for
kau/kawad (dà)	move to another place, alter position of
nūnà [5]	point out, show
tàimakà (i/ē)	help, assist
yankà	cut (up), slaughter

Particles

| kàm | (emphasis particle) at least, at any rate, as for . . . |

---

[4] Typical examples of the way **hanà** is employed are : **yā hanà ni/minì aikì** = *he kept me from working* or *he kept me from getting a job ;* **kadà kà hanà masà àbinci** = *don't refuse him food ;* **an hanà shân giyà** = *beer drinking is proscribed.*

[5] An indirect object is very frequent with **nūnà**, e.g. **yā nūnà minì** = *he showed me ;* **nā nūnà masà hanyà** = *I showed him the road ;* **tā nūnà wà yārò àbincinsà** = *she showed the boy his food ;* but **yā nūnà ƙarfinsà** = *he showed his strength.*

wàtò   that is, . . . (the preceding
                                statement is then re-
                                phrased to clarify it),
                                namely, viz.

Important Phrases

kèken dinkì   sewing machine
sai kà cê   like, as if
sai kà ganī   you have to see it (to believe
                                it)
shā wàhalà   have (*lit.* drink) difficulty,
                                suffer

EXERCISES

Translate into English :

1. **Yā kàmātà ìn yankà wannàn yādì. Dàuki àlmakàshī
   kà tàimàkē nì.**
2. **Shī bà mùtumìn kirkì ba nè. Yanà sô yà hanà àbōkīnā
   aikì.**
3. **Dà ya shìga bukkàrsà sai ya zaunà, ya fārà dinkì.**
4. **Zân jirā shì. Wàtò, zân dākàtā nân sai yā dāwō.**
5. **Àkwai àlāmà zā kà shā wàhalà nân ìdan bà kà kawad
   dà kāyankà dà wuri ba.**

Translate into Hausa :

1. Sew me a good (looking) gown. I am going to the
   dance tomorrow.
2. I want you to help me to move my sewing machine to
   another stall.
3. As for me I will wait for him here—perhaps he will
   come after a while.
4. I didn't show him your watch. They say he saw it on
   your wrist (arm).
5. He hasn't eaten yet. Why ? Because I refused him
   food until you arrived.

Dialogue

Hārūnà : Sànnu maɗìnkī !

Gàmbo : Af Hārūnà ! Barkà dà yâmmā.

Hārūnà : Barkà kàdai. Ìnā aikì yâu ?

Gàmbo : Aikì, ai bā yà ƙārèwā.

Hārūnà : Mādàllā. Hakà a kè sô.

Gàmbo : Gàskiyarkà. Kanà yāwò à kàsuwā nè ?

Hārūnà : Ā'à. Dā mā inà nēman bukkàrkà.⁶

Gàmbo : Tô. Rân nan na kau dà kāyānā zuwà nân.

Hārūnà : Dà kyâu. Dā kanà cikin bukkà ta cìyāwà àmmā wannàn ta kwānò ⁷ cē.

Gàmbo : Hakà nē. Nā yi sā'à kè nan.

Hārūnà : Mādàllā. Zā kà iyà kà ɗinkà minì waɗansu tufāfī nē ?

Gàmbo : Ai sàna'àtā cè. Wànè irì nē ka kè sô ?

Hārūnà : Inà bùkātàr gàjēren wàndō gùdā biyu dà bàbbar rìgā kumā.

Gàmbo : Tô bâ lâifī. Kā zō dà yādì nē ?

Hārūnà : Ī. Gà kàkī na yîn wandunà dà farin yādì na yîn rìgā. Nawà nē kuɗin ɗinkì ?

Gàmbo : Dukà zâi kai sulè àrbà'in dà biyar—wàtò, nairà huɗu dà sulè bìyar kè nan.

Hārūnà : Kâi, yā yi yawà ! In bà kà yàrda dà nairà huɗu ba, sai in nèmi wani.

Gàmbo : Tô nā yàrda. Àjìyè yādìn cân.

Hārūnà : Dà kyâu. Sai yàushè zân zō ìn kàrɓā ?

Gàmbo : Sai gòbe ai. Bà zân iyà gamà ɗinkìnsù dukà yâu ba.

Hārūnà : Tô, sai gòbe kè nan.

Gàmbo : Yâuwā, sai gòbe.

---

⁶ The addition of **mā** to **dā** completely alters the meaning from *formerly (but no longer)* to *formerly too*, i.e. *anyway, in any case, all along.*

⁷ I.e. made of corrugated iron or aluminium roofing materials.

Lesson 30

Prefixes and Suffixes

1. Hausa employs a number of prefixes and suffixes to change basic forms of words into words with more specialized meanings. Certain prefixes and suffixes have already been described (see Lessons 25 and 28), but several others are common enough to warrant mention here.

2. **Bà-** = *place of origin, profession.*

(*a*) Certain nouns may be prefixed with **bà-** in the singular with the resultant form indicating the *place of origin* of the person referred to. The masculine forms usually end in **-ề** with initial and final low tones (all other tones high). These words have feminine and plural forms as well, as illustrated below.

(Kanồ)	Bàkanề/Bàkanồ, Bàkanùwā, Kanāwā	Kano person
(Hausā)	Bàhaushề, Bàhaushìyā, Hàusàwā	Hausa person
(Tūrai)	Bàtūrề, Bàtūrìyā, Tùràwā/Tūrāwā	European person
	Bàfàransì, Bàfàransìyā, Fàrànsâi	Frenchman
	Bàfilācề, Bàfilātà, Filằnī	Fulani person

(*b*) Other nouns may be prefixed with **bà-** in the singular to form nouns indicating the *occupation* of the person referred to. The tone rules are usually the same as those above, but the final vowel of the masculine form varies. Feminine forms are not common (nor are women who have these occupations).

	bàdūkù, dùkàwā [1]	leatherworker
(fādà, *chief's palace, court*)	bàfādà/bàfādè, fàdàwā	courtier
(sarkī, *chief*)	bàsarākè, sarākunà/ sàràkai [2]	office-holder under a chief

3. The noun ɗā, *son*, is widely used (in the form ɗan ; *f.* 'yar ; *pl.* 'yan) as a prefix (although it is written as a separate word) in the following senses :

(*a*) To indicate *place of origin* :

ɗan Kanò, 'yar Kanò, 'yan Kanò	Kano person
ɗan ƙasā, 'yan ƙasā	local inhabitant(s) of a country, son(s) of the soil

(*b*) To indicate *occupation* :

ɗan kàsuwā, 'yar kàsuwā, 'yan kàsuwā	market trader
ɗan tēbùr, etc.	petty market trader (who displays his goods on a table)

(*c*) As a *diminutive* :

ɗan yārò	little boy
'yar kàsuwā	small market
'yan kāyā	small belongings
cikin ɗan lōkàcī	in a short time

---

[1] These may have originated from a place called **Dùkù**.

[2] These plurals are also employed for **sarkī**, but there is seldom any confusion of meaning since any given town or region has only one **sarkī**.

(d) In certain *stylized expressions :*

ɗan sàndā, 'yan sàndā	Government policeman (*lit.* son of a stick)
ɗan dòkā, 'yan dòkā	N.A. (= Native or Local Authority) policeman (*lit.* son of an order)
ɗan Adàm, 'yan Adàm	human being (*lit.* son of Adam)
'yar cikī	type of gown

(e) ɗan (never 'yar or 'yan) is used with verbs (with or without kàɗan) signifying *a little (bit)* :

Nā ɗan dākàtā (kàɗan).	I waited a bit.
Yā ɗan tūrĕ shi.	He pushed it a little.
Sai kà ɗan ragè kuɗinsà.	You should lower the price a bit.

4. Various types of nouns may be formed from verbs by employing a **ma-** prefix with or without an **-ī** suffix :

(a) Nouns signifying the *agent or doer of an action* are formed by prefixing the **ma-** and (usually) suffixing an **-ī**. The tones on the masculine form are high-low for two-syllable words, high-low-(low-)high for three- and four-syllable words. Feminine (sometimes) and plural (usually) forms of these words also occur. Forms having the **-ī** (high tone) suffix take a ' referential ' **-n** before a modifying noun or pronoun, e.g. **masòyin Sāratù, masòyinkà** ; the others do not, e.g. **majì dāɗī**.

(**fi,** **mafì/mafìyī,** *pl.* **mafìyā**	
surpass) surpassing, exceeding, e.g. :	
Wannàn mafì kyâu	
nē.	This is the best one.
mafì tsàdā	more expensive

(sȯ, *want,* masȯ ³/masȯyī, masōyìyā, masȯyā
   love) one who likes or loves, e.g. :
      Masȯyinkà bā yà Your close friend
      ganin aibùnkà. doesn't see your
                          faults.
      masȯyin Sāratù one who loves Sarah
      masȯyin shìnkāfā one who likes rice

(ji, *hear,* majì/majìyī, majìyìyā, majìyā
   feel) hearer, feeler, e.g. :
      majì dādī happy person

(rasà, maràs/maràshī, marashìyā, maràsā
   lack) lacking in . . ., e.g. :
      maràshin hankàlī, senseless
      (See also Lesson 23, section 6.)

(àikā, ma'àikī, ma'àikā
   send) messenger ⁴

(aikàtā, ma'àikàcī, ma'aikacìyā, ma'àikàtā
   do work) worker

(ɗinkà, maɗìnkī, maɗinkìyā, maɗìnkā
   sew) tailor

(fâutā, *cut* mahàuci, mahàutā
   up meat) butcher, meat-seller

(haifù mahàifī, mahaifìyā, mahàifā
   give parent
   birth)

(haukàcē, mahàukàcī, mahaukacìyā, mahàukàtā
   go mad) madman

(ƙērà, maƙèrī, maƙèrā
   forge) blacksmith

---

³ The short form **masȯ** is regularly employed with the meaning
tending toward to denote the intermediate points of the compass, e.g.
arēwā masȯ gabàs = *north-east,* **kudù masȯ yâmma** = *south-west,* etc.

⁴ The meaning here is passive, i.e. one who is sent (compare
macìyī = (i) *glutton,* (ii) *dependent* (i.e. *one fed by you*)). The word is
mainly used of the Prophet in the expression **Ma'àikin Allà,** *God's
Messenger.*

(b) Nouns signifying a *place* where the activity indicated
by the original verb is performed are also formed by
prefixing **ma-**. The ending may be either **-ā** or **-ī**.
The tones on the singular form are all high.

(aunà,
  measure,
  weigh)
	ma'aunā, mà'àunai	place where corn is
		sold

(ajìyē, *set* *aside*)	ma'ajī, mà'àjìyai	storehouse
(dafà, *cook*)	madafā/madafī, màdàfai	kitchen, cooking- place
(fàutā, *cut* *up meat*)	mahautā, màhàutai	place where meat is sold
(karàntā, *read*)	makarantā, màkàràntū	school

(sàllàtà,
  perform
  a **sallà**)
	masallācī,
	màsàllàtai
		mosque, place of
		Muslim prayers

(c) Nouns signifying a *tool* or *implement* involved in the
action indicated by the original verb are formed by
prefixing **ma-** and suffixing **-ī**. The tones on the
masculine form are all high.

(aunà,
  measure,
  weigh)
	ma'aunī, mà'àunai	any measure, scales

(būdè, *open*)	mabūdī, màbùɗai	key
(gìrbā, *reap*)	magirbī, màgìrbai	type of harvesting tool
(gwadà, *measure*)	magwajī, màgwàdai	measuring rod

(kaɗà,
  beat a
  drum)
	makaɗī, màkàɗai	drum stick

5. A **-ancī** (sometimes **-cī**) suffix is employed with ethnic terms to indicate the *language (and customs) of* .... All tones are high.

(**Tūrai,** Europe)	**Tūrancī**	European language (in Nigeria this usually means English)
(**Kanò,** Kano)	**Kanancī**	language (dialect) of Kano
(**Zazzàu,** Zaria)	**Zazzagancī**	language (dialect) of Zaria
(**Bàlārabè,** Arab)	**Lārabcī**	Arabic language

A rather humorous (but acceptable) term to designate the mixture of Hausa and English in which many bilinguals converse has recently come into currency.

It is :

> **mālamancī**   (from **mālàm,** *educated person*)

So, too :

> **bībīsancī**   (from B.B.C., *the Hausa of the B.B.C. Hausa broadcasts*).

6. Certain abstract nouns may be formed from more definite nouns by using the following suffixes :

(*a*) **-ntakà, -antakà** = *the quality of being* .... The tones are low-low-high-low :

(**bēbē,** *deaf mute*)	**bèbàntakà**	deaf-muteness
(**mùtûm,** *person*)	**mùtùntakà**	human nature (with its frailties)
(**gwaurō,** *wifeless man*)	**gwàuràntakà**	state of wifelessness

(shēgè, *bastard*) [5]   shègàntakà   impudence,
                                                            rascality
(yārò, *boy*)   yàràntakà   childishness

(b) -ntà, -ncì, -tā, -ntā = *that possessed by* . . . :

(gwànì, *expert*)   gwànintà   skill
(ƙànƙanè, *a little*)   ƙanƙantà   smallness
(mùtûm, *man*)   mutuncì   manliness, self-
                                                            respect, integrity

(bāwà, *slave*)   bàutā   slavery
(gàjērē, *a short*   gajartà   shortness
     thing)
(angò,   angwancì   state of being a
     bridegroom)   bridegroom
(ādàlī, *just*   ādalcì   justness,
     person)   righteousness
(mūgù, *evil thing*)   mùgùntā [6] wickedness

7. Nouns may be formed from certain verbs by using the
following suffixes :

(a) -ayyà = *repetition* and/or *reciprocity, settled attitude* :

(bùgā, *hit*)   bùgayyà   exchanging blows
(sō, *love*)   sòyayyà   mutual love
(jā, *pull*)   jàyayyà   controversy, dispute
(ji, *hear*)   jìyayyà   being on good terms,
                                                            mutual trust

(àurā, *marry*)   àuràtayyà intermarriage
(ƙi, *hate*)   ƙìyayyà   mutual hatred
(bi, *follow, obey*)   bìyayyà   obedience, loyalty

(b) -au = *person or thing characterized by* :

(màntā, *forget*)   màntau   forgetful person
(màkarà, *be late*)   màkàrau   dilatory person

[5] This term is used in Hausa (as in English) as a term of abuse.
Note that the meaning of the derived form is taken from the figura-
tive (rather than the literal) meaning of the original noun.
[6] Note the shortening of the first -u- here.

VOCABULARY

Nominals

ɗilā (*pl.* ɗilōlī)	jackal
gìndī	base, bottom, buttocks, foundation
girbì	harvest
guntū (*f.* guntuwā, *pl.* guntàyē)	short (thing)
gwànī (*f.* gwànā, *pl.* gwanàyē)	expert
gwànintà	skill, expertise
hànkākà (*m.*) (*pl.* hànkàkī)	crow
kallō	watching, looking at
kûnnē (*pl.* kunnuwà)	ear(s)
mabūɗī (*pl.* màbùɗai)	key
macìjī (*pl.* màcìzai) [7]	snake (*lit.* ' biter ')
mahàucī (*pl.* mahàutā)	butcher, meat-seller
mahàukàcī (*pl.* mahàukàtā)	madman
màimakon	instead of, in return for (from màimakō, *substitute*)
makàɗi (*pl.* makàɗā)	drummer
maƙèrī (*pl.* maƙèrā)	blacksmith
sàndā (*pl.* sandunà)	stick, force
shìnkāfā (*f.*)	rice

Verbals

aunà	measure, weigh
cìzā (i/ē)	bite
dòkā (*v.n.* dūkà)	beat, strike, thrash
fāɗō	fall down (here)
gìrbā (i/ē)	reap, harvest
kasà	arrange in heaps, dispose (with kûnnē = *listen*)
màkarà	be late

[7] This plural, note, is irregular (it should be macìzā). Also the verb used of a snake biting is usually sàrā, not cìzā.

o

rasà	lack, be short of, lose
rērà	(with **wāƙà** = *compose and sing*)
sàrā (i/ē)	chop down (a tree), (snake) bite
tūrè	push, knock over

Particles

kaɗai	only
ƙùrùnƙus	the story is over !
shēgè !	damn it ! (very strong swear-word, *lit.* ' bastard ')

Important Phrases

arèwā masò yâmmā	north-west
ɗan sàndā (*pl.* **'yan sàndā**)	Government policeman
kasà kûnnē	prick up one's ears, dispose one's ears to listen
nā rasà yaddà zân yi	I don't know what to do
rērà wāƙà	(compose and) sing a song
'yan ƙasā	' sons of the soil '

EXERCISES

Translate into English :

1. **Macìjī yā sàri ma'àikī àmmā likità yā bā shì māgànī har yā warkè.**
2. **Shī bà Bàhaushè ba nè, Bàfilācè nē. Àmmā duk dà hakà yā iyà Kanancī.**
3. **Zāriyà kudù masò yâmmā ta kè dà Kanò. Kàtsinà, arèwā masò yâmmā ta kè dà ita.**
4. **Dā zā mù yi aikìmmù tàre àmmā shī yā màkarà. Sabòdà hakà nā rasà àbin dà zân sayar à kàsuwā.**
5. **Mūsā gwànī nè. Bâ wandà ya iyà irìn wannàn aikì sai shī kaɗai. Yā kàmātà mù nèmē shì màimakon Audù.**

Translate into Hausa :

1. He's a forgetful person. Don't tell him to do anything for you.
2. In a short time all the workers had left. I didn't know what to do.
3. Bring the key here. Let me open the door.
4. I waited a bit until the drummers began to pay attention.
5. I think if his wife sings a song the chief will be surprised.

Fable

Dilā Sarkin Dàbārà [8]

Wata rānā wani hànkākà yanà yāwò. Yanà nēman àbîn dà zâi ci. Sai ya ga wani guntun nāmà à ƙasà kusa dà wani dūtsè. Ya sàuka, ya sâ bàkī ya ɗaukà. Ya tāshì samà dà nāmàn à bàkinsà ya sàuka bisà wani itàcē.

Àshē dilā yanà kallonsà—yā ga duk àbîn dà hànkākà ya yi. Dilā, kumā, yanà jîn yunwà. Yanà sô yà sàmi nāmàn. Sai ya yi dàbāràr dà zâi sāmù.[9]

Sai dilā ya tàfi gindin itàcē, ya gai dà hànkākà. Ya cè masà, ' Kâi, rân nan na ji kanà rērà wāƙà. Muryàrkà, kùwā, dà dāɗī ta kè ainùn. Sai yàushè zân sākè jîn wāƙà irin tākà kumā ? '

Hànkākà, dai, ya kasà kûnnē. Àbîn dà dilā ya fàɗā ya yi masà dāɗī. Dà ya ji hakà sai ya màntā dà àbîn dà kè cikin bàkinsà. Ya būɗè bàkinsà. Zâi rērà wāƙà kè nan.

Shī kè nan ! Sai nāmàn ya fāɗō. Dilā ya ɗaukà, ya cè, ' Mādàllā '. Ya tàfi dà shī. Kùrùnƙus !

---

[8] See *Ka Koyi Karatu*, page 9, for another version of this story.
[9] ' He made a plan to get it.'

Part Three

Reference

Lesson 31

Greetings II

1. In Lesson 4 a number of the most common greetings were introduced. It is the aim of this lesson to provide the student with a much longer (though still by no means complete) list of typical greetings than was necessary earlier in the course.

2. General greetings :

Greeting		*Reply*	
sànnu	hello	yâuwā, sànnu	hello
		sànnu dai	hello
		sànnu kàdai	hello
sànnu-sànnu	hello	(same replies as for sànnu)	
sànnunkù	hello (to several)	(same replies as for sànnu)	
sànnunkì	hello (to a woman)	(same replies as for sànnu)	
lāfiyà ?	are you well ?	lāfiyà	all's well
		lāfiyà lau	very well
		lāfiyà ƙalau	very well
		lāfiyà dai	all's well
		lāfiyà, bâ kōmē	all's well
ìnā gàjiyà ?	how's your tiredness ?	bâ gàjiyà	all right
		bābù gàjiyà	all right
		gàjiyà dà sauƙī	it's better
		àlhamdùlìllāhì	all's well

Greeting		Reply	
		gàjiyà tā bi lāfiyà	the tiredness is only tempo- rary [1]
ìnā làbārì ?	what's the news ?	(làbārì) sai àlhērì	all's well
		lāfiyà	all's well

3. Situational :

Greeting	Reply
ìnā aikì ? how's (your) work ?	aikì dà gòdiyā with thankfulness àlhamdùlìllāhì thank God (for it) mun gōdè Allà we thank God (for it)
sànnu [2] dà aikì greetings at work	(same replies as for sànnu)
sànnu [2] dà zuwà greetings on arriving	(same replies as for sànnu)
maràbā dà zuwà greetings on arriving	(same replies as for sànnu)
maràbā welcome	(same replies as for sànnu)
sànnu [2] dà hūtàwā greetings at rest	(same replies as for sànnu)
sànnu dà àniyà greetings in (your) effort	(same replies as for sànnu)

[1] Literally, ' tiredness has alternated with well being '.

[2] **Barkà** is frequently substituted for **sànnu** in these (and other) contexts. The two words are equivalent in meaning, but **barkà** usually implies a greater familiarity between the greeters and tends to be used to the exclusion of **sànnu** between close friends. The usual reply to a greeting with **barkà** in it is **barkà dai**.

Greeting	*Reply*
sànnu dà ƙòƙarī	
greetings in (your) effort	(same replies as for **sànnu**)
sàlāmù àlaikùn	**yâuwā, àlaikà sàlāmù**
(on entering a compound)	(reply)
	m̀hm̂ (reply)
gāfarà	**yâuwā, barkà dà zuwà**
(woman entering	greetings on arrival
compound)	
gāfarà dai	**yâuwā, barkà dà zuwà**
(woman entering	greetings on arrival
compound)	

4. Time of day :

Greeting	*Reply*
ìnā kwānā ?	
how did you sleep ?	(same replies as for **lāfiyà ?**)
kwal lāfiyà ?	
how did you sleep ?	(same replies as for **lāfiyà ?**)
barkà dà kwānā	**barkà dai** greetings
greetings in the a.m.	
kā tāshì lāfiyà ?	
did you get up well ?	(same replies as for **lāfiyà ?**)
kā kwāna lāfiyà ?	
did you sleep well ?	(same replies as for **lāfiyà ?**)
ìnā wunì ?	
how's (your) day ?	(same replies as for **lāfiyà ?**)
ìnā yinì ?	
how's (your) day ?	(same replies as for **lāfiyà ?**)
barkà dà rānā	**barkà dai** greetings
greetings (at noon)	
barkà dà yâmmā	**barkà dai** greetings
greetings (in late p.m.)	
barkà dà darē	**barkà dai** greetings
greetings (at night)	

5. Personal :

Greeting	Reply
kanà lāfiyà ?	
are you well ?	(same replies as for **lāfiyà ?**)
inā gidā ?	
how's (your) family ?	(same replies as for **lāfiyà ?**)
inā iyālì ?	
how's (your) family ?	(same replies as for **lāfiyà ?**)
inā mutànenkà ?	
how's your family ?	(same replies as for **lāfiyà ?**)
gidankà lāfiyà ?	
how's your family ?	(same replies as for **lāfiyà ?**)
iyālìnkà lāfiyà ?	
how's your family ?	(same replies as for **lāfiyà ?**)
mutànenkà lāfiyà ?	
how's your family ?	(same replies as for **lāfiyà ?**)
inā yârā ?	
how are (your) children	(same replies as for **lāfiyà ?**)
yârā lāfiyà ?	
how are (your) children ?	(same replies as for **lāfiyà ?**)
yàyà yârā ?	
how are (your) children ?	(same replies as for **lāfiyà ?**)
inā uwargidā ?	
how's (your) wife ?	(same replies as for **lāfiyà ?**)
rânkà yà daɗè [3]	m̀hm̀ (reply)
greetings (to social superior)	
yàyà jìkī ? [4]	**(yanà) dà saukī**
how's (your) illness ?	it's better
sànnu	**yâuwā**
greetings (in misfortune)	thanks
Allà yà bā dà saukī	**àmin**
may God make (you) well	may it be so

[3] This greeting is used especially to a chief or other important person.

[4] Literally : *how's (your) body ?*

Greeting	*Reply*
Allå yà sawwàƙē [5]	**àmin**
may God lighten (your) trouble	may it be so
Allå yà ji ƙansà [6]	**àmin**
may God have mercy on him (may his soul rest in peace)	may it be so

6. Seasonal :

Greeting	*Reply*
inā gùmī ?	**lōkàcinsà nē**
how's the heat ?	it's the time for it
	kwànàkinsà nē
	it's the season for it
	kâi, yā yi yawà !
	there's a lot !
	dà sauƙī
	it's eased off
inā ruwā ?	(same replies as for **inā gùmī ?**)
how's the rain ?	
	ruwā yā yi gyārā
	the rain has helped
	(same replies as for **inā aikì ?** but substitute **ruwā** for **aikì** in first reply)
inā sanyī ?	(same replies as for **inā gùmī ?**)
how's the cold ?	
yàyà ka ji dà ɗārī ?	(same replies as for **inā gumī ?**)
how's the cold ?	
barkà dà sallà	**barkà dai**
greetings (during holidays)	greetings

[5] Or, less commonly, **sauƙàƙē**.
[6] Employed with reference to a dead person.

7. Parting greetings :

Greeting	*Reply*
sai an jimà [7]	**yâuwā, sai an jimà**
see you later	okay, see you later
	yâuwā, mun jimà dà yawà
	okay, we'll wait
sai gòbe	**yâuwā, sai gòbe**
see you tomorrow	okay, see you tomorrow
	tò Allà yà kai mù
	may God bring it about
sai dà sāfē	**yâuwā, sai dà sāfē**
until morning	okay, until morning
	tò Allà yà kai mù
	may God bring it about
sai dà yâmmā	**yâuwā, sai dà yâmmā**
until evening	okay, until evening
sai wani lōkàcī	**yâuwā, sai wani lōkàcī**
see you sometime	okay, see you sometime
sai wani sā'ì	**yâuwā, sai wani sā'ì**
see you sometime	okay, see you sometime
sai wata rānā [8]	**yâuwā, sai wata rānā**
see you sometime	okay, see you sometime
sai kā dāwō	**yâuwā, sai nā dāwō**
until you return	okay, till I return
sàuka lāfiyà	**tò Allà yà sâ**
may you arrive safely	may God make it so
(kà) gai dà gidā	**tò sâ ji** [9]
greet your family	okay, they'll hear
(kà) gai minì dà Audù	**tò yâ ji** [9]
greet Audu for me	okay, he'll hear

[7] Literally ' until one has waited a while '.

[8] **Sai wata rānā** usually implies less expectation of seeing the person again than does either of the two preceding greetings.

[9] Future 2 (see Lesson 16) is invariably used in this formula.

8. Miscellaneous expressions often employed in greeting situations :

tồ	okay, well
mādàllā	fine, splendid, thank you (*lit.* praise God)
yâuwā	(reply) okay, fine
àlbishìrinkà !	I've brought you good news !
gōrồ	(reply to **àlbishìrinkà**) = (I'll give you) a kolanut (if you tell me)
bismìllāhì	(formula said before beginning an action, *e.g.* eating, starting work— *lit.* in the name of God)
bìsmillà !	go ahead and start (whatever is to be done) !
in Allà yā yàrda	if God wills
in shā Àllā(hù)	if God wills

Lesson 32

Numbers

1. In Lesson 11 the numbers 1–22 and several related expressions were introduced. It is the purpose of this lesson to list Hausa numbers in greater detail than in Lesson 11.

2. Cardinal numbers:

1	ɗaya	12	(gōmà) shâ biyu
2	biyu	13	(gōmà) shâ ukù
3	ukù	14	(gōmà) shâ huɗu
4	huɗu	15	(gōmà) shâ bìyar
5	bìyar	16	(gōmà) shâ shidà
6	shidà/shiddà	17	(gōmà) shâ bakwài
7	bakwài	18	àshìrin biyu bābù *or* (gōmà)
8	takwàs		shâ takwàs
9	tarà	19	àshìrin ɗaya bābù *or* (gōmà)
10	gōmà		shâ tarà
11	(gōmà) shâ ɗaya	20	àshìrin

All numbers above 20 employ **dà**, rather than **shâ**, in compound numerals, e.g. àshìrin dà ɗaya, àshìrin dà biyu, tàlàtin dà ɗaya, etc.

20	àshìrin	90	càsà'in [1]
30	tàlàtin	100	ɗàrī
40	àrbà'in	200	mètan/ɗàrī biyu
50	hàmsin	300	ɗàrī ukù
60	sìttin	400	ɗàrī huɗu/àrbàminyà
70	sàbà'in	500	ɗàrī bìyar/hàmsàminyà
80	tàmànin	1000	dubū/alìf/zambàr

[1] **Tàsà'in, tis'in, tàmànin dà gōmà** and **ɗàrī bâ gōmà** are also used for 90.

3 000   **dubū ukù**   1 000 000   **mìlyân, zambàr dubū**
10 000   **zambàr gōmà**

When more than one term is listed above, the first is
the most common.   The term **zambàr** is ordinarily
reserved for use in numbers above 9000.

Numbers between those listed above are formed in a
regular manner with **dà**, e.g. **hàmsin dà biyu** (52), **mètan
dà shidà** (206), **ɗàrī bìyar dà gōmà** (510), **ɗàrī takwàs dà
sàbà'in dà ukù** (873), **dubū bakwài dà ɗàrī huɗu dà
càsà'in dà ɗaya** (7491), **dubū ɗaya** (*or* **gùdā**) **dà biyu**
(1002), **mìlyân gùdā dà dubū bìyar dà ɗàrī tarà dà gōmà
shâ takwàs,** etc. (1005, 918).

The *year 1973* is **dubū ɗaya dà ɗàrī tarà dà sàbà'in dà
ukù.**

3. The term for *zero* is **sifìrī.**

4. See Lesson 11, section 6, for the formation of *ordinal
numbers.*

5. See Lesson 11, section 7, for the use of **gùdā** with
numbers.

6. *Addition* employs **dà,** e.g. :

Ukù dà ukù nawà (nē) ?
  Shidà nē.   3 and 3 are how many ? 6.
Shâ biyu dà àshìrin ɗaya bābù   12 plus 19 are how many ?
  nawà (nē) ? Tàlàtin dà ɗaya.   31.

7. *Subtraction* employs . . . **bābù, dàgà** *or* **ɗēbè/fitad dà** . . .
dàgà cikin, e.g. :

Gōmà, huɗu bābù nawà (nē) ?   10 minus 4 is how many ?
  Shidà.   6.

Biyu dàgà shidà nawà (nē) ?
Huɗu.

2 from 6 (leaves) how many ? 4.

À ɗēbè bìyar dàgà cikin tàlàtin dà huɗu, nawà (nē) ya ragè ? Tàlàtin ɗaya bābù.

Take 5 from (in) 34, how many remain ? 29.

8. *Multiplication* employs **sàu,** *times,* e.g.:

Ukù sàu ukù nawà (nē) ? Tarà. $3 \times 3 = ?$ 9.

Shâ bìyar sàu huɗu sìttin nè. $15 \times 4 = 60.$

9. *Division* employs **shìga** and **sàu,** e.g. :

Shidà zâi shìga àshìrin dà huɗu sàu nawà ? Huɗu.

6 goes into 24 how many times ? 4.

Sàu nawà gōmà zâi shìga mètan ? Àshìrin.

How many times does 10 go into 200 ? 20.

10. *Fractions* are expressed as follows :

$\frac{1}{2}$ is **rabì.** $\frac{1}{4}$ is **kwatà** or **rubù'ì.**
Other fractions are usually described as, e.g. :

$\frac{1}{3}$ is **sulùsī** *or* **ɗaya bisà ukù** *or* **ɗaya dàgà cikin ukù**
$\frac{2}{5}$ is **biyu bisà bìyar** *or* **biyu dàgà cikin bìyar**
$\frac{3}{8}$ is **ukù bisà takwàs** *or* **ukù dàgà cikin takwàs**
$\frac{1}{10}$ is **ushùrī** *or* **ɗaya bisà gōmà** *or* **ɗaya dàgà cikin gōmà,**
etc.

11. Percentages are expressed as follows :

$10\% =$ **gōmà bisà ɗàrī** (*lit.* 10 on/over 100), etc.

(25) **Yâu dà gòbe shī ya sâ àllūrà ginìn rījìyā.** (Doing a thing) little by little this made it possible for the needle to dig a well. (*i.e.* Perseverance wins out.)

(26) **Zuwà dà wurì yā fì zuwà dà wuri.** Coming with some money (*lit.* a cowrie) is better than coming in good time. (*i.e.* It is better to arrive late with even a small gift than to arrive early with nothing.)

(*d*) Proverbs stating facts of life :

(27) **Darē rìgar mūgù.** Night-time (is) the cloak of evil.

(28) **Don hannunkà yā yi d'òyī, bā kà yankèwā kà yar.** Because your hand has become foul smelling, you wouldn't cut it off and discard it. (*i.e.* One cannot but pardon the faults of one's dependants.)

(29) **Gàba dà gàbantà.** (Everyone) in front has (someone) in front of him. (*i.e.* Even the greatest has someone greater than him.)

(30) **Jìkī magàyī.** The body (is) the informer. (*i.e.* Let your strength be your guide—don't overdo things.)

(31) **Kōmē nīsan darē gàrī yâ wāyè.** No matter how long the night, morning will come. (*i.e.* Every cloud has a silver lining.)

(32) **Kurùm mā màganà cē.** Even silence is speech. (*i.e.* Silence may be significant.)

(33) **Làbārìn zūcìyā à tàmbàyi fuskà.** (For) the news of the heart one should ask the face. (*i.e.* One's face shows what is in one's heart.)

(34) **Tsōhon dōkì mài sànē.** An old horse (is) a knowing one.

(35) **Wànzāmì bā yà sôn jàrfā.** The tatooer (*lit.* barber) doesn't like (to be) tatooed. (*i.e.* One who cheats/ hurts others doesn't like it when the tables are turned on him.)

(*e*) Proverbs dealing with cause and effect, remedy, result :

(36) **Àlbarkàcin kàzā ƙàdangarè ya shā ruwan kaskō.** Thanks to the chicken the lizard drank water from a bowl. (*i.e.* Some gain advantages through no virtue of their own.)

(37) **Mài nāmà ya kàn nèmi wutā.** The one who (already) has meat will look for fire. (*i.e.* A person doesn't seek a thing unless he already has a reason for needing it.)

(38) **' Mù jē mù ganī ' māgànin maƙàryàcī.** ' Let's go see (it) ' (is) the remedy for a liar.

(39) **Tsūtsàn nāmà, ita mā nāmà cē.** The maggot in the meat is itself meat. (*i.e.* It's all the same.)

(40) **Ùngùlū bā tà sàukā banzā.** The vulture doesn't descend without reason. (*i.e.* A (dire) effect does not come about without a cause.)

(41) **Yārò bài san wutā ba sai tā ƙōnà shi.** A child doesn't know fire until it burns him.

(*f*) Miscellaneous proverbs involving comparison :

(42) **Àbōkin sarkī, sarkī nè.** A chief's friend (is) a chief. (*i.e.* The friend of a person in high position shares the advantages of that position.)

(43) **Àlhērì gadon barcī nè.** Kindness is a bed to sleep on. (*i.e.* Doing a favour is a good investment.)

(44) **Allà shī nè sarkī.** God is the Chief (of chiefs). (*i.e.* God is over all.)

(45) **Dà tsìrārà gāra baƙin bàntē.** Rather than nakedness better a black loincloth. (*i.e.* Half a loaf is better than none.)

(46) **Dūniyà màcè dà cikì cē.** The world is a pregnant woman. (*i.e.* No one knows what will come of the pregnancy—a boy, a girl, alive, dead, *etc.*)

(47) **Ganī yā fi (or yā kòri) jî.** Seeing is better than (or chases away) hearing. (*i.e.* Seeing is believing.)

(48) **Gàskiyā tā fi kwabò.** Truth is better than money (*lit.* a penny). (*i.e.* Honesty is the best policy.)

(49) **Gīwā à gàrin wani zōmō.** An elephant in another's town (is but) a rabbit. (*i.e.* A person who is important in his own town is just another ordinary person in another town.)

(50) **Harbì à wutsiyà yā fì kuskurè.** Shooting (something) in the tail is better than missing (completely). (*i.e.* Half a loaf is better than none.)

(51) **Jìkī yā fì kûnnē jî.** The body is better at sensing/hearing than the ears. (*i.e.* If one refuses to listen to advice he will be taught by hard knocks.)

(52) **Kàmā dà Wānè bà Wānè ba.** Like So-and-so (is) not So-and-so. (*i.e.* The similarity of two things is far from saying that they are the same.)

(53) **Kō bà à gwadà ba lìnzāmì yā fì bàkin kàzā.** Even though no measurement is taken (one can see that) a bridle is too big for the mouth of a chicken. (*i.e.* Such-and-such is completely obvious.)

(54) **Lāfiyàr jìkī arzìkī nè.** Health is wealth.

(55) **Rashìn sanì yā fì darē duhù.** Lack of knowledge is darker than night time. (*i.e.* There is nothing worse than ignorance.)

(56) **Sāmù yā fì iyàwā.** Possessing (something) is better than expertise (in using it). (*i.e.* Possession is nine points of the law.)

(*g*) Proverbs for more specialized situations :

(57) **Aikìn banzā màkāhò dà wàiwàye.** (It is) worthless work (for) a blind man to turn his head to look. (*i.e.* An illustration of a supreme waste of effort.)

(58) **Ā nèmi jinī gà fàrā ?** Would one seek blood from a locust ? (*i.e.* You can't get blood from a stone.)

(59) **Bâ dāmā tēshàn Kanò.** The Kano railway station is impossible. (*i.e.* Not a chance anywhere.)

(60) **Banzā tā kòri wòfī.** A worthless one has chased away a useless one. (*i.e.* Two villains queered each other's pitch.)

s

(61) **In nā yi makà rānā, kadà kà yi minì darē.** If I make
daylight for you, don't you make night for me. (*i.e.*
If I do good to you, don't you repay me with evil.)

3. *Riddles* are a common form of Hausa word game.
Riddles are typically presented as statements (rather
than as questions). If the answerer is stumped by the
riddle he will reply **Nā bā kà gàrī,** *I give up* (lit. *I give you
the town*). He is then told the answer.

4. The following short list of riddles is taken largely from
G. Merrick, *Hausa Proverbs*, London, 1905 :

(1) **Rìgātā gùdā ɗaya, àljīfuntà ɗàrī.** *Answer* : **Gidan
gàrā.** I have only one gown (but it has) 100 pockets.
Answer : An anthill.

(2) **Bàba nà ɗākì, gēmùnsà nà wàje.** *Answer* : **Wutā dà
hayāƙī.** Father is in the hut (but) his beard is outside. *Answer* : Fire and smoke. (*i.e.* Fires are built
inside of huts for warmth. As the smoke streams out
through a door, window or through a grass roof it
resembles a white beard.)

(3) **Hanyà ɗaya tā ràbu biyu.** *Answer* : **Wàndō.** A
single path divides into two. *Answer* : Trousers.

(4) **Shānuntà ɗàrī, maɗaurintà ɗaya.** *Answer* : **Tsintsiyā.** Its cattle number 100 (but) it only has one
rope/string (*lit.* tyer.) *Answer* : A broom. (*i.e.* A
single string ties 100 or more pieces of grass together
to form a broom.)

(5) **Kàsuwā tā ci tā wātsè, tā bar kàrē kālā.** *Answer* :
Harshè. The market was held and broke up, it left
a dog gleaning. *Answer* : The tongue. (*i.e.* After a
person finishes eating his tongue goes wandering
around in his mouth picking up the remaining food.)

(6) **Gōɗìyātā tanà dà cikì. Bā nà hawan gōɗìyâr, sai cikì
na kè hawā.** *Answer* : **Ɗākì dà gadō à cikì.** My mare

is pregnant. I don't ride the mare, (I) only ride the unborn foal. *Answer* : A hut with a bed in it.

(7) **Rawànin sarkī yā fàskàri naɗèwā.** *Answer* : **Hanyà.** The chief's turban was impossible to wind around (his head). *Answer* : A road.

(8) **Ɗākìn sauràyī bābù ƙōfà.** *Answer* : **Kwai.** The hut of a young man has no doorway. *Answer* : An egg.

(9) **Nā wankè ƙwaryāta. Nā jē gabàs, nā jē yâmmā, nā dāwō, bà tà būshè ba.** *Answer* : **Harshèn kàrē cikin bàkinsà.** I washed my calabash. I went to the east, I went to the west, I returned, it hadn't dried. *Answer* : A dog's tongue in its mouth.

(10) **Ukù-ukù, gamà gàrī.** *Answer* : **Murfù.** Three each, the town (is) complete. *Answer* : The three stones on which pots are set over fire = a local kind of stove. (*i.e.* No town is complete without cooking places.)

Lesson 41

Additional Conversations

1. It has been possible to include only a limited number of typical dialogues in the regular lessons. A larger selection, arranged topically appears below. Full translations are not given. Where explanation is necessary an asterisk (*) appears referring the student to section 8, *Notes*, at the end of this lesson.

2. Additional greeting conversations :

(*a*) **Audù** meets **Mūsā** :

    Audù : Sànnu.
    Mūsā : Sànnu dai.
    Audù : Lāfiyà ?
    Mūsā : Lafiyà lau.
    Audù : Ìnā gàjiyà ?
    Mūsā : Bâ gàjiyà.
    Audù : Ìnā làbārì ?
    Mūsā : Làbārì sai àlhērì.
    Audù : Ìnā ìyālìnkà ?
    Mūsā : Lāfiyà dai.
    Audù : Tô mādàllā.
    Mūsā : Kanà lāfiyà ?
    Audù : Lāfiyà, bâ kōmē.
    Mūsā : Mutànenkà lāfiyà ?
    Audù : Lāfiyà ƙalau.
    Mūsā : Ìnā aikì ?
    Audù : Àlhamdùlillāhì
    Mūsā : Mādàllā, sai an jimà.
    Audù : Yâuwā, mun jimà dà yawà.

(*b*) **Mammàn** meets **Sulè** resting in the heat of the day :

Mammàn : Sànnu dà hūtàwā.
Sulè : Yâuwā, maràbā dà zuwà.
Mammàn : Ìnā wunì ?
Sulè : Lāfiyà.
Mammàn : Ìnā gùmī ?
Sulè : Ai lōkàcinsà nē.
Mammàn : Gàskiyarkà.
Sulè : Kā zō lāfiyà ?
Mammàn : Lāfiyà dai.
Sulè : Gidankà lāfiyà ?
Mammàn : Kalau.
Sulè : Mādàllā, zō kà zaunà.
Mammàn : Ā'à, zâ ni kàntī.
Sulè : Tò bâ lâifī, sai kā dāwō kè nan.
Mammàn : Yâuwā, sai nā dāwō.

(*c*) **Bellò** visits **Jàtau** (who has been sick) at the latter's home :

Bellò : Sàlāmù àlaikùn.
Jàtau : Yâuwā, shìgō Bellò.
Bellò : Mādàllā, kanà lāfiyà ?
Jàtau : Lāfiyà dai.
Bellò : Ìnā gidā ?
Jàtau : Lāfiyà.
Bellò : Mutànenkà lāfiyà ?
Jàtau : Lāfiyà dukà.
Bellò : Tô, yàyà jìkī ? *
Jàtau : Kâi, jìkīnā yanà dàmuwā * sòsai !
Bellò : Kâi, sànnu ! Cīwòn cikì nē ?
Jàtau : Ā'à, ƙafà cē.
Bellò : Kâi, Allà yà bā dà sauƙī.
Jàtau : Āmin.

3. Conversations dealing with foodtime :

(a) Bàtūrè and his cook Àlī :

Bàtūrè : Àbinci yā yi ?
Àlī : Yā yi.
Bàtūrè : Tò dà kyâu.
Àlī : Kanà sô ìn kāwō shì ?
Bàtūrè : Ī, àmmā bàri ìn wankè hannū tùkùna.
Àlī : Tô, zân dākàtā kàɗan.
Bàtūrè : Kâi, nā ji yunwà yâu.
Àlī : Tò bâ lâifī, nā shiryà àbinci dà yawà.
Bàtūrè : Dà kyâu, mè ka shiryà ?
Àlī : Nāmàn sānìyā dà wākē dà dànkalì.
Bàtūrè : Mādàllā, kàwō sù.
Àlī : Tô, inà zuwà.*
Bàtūrè : Zā mù yi bàƙī * gòbe.
Àlī : Tô, zân jē kàsuwā dà sāfē.
Bàtūrè : Dà kyâu, à sàyi ìsasshen * nāmà.
Àlī : Tô, wànè irì nē ka kè sô ?
Bàtūrè : Na kàzā yanà dà àràhā yànzu ?
Àlī : Ai dāma-dāma * yànzu.
Bàtūrè : Tô zā kà yi burōdì * kumā ?
Àlī : Ā'à, nā yī shì yâu.
Bàtūrè : Dà kyâu. Kâi, nā ƙōshi ! *
Àlī : Mādàllā, bàri ìn kāwō kòfī.*
Bàtūrè : Tò dà kyâu.

(b) Àliyù and Hasàn drinking tea :

Àliyù : Bàri mù zaunà mù shā tî.*
Hasàn : Tô, bâ lâifī.
Àliyù : Gà sukàr * dà madarā nân.
Hasàn : Tò ɗèbō * minì sukàr kàɗan kawài.
Àliyù : Àshē, bā kà sônsà dà zāƙī * ?
Hasàn : Ī, bâ dāɗī hakà.
Àliyù : Ai bàn yàrda ba.
Hasàn : Kanà sôn sukàr dà yawà ?

Àliyù : Sòsai !
Hasàn : Tô bâ lâifī.
Àliyù : Gằ bìskitì * kumā.
Hasàn : Tô, nā gōdè.

4. Conversations on the road :

(a) Ìsā meets Garbà on the way to market :

Ìsā : Sànnu Garbà, ìnā zuwà ? *
Garbà : Ai, zâ ni kàsuwā.
Ìsā : Tô, bàri mù jē tàre.
Garbà : Mādàllā, mè zā kà yi à kàsuwā ?
Ìsā : Zâ ni ìn gai dà ɗan'uwāna.
Garbà : Tô dà kyâu. Dàgà gàrī ya kè ?
Ìsā : Ā'à, dàgà ƙauyè * nē, àmmā yanà zuwà kàsuwā kullum.
Garbà : Dà kyâu.
Ìsā : Sàyē zā kà yi ?
Garbà : Wàtàkīlà. Zân nèmi ƙōtàr * fartanyà.
Ìsā : Tākà tā tsūfa nè ?
Garbà : Ī, tanà sô tà karyè.*
Ìsā : Lallē, yā kàmātà à sàmi sābuwâr.

(b) Daudà takes a trip in a lorry * :

(i) Bargaining for the price with the driver :

Daudà : Dirēbà, inà sô ìn tàfi Kanò.
Dirēbà * : Tô, kàwō sulè bakwài.
Daudà : Habà !, Dâ mā kuɗinsà sulè shidà nē.
Dirēbà : Bà cikin kyàkkyāwar mōtà kàmar wannàn ba.
Daudà : Ôhō. Zân nèmi wani dirēbà.
Dirēbà : Zā kà biyā shidà dà sīsì nē ?
Daudà : Bābù ! In bà shidà ba, zâ ni nēman wani.
Dirēbà : Tô, kàwō kuɗī. Shìga dà saurī, zân bugà * yànzu.

(ii) On the road, chatting with the motor boy :

Daudà :   Kâi, wannàn mōtà tā iyà gudù !
Kàren Mōtà * :   Sòsai ! Wannàn dirēbà tsōfon
                  hannū * nè.
Daudà :   Yā daɗè yanà aikìn dirēbà nē ?
Kàren Mōtà :   Hakà nē—wajen shèkarà
                  àshìrin.
Daudà :   Kâi ! Wannàn mōtà tāsà cē ?
Kàren Mōtà :   Ī mànà ! Yanà dà mōtà ukù.
Daudà :   Àshē ? Àmmā yā arzùtā ! *
Kàren Mōtà :   Gàskiyarkà.   Ai, yā yi hajì *
                  bàra.
Daudà :   Tabdì ! Dà mōtàrsà ?
Kàren Mōtà :   Ā'à, dà jirgin samà.
Daudà :   Àshē ?
Kàren Mōtà :   Ī, anà cê dà shī, ' Àlhajì Jirgin
                  Samà.' *

(iii) Stopping for a ' rest stop ', talking with fellow
      passenger Bàlā :

Daudà :   Bàri mù sàuka mù hūtà.
Bàlā :   Tô, zā ni dājì in yi fitsārī * tùkùna.
Daudà :   Tô, zân nèmi ràkē.*
Bàla :   Dà kyâu, à sayō minì na tarō.

(iv) Starting again, the driver and the motor boy :

Dirēbà :   Tô, à kirāwō * fasanjōjī.*
Kàren Mōtà :   Tô, sunà nan.
Dirēbà :   Dukànsù ?
Kàren Mōtà :   Sai ɗaya. Kai ! Zō maza !
Dirēbà :   Yàyà yànzu ?
Kàren Mōtà :   Shī kè nan, bùgà mâi ! *

(v) Back on the road, Daudà and Bàlā :

Daudà :   Kâi, hanyàn nan tā ɓàcì ! *
Bàlā :   Lallē. Àkwai gàngarà * dà yawà.

Daudà : Ī, dà santsī * kumā.

Bàlā : Hakà nē, ruwan samà nē ya ɓatà * ta.

Daudà : Har, wai, wani kògī yā cìka yā kwāshè gadà.*

Bàlā : Ī, àmmā an gyârtā.*

Daudà : A'a, mōtà ta tsayà !

(vi) Stuck on a slippery hill, the driver and motor boy giving orders :

Dirēbà : Kàren mōtà ! Sâ wejì ! *

Kàren Mōtà : Tô, nā sâ.

Dirēbà : Kōwā yà sàuka yà tūrà.*

Kàren Mōtà : (to passengers) Sàuka ! Sàuka !

Dirēbà : Tô, tùra !

Kàren Mōtà : Tô, bùga !

Shī kè nan, tā fìta.

(to passengers) Kù hau ! Kù hau !

(to driver) Tô, bùga !

5. Conversations at work :

(a) On the farm—when to plant :

Sà'īdù : Kâi, ruwā * yā fārà zuwà sòsai !

Nūhù : Gàskiyarkà, zân fārà shūkà gòbe.

Sà'īdù : Àshē, bà kà sōmà * ba tùkùn ?

Nūhù : Ī, nā yi ɗan lattì * bana.

Sà'īdù : Ìnā dàlīlì ?

Nūhù : Ai uwātā tā ràsu * sātin nàn.

Sà'īdù : Kâi, sànnu ! Mātankà fà ? Sun màkarà kumā ?

Nūhù : Ā'à, sun sōmà tun dà wuri.

Sà'īdù : Dà kyâu, bà zā kù ji yunwà * ba.

Nūhù : Hakà nē.

(b) On the farm—Nigerian versus Western hoes :

Bàtūrè : Nī, bàn taɓà aikì dà irìn tākù fartanyà ba.

Hārūnà : Àshē ? Bābù irìntà à ƙasarkù ?
Bàtūrè : Ī, irìn tāmù tanà dà dōguwar ƙōtà * nē.
Hārūnà : Hakà nē. Don mè bà à kāwō sù nân ba ?
Bàtūrè : Ai, an kāwō, àmmā bâ su dà àmfànī.
Hārūnà : Àshē ?
Bàtūrè : Ī. Dōguwar ƙōtàrsù ta kàn karyè * dà
         saurī.
Hārūnà : Sabò dà taurin * ƙasā kè nan ?
Bàtūrè : Hakà nē.
Hārūnà : Ai, wàtàkīlà à ƙasarmù irìn tāmù tā fi
         kyâu.
Bàtūrè : Sòsai.
Hārūnà : Àmmā aikì dà irìn tāmù dà wùyā.
Bàtūrè : Gàskiyā nè—sai à sùnkwìye.*
Hārūnà : Hakà nē—har wani sā'ì mùtûm zâi ji
         cīwòn bāyā.
Bàtūrè : Kâi, mutànenkù sunà shân wàhalà !
Hārūnà : Ai dōlè nē. In bābù nōmā, bābù àbinci.
Bàtūrè : Gàskiyarkà—kō à ƙasarmù hakà ya kè.

(c) On the farm—anticipating harvest :

Yàƙubù : Dà yàrdar Allà * hatsimmù * zâi yi kyâu
         bana.
Bàtūrè : Gàskiyarkà, ya tsìra sòsai.
Yàƙubù : Har jân * yā fārà nūnā * yànzu.
Bàtūrè : Zā à yi girbìnsà à watàn Sàtumbà kō ?
Yàƙubù : Ā'à, sai ruwā yā ɗaukē * tùkùn.
Bàtūrè : Tô, sai Òktōbà kè nan.
Yàƙubù : Hakà nē. Anà girbìnsà sā'ì ɗaya dà gērō.*
Bàtūrè : Tô, ƙarar dāwà fà ?
Yàƙubù : Ai ƙarâr, sai Nùwambà.
Bàtūrè : Àmmā ita cè mài kyânsù kō ?
Yàƙubù : Sòsai ! Farâr tā fi dukà dāɗī.
Bàtūrè : Ràwayà * fà—an fi sôntà * dà jā ?
Yàƙubù : Ī, àmmā bà tà kai ƙarâr ba.
Bàtūrè : Yàushè a kàn gìrbē tà ?

Yàƙubù : Wajen farkon Nùwambà nē.
Bàtūrè : Kâi, kunà shân aikì dà kàkā.*
Yàƙubù : Gàskiyā nè. Àmmā munà sāmùn hūtū kàɗan dà rānī.*
Bàtūrè : Bābù aikì dà rānī ?
Yàƙubù : Ā'à, àkwai dà yawà, àmmā sai na gidā.*
Bàtūrè : Tò bâ lâifī.

(d) At the office—Gàmbo is a clerk (àkàwū), Sulè and Yūsufù are messengers (māsinjà).

(i) Gàmbo : Sulè !
Sulè : Nà'am.
Gàmbo : Zō kà kai wannàn wàsīƙà fàs ōfìs *
Sulè : Rânkà yà daɗè !
Gàmbo : Gà sulè biyu. Kà sayō kân sarkī * na āhù-āhù kà sâ biyu à kân wàsīƙàr.*
Sulè : Tò shī kè nan ?
Gàmbo : Shī kè nan.

(ii) Gàmbo : Yūsufù, kàwō littāfìn ràsît.*
Yūsufù : Tò, ngō.*
Gàmbo : Tò, yànzu kà jē kàntin littàttàfai,* kà sayō sābon irìnsà.
Yūsufù : Tò, nawà nē kuɗinsà ?
Gàmbo : Yanà tsàkānin sulè ukù dà sulè huɗu. Gà sulè huɗu.
Yūsufù : Tò, shī kè nan ?
Gàmbo : Shī kè nan.

(iii) Sulè : Nā dāwō. Gà kân sarkī.
Gàmbo : Tò. Yànzu kà kai wannàn takàrdā * zuwà bàbban àkàwū à Jànhôl *— sūnansà Àlī.
Sulè : Tò.
Gàmbo : In kā kai tà cân sai kà biyō ta kàntin littàttàfai kà sayō minì kwalbar jar tàwadà.* Gà sulè.

Sulè :   Tô.
Gàmbo :   In kā ga Yūsufù cân kà cê masà yà
              dāwō dà wuri. Inà bùkātàrsà.
Sulè :   Tò nâ yi.
Gàmbo :   Shī kè nan.

6. Conversations dealing with health :

(a) Sùlèmānù meets Būbà on the path :

Sùlèmānù : Ìnā zâ ka àbōkī ?
Būbà :   Ai, zâ ni asìbitì ìn shā māgànī.
Sùlèmānù : Àshē ? Bā kà dà lāfiyà nē ?
Būbà :   Ĩ, bàn yi barcī ba yâu * kō kàɗan.
Sùlèmānù : Zàzzàɓī nè ?
Būbà :   Ĩ, dà cīwòn kâi.
Sùlèmānù : Kâi, bâ kyâu !
Būbà :   Hakà nē. Dã yanà zuwà lōtò-lotò kawài
              àmmā yànzu nā yi kwānā ukù bàn
              ràbu * dà shī ba.
Sùlèmānù : Likità zâi bā kà àllūrà nē ?
Būbà :   Wàtàkīlà. Hakà na kè sô.
Sùlèmānù : Allà yà sawwàƙē ! *
Būbà :   Āmin.

(b) Lawàl is chatting with Dōgo :

Lawàl :   Uwargidankà tā yi cikì * nē ?
Dōgo :   Hakà nē. Tanà dà na * watà bìyar.
Lawàl :   Mādàllā. Na farkō nè ?
Dōgo :   Ā'à, ta yi wani bàra àmmā yā zubè.*
Lawàl :   Tô, àmmā lāfiyà ta kè yànzu ?
Dōgo :   Ai dāma-dāma.* In Allà yā yàrda zā tà haifù
              lāfiyà.
Lawàl :   Tò Allà yà sâ.
Dōgo :   Āmin.

(c) **Àbūbakàr** has come to the doctor with a complaint :

Àbūbakàr : Kâi, likità, cikìnā yanà dāmùnā *
     ƙwarai !
Likità : Kâi, sànnu ! Yàushè nē ya sōmà ? *
Àbūbakàr : Ai yā daɗè—kàmar sātī biyu.
Likità : Tô. Kwàntā * à tēbùr nân mù dūbà.
Àbūbakàr : Tô.
Likità : Kanà zāwò * nē ?
Àbūbakàr : Ā'à. Ai cikì yā ɗaurè.*
Likità : Tô. In nā taɓà nân, dà zāfī * nè ?
Àbūbakàr : Ā'à, bài fi na * sauran cikì ba.
Likità : Tô, kā iyà tāshì yànzu. Kà jē kà cikà
     wannàn kwalbā dà fitsārī,* kà cikà
     wannàn dà bāyan gidā, kà bar sù nân,
     kà dāwō gòbe.
Àbūbakàr : Tô.
Likità : Shī kè nan, sai gòbe wàrhakà.*
Àbūbakàr : Yâuwā, sai gòbe.

7. Conversations dealing with weather :

(a) **Ìmâm** and **Sambò** sitting outside the latter's home :

Ìmâm : Kâi, gìzàgìzai * sun yi yawà.
Sambò : Ai, dàmunā tā kusa.*
Ìmâm : Gàskiyarkà, watàn Afrìl nē.
Sambò : Inà bègē * dàmunā zā tà yi kyâu bana.
Ìmâm : Nī mā hakà. Bàra ruwā bài yi sòsai ba.
Sambò : Har hatsin * wasu yā ƙōnè.*
Ìmâm : Hakà nē. Sabò dà wannàn waɗansu sunà
    jîn yunwà yànzu.
Sambò : Waɗansu mā sun ci bāshì dòmin hātsinsù
    yā kāsà.*
Ìmâm : Gàskiyarkà. Àmmā in Allà yā yàrda àbîn
    zâi gyàru * bana.
Sambò : Allà yà sà.

(*b*) **Àdàmu** explains Nigerian seasons to a European :

Bàtūrè : À ƙasarmù ruwā yanà zuwà kōwànè
lōkàcī.

Àdàmu : Àshē ? Bà hakà ya kè à wurimmù ba.

Bàtūrè : Yàyà ?

Àdàmu : Sai dà dàmunā nè mu kè sāmùn ruwā.

Bàtūrè : Bābù ruwā dà rānī ?

Àdàmu : Kō kàɗan.

Bàtūrè : Dà bazarā * fà ?

Àdàmu : Ai wani sā'ì àkwai ruwā kàɗan dà bazarā.

Bàtūrè : Tô, àmmā bâ yawà kō ?

Àdàmu : Wani lōkàcī zâi zō dà ɗan yawà.

Bàtūrè : Àshē ?

Àdàmu : Ì, àmmā an jimà sai yà ɗâukē.*

Bàtūrè : Tô, ìdan an shūkà dà bazarā zâi yi * nè ?

Àdàmu : Wàtàkīlà, àmmā yawancin lōkàcī bā yà yî.

Bàtūrè : Mài shūkà zâi shā wàhalà kō ?

Àdàmu : Hakà nē. Àbinsà sai yà lālàcē.*

Bàtūrè : Kâi, wannàn bâ kyâu !

Àdàmu : Gàskiyarkà, àmmā lâifin kânsà * nē.

8. Notes on asterisked items from the conversations
presented in sections 2–7 of this lesson :

2 (*c*)	**yàyà jìkī ?**	how's (your) illness (*lit.* body) ? (see Lesson 31, section 5)
	dàmuwā	the verbal noun from **dàmu**
3 (*a*)	**inà zuwà**	I'm coming (*i.e.* just a minute and I'll have it done)
	yi bàƙī	have guests
	ìsasshē	enough (from **isa,** *be enough*)
	dāma-dāma	a bit better (than formerly)
	burōdì/brōdì	bread, rolls
	ƙòshi	have become full (of food)
	kòfī	coffee
3 (*b*)	**tî**	tea

	sukàr	sugar
	ɗēbō	dip out (into my cup) (from **dībā,** *extract, draw out*)
	zāƙī	sweetness
	bìskitì	biscuit (British English), cookie (American English)
4 (*a*)	**inā zuwà = inā zâ ka**	
	ƙauyè	village, suburb
	ƙōtà	handle (of hoe, axe, *etc.*)
	karyè	snap, break (as a stick breaks)
4 (*b*)	in a lorry	lorries are the ordinary means of transportation for people as well as goods over large areas of Nigeria. There are buses and other passenger vehicles in and between certain large urban centres as well.
4 (*b*) (i)	**dirēbà**	driver
	bugà	start (the engine), start (driving)
4 (*b*) (ii)	**kàren mōtà**	motor boy (*lit.* motor dog). He is the person responsible to see that loads, people, etc., are all in place before the lorry starts, to inform the driver if anything goes wrong, to put wedges behind the wheels when the lorry stops, (sometimes) to collect the fares, etc.
	tsōfon hannū	' old hand ', experienced person
	arzùtā	has become wealthy
	hajì	pilgrimage to Mecca
	Àlhajì Jirgin Samà	an Alhaji who has made the pilgrimage by aeroplane. (The title is used humorously.) Alhaji is the title given to anyone who has made the pilgrimage.

4 (b) (iii)	fîtsārī	urinate. It is not considered in-delicate for a person to state that the reason for his going off is to urinate.
	ràkē	sugarcane
4 (b) (iv)	kirāwō	call here (the **-ō** form of **kirā**)
	fasanjōjī	the plural of **fasànjà** = passenger
	bùgà mâi	start going ! (*lit.* hit the petrol, ' step on the gas ')
4 (b) (v)	ɓācì	is ruined, spoiled
	gàngarà	bumpiness
	santsī	slipperiness
	ɓātà	ruin, spoil
	gadà	bridge (from English ' girder ')
	gyârtā	= **gyârà,** fix, repair
4 (b) (vi)	wejì/wajì	wedge. Each lorry carries two or more wooden blocks (usually approximately four inches square with one end whittled down to form a handle) which the motor boy puts behind (or in front of) the rear wheels whenever the lorry is stopped, to keep it from rolling.
	turà	push
5 (a)	ruwā	in a context such as this it means *rain*
	sōmà	= **fārà,** begin, start
	lattì	late
	ràsu	died (the **-u** form of **rasà,** lack)
	ji yunwà	here it means *go hungry, starve*
5 (b)	ƙōtà	handle (of hoe, axe, *etc.*—see also under 4 (a) above)
	karyè	snap, break (as a stick—see also under 4 (a) above)

	taurī	hardness, toughness
	à sùnkwìye	stooped over
5 (c)	dà yàrdar	
	Allà	by God's grace
	hatsī	grain
	jân	red variety of guinea corn—the earliest maturing and lowest prestige type of guinea corn
	nǜnā	ripening
	ɗâukē	(rain) stops
	gērō	early maturing variety of millet
	ràwayà	yellow variety of guinea corn
	fi sô	prefer
	kàkā	harvest season
	rānī	dry season
	na gidā	work at home (e.g. repairing the huts, re-roofing, making new mats, etc.)
5 (d) (i)	fâs ōfìs	post office (also called **gidan wayà** = home of the telephone/telegraph)
	kân sarkī	postage stamp (lit. head of the king)
	wàsīƙà	letter
5 (d) (ii)	ràsît	(**littāfin ràsît** = receipt book)
	ngō/ungō	here, take it !
	kàntin littàttàfai	bookstore, bookshop
5 (d) (iii)	takàrdā	letter (lit. paper)
	Jànhôl/Jàn hwâl	John Holt canteen (name of a prominent commercial firm)
	jar tàwadà	red ink
6 (a)	yâu	the Hausa day begins at 6 p.m. Thus, *I didn't sleep today* in Hausa is *I didn't sleep last night* in English.

T

	ràbu	be separated (**-u** form of **rabà,** *separate, divide*)
	Allà yà sawwàḙē	may God lighten (your) trouble (see Lesson 31, section 5)
6 (*b*)	**yi cikì**	become pregnant
	na	(*i.e.* pregnancy of)
	zubè	(pregnancy) aborted
	dāma-dāma	better than before (at least)
6 (*c*)	**yanà dāmừnā**	it is bothering me
	sōmà = **fàrà**	(see also under 5 (*a*) above)
	kwàntā	(from **kwântā,** *lie down*) lie down !
	zāwò	diarrhoea
	cikì yā ɗaurè	I'm constipated (*lit.* stomach has tied up)
	dà zāfī	is there pain ? (**zāfī** = heat, pain)
	na	*i.e.* pain of
	fitsārī	urine (see also under 4 (b) (iii) above)
	(gòbe) wàrhakà	at this time (tomorrow) (see Lesson 33, section 2)
7 (*a*)	**gìzàgìzai**	(plural of **girgijè,** *raincloud*) clouds
	kusa	is close (verb form of the noun **kusa,** *close*)
	bègē	a noun meaning *hope*
	hatsī	grain (see also under 5 (*c*) above)
	ḙōnè	burn (*i.e.* from the heat of the sun and lack of moisture)
	kāsà	run short, fall short
	gyàru	be repaired, corrected (**-u** form from **gyārà,** *fix, repair*)
7 (*b*)	**bazarā**	hot, muggy season (March–April) just before the rains come

ɗâukē	(rain) stops (see also under 5 (c) above)
zâi yi ?	will it mature ?
lālàcē	spoil (= **ɓācì** under 4 (b) (v) above)
lâifin kânsà	his own fault

Lesson 42

Additional Texts

1. Several fables have already been introduced as conversational materials in the foregoing lessons (see Lessons 20, 23, 26, 27, 30). Several more are introduced below. Since some version of each of these has already appeared in print (usually minus any indication of tone and vowel length) a reference to these is given for each text.

2. Màkāhò Mài Fìtilà

Wani sauràyī yanà yāwò dà dàddarē sai ya hàngi wani mùtûm dà fìtilà à hannunsà. Dà sukà gàmu ya ga—àshē, màkāhò nē!

Sai ya cè, ' Kai, màkāhò, kanà hàukā nè ? Mè ya kai kà yāwò dà fìtilà ? Darē dà rānā bà duk ɗaya su kè gàrē kà ba ? '

Màkāhò ya cê, ' Ai, duk ɗaya nè mànà ! Har, in dà darē nè nâ fī kà ganī. Fìtilàn nan, nā rìƙè ta bà don kâinā ba nè, àmmā don irìnkù nē—màsu idò àmmā maràsā hankàlī—don kù gan nì dà dàddarē, kadà kù tūrè ni ! '

Notes :

See *Ka Kara Karatu*, NORLA (now Gaskiya Corporation), 1954, page 4. See also Abraham, R. C., *Hausa Literature*, 1959, page 37.

màkāhò	blind man
saurayī (*pl.* sàmàrī)	young man
dà dàddarē = dà darē	at night

hàngā (i/ē)	see from a distance
hàukā	going mad
duk ɗaya	it's all the same
irìnkù	the likes of you
màsu idò	able to see (*lit.* possessing eyes)
tūrè	knock over

3. Dilā da Zalɓè

Wata rānā dilā yanà cîn kàzā, sai wani ƙàshī mài tsìnī ya kākàrē masà à màƙōgwàrō. Ya bi nân, ya bi cân, yanà nēman wandà zâi cirè masà ƙàshîn. Ya cê duk wandà ya cirè masà, zâi bā shì lādā.

Tô, sai zalɓè ya zō, ya cè shī zâi yi. Dilā ya būɗè bàkī, zalɓè ya sâ kânsà, ya cirō ƙàshîn.

Dilā ya jūyà, zâi yi tàfiyàrsà, sai zalɓè ya cê, 'Ìnā lādāna ? '

Dilā ya amsà, ya cè, ' Ai, lādankà kè nan : kā sâ kânkà cikin bàkin dilā, kā fìta lāfiyà ! '

Notes :

See *Ka Kara Karatu*, NORLA (now Gaskiya Corporation), 1954, page 7. See also Abraham, R. C., *Hausa Literature*, 1959, page 37.

zalɓè	common grey heron
ƙàshī	bone
tsìnī	sharp point
kākàrē	become jammed
màƙōgwàrō	throat
ya bi nân, ya bi cân	he went hither and thither
cirè	pull out
duk wandà	whoever
lādā	reward
cirō	pull out (-ō form of cirè)
jūyà	turn (*i.e.* turned to go)
lādankà kè nan	this is your reward

4. Kwàɗī Biyu

Waɗansu kwàɗī gùdā biyu sukà fāɗà cikin ƙwaryar madarā, sukà kāsà fìtā. Sunà ta iyò, sunà ta iyò, bâ dāmā. Anà nan, sai ɗayansù ya gàji, ya cê, ' Yâu kwānānā ya ƙārè.' Ya bar ƙòƙarī, ya nutsè, ya mutù.

Ɗayân, mā, ya yi ta yî. Mòtsinsà kumā, ya sâ mâi ya tàru, ya yi cūrì. Sā'àn nan ya hau bisà cūrìn mân, ya yi tsallē, ya fìta.

Allà ya cê, ' Tàshi ìn tàimàkē kà.'

Notes :

See *Ka Kara Karatu*, NORLA (now Gaskiya Corporation), 1954, page 4. See also Abraham, R. C., *Hausa Literature*, 1959, page 37.

kwàɗī (*sing.* **kwàɗō**)	frogs
kāsà	run short, fall short
ta	in the process of
iyò	swimming
bâ dāmā	it is/was impossible (**dāmā** = chance, opportunity)
anà nan	after awhile
nutsè	vanish (under water)
yi ta yî	keep on trying
mòtsī	movement, motion, activity
mâi	= **mân shānū**
tàru	gather together, collect (**-u** form of **tārà**, *gather, collect*)
cūrì	a ball
sā'àn nan	then . . .
tsallē	a jump

5. Mūgùn Àlƙālī

Akà kai wani ƙārā wurin àlƙālī, akà yi shàrì'à. Àlƙālī ya ga wandà akà yi ƙārarsà bâ shi dà gàskiyā, ya cê masà, ' Kanà dà màganà ? '

Mùtumìn ya cê bā yằ dà màganà àmmā à ɓòye yā
kwatàntà ukù dà hannunsà. Dà àlƙālī ya ga mùtumìn
ya kwatàntā dà hannunsà hakà ya yi tsàmmānì zâi bā
shì awākī ukù nē. Sai ya yankè shàrī'à, sukà tāshì.

Dà mùtumìn ya kōmà gidā, ya aikō wà àlƙālī dà
kàbēwà gùdā ukù. Dà ganin hakà àlƙālîn ya kirāwō
mùtûm, ya cê masà, ' Kai, dai, munāfùkī nè, kā cùcē nì !
Allà wadankà ! Tàshi, tàfi ! '

Dà mùtumìn ya fìta wàjē, ya cê, ' M̂, wànzāmì bā yằ
sôn jàrfā.'

Notes :

See *Ka Ƙara Karatu*, NORLA (now Gaskiya Corporation), 1954, page 6.   See also Abraham, R. C., *Hausa
Literature*, 1959, page 37.

àlƙālī	judge
shàrī'à	administration of justice
wandà akà yi ƙārarsà	the accused
à ɓòye	hidden (from ɓòyè, *hide*)
kwatàntā	indicate, compare (here, the man held up three fingers)
yankè shàrī'à	pass sentence, give the verdict
aikō . . . dà	send to (-ō form of aikà, *send*)
kàbēwà	pumpkin
dà ganin hakà	when he saw this
kirāwō	call (here) (the -ō form of kirā, *call*)
munāfùkī	hypocrite, traitor
cùtā (i/ē)	cheat
Allà wadankà	may God curse you !
m̂	(exclamation of slight surprise)
wànzāmì	barber (who shaves people's heads, performs scarification, tattoos, *etc.*)
jàrfā	tattoo marks
wànzāmì . . .	for the meaning of this proverb see Lesson 40, proverb 35

6. Kwàɗī dà Shānū

Waɗansu kwàɗī sunà kīwò à fàdamà, sai sukà hàngi bìjìmai gùdā biyu sunà faɗà. Sai ɗayansù ya cê, 'Kâi! Faɗà ɗîn nan fa, dà ban tsòrō! Mū, waɗàndà bā mù dà ƙarfī, yàyà zā mù yi dà kâmmù?'

Wàncan, kumā, ya cê, 'Kâi, ìnā ruwansù dà mū? Sunà yī tsàkāninsù kawài, don duk wandà ya fi ƙarfī tsàkāninsù yà gājè mātan shānûn dà kè cikin garkèn nân. Ai, bā sà kùlā dà irìmmù ƙanānā.'

Na farkō, mā, ya amsà cêwā, 'Hakà nē. Nā sanì, kōmē nāsù dàban ya kè dà nāmù. Àl'àdun zamansù bà ɗaya su kè dà nāmù ba. Àmmā fa, duk dà hakà, kō dà su kè dà nīsa yànzu, wandà ya kāsà cikinsù zâi shèƙà dà gudù, bà zâi kùlā dà kōmē ba sai kânsà. Wàtàkīlà zâi zō yà tattàkē mu cikin gudù. Lallē, faɗànsù yā shàfē mù!'

Àshē gàskiyā nè akà cê, 'Ìdan mânya-mânyā sunà faɗà kō talakāwā su kàn shā wàhalà.'

Notes :

See *Al'mara*, Oxford University Press and Gaskiya Corporation, 1952, page 4.

kīwò	grazing, searching for food; tending animals
fàdamà	marshy ground
bìjimī/bàjimī (*pl.* bìjìmai/bàjìmai)	big bull
faɗà	fighting, arguing
fa	(emphasis particle or insert) indeed
ban tsòrō	frightening, terrifying (*lit.* giving fear)
wàncan	the other one, the one in question
ìnā ruwansù ?	what do they care ? (**bā ruwansà** it is none of his concern ; **ìnā ruwankà ?** what business is it of yours ?)

gājè	inherit (-è form of gàdā, *inherit*)
garkè	herd, flock
kùlā dà	pay attention to
kōmē nāsù	everything about them
àl'ādà (*pl.* àl'àdū)	custom
àl'àdun zamansù	their way of life
ɗaya	here it means *same*
kō dà	even though
sheƙà dà gudù	take to (his) heels
tattàkē	trample under foot (from tākà, *tread on, walk along*)
mu	a direct object pronoun is high after a high-low-high tone verb
shàfā (i/ē)	affect, wipe
mânya-mânyā	the influential/wealthy of the world

7. Farkē dà Birai

An yi wani farkē, àttājìrī. Wata rānā ya ɗàuki hūlunàn dàrā gùdā gōmà zâi kai kàsuwā. Yanà kân hanyà sai ya rātsè gìndin wani itàcē don yà hūtà. Dà ya ji barcī yanà nēman kāmà shi, sai ya sâ duk hūlunàn à bisà kânsà—ɗaya bisà ɗaya—māgànin ɓàràyī kè nan. Shī kè nan, barcī ya kwāshè shi har dà minshārī.

Cân sai waɗansu birai sukà biyō ta wurîn dà farkên nan kè barcī, sukà gan shì. Tô, kun san halin birai dà sôn wàsā. Sai birì gùdā ya laɓàɓā, ya zārè hùlâd dà kè bisà, ya sâ à kânsà. Sauran birai, kumā, dà ɗai-ɗai sukà yi hakà. Sukà bar farkē dà tsōhuwar hùlarsà kawài. Sukà hayè kân itàcē, sukà zaunà, sunà kallonsà.

Farkē ya farkà bai ga hūlunànsà ba. Ya ɗagà kâi samà, sai ya yi arbà dà ɓàràyinsà à kân itàcē! Haushī ya kāmà shi. Ya cirè hùlâd dà kè kânsà, ya wurgar! Nan dà nan birai, kumā, sukà kwàikwàyē shì, sukà yi ta wurgō tāsù ƙasà. Mhm! Mādàllā! Farkē ya tsincè kāyansà, ya tàfi yanà farin cikì.

Notes :

See *Mu Koyi Hausa*, Gaskiya Corporation, 1960.

farkē/falkē	itinerant trader
birì (*pl.* birai)	monkey
àttājirī	wealthy trader
hùlā (*pl.* hūlunà)	hat, cap
dàrā	fez (**hùlad dàrā** = *fez*)
rātsè	turn aside, swerve (*e.g.* from a road)
daya bisà daya	one on top of the other
6àrāwò (*pl.* 6àràyī)	thief
minshārī	snoring
cân	used this way **cân** = *later*
biyō ta wurîn . . .	came by the place . . .
halī	character, temperament
sôn wàsā	playfulness (*lit.* liking playing)
la6à6ā	sneak up on
zarè	grab
dà dai-dai	one by one
hayè	climb (**hayè kân itàcē** = *climb up into the tree*)
dagà	lift up
yi arbà	come upon unexpectedly
haushī	vexation, anger
cirè	pull (thing) off, pull (thing) out
wurgar	throw (violently) (**-ar** form of **wurgà**, *throw*)
kwàikwayà(i/ē)	imitate
wurgō	throw down (**-ō** form of **wurgà**, *throw*)
m̀hm̂	exclamation of approval of an action
tsincè	pick up, find by chance (*e.g.* along the road) (**-è** form of **tsìntā**, *pick up*)
farin cikì	happiness (*lit.* white stomach)

Lesson 43

Bibliography

1. Publication of materials in and on Hausa started well
before the beginning of the twentieth century. The first
important grammar of the language was published by
J. F. Schön in 1862, followed by his Hausa dictionary in
1876,[1] and by 1911 it was possible for Struck to produce a
bibliography of Hausa which lists 227 items.[2] An
excellent survey of early writings in Hausa is P. E. H.
Hair, *The Early Study of Nigerian Languages* (Cambridge
University Press, 1967).

In addition to a substantial number of books and
articles by Europeans, Hausa students are fortunate to
have at their disposal a large number of publications
in Hausa. The contents of these publications include
fables, history, biography, proverbs, poetry, geography,
nature study, religious materials and much more. The
abundance of such material is due largely to the efforts
of the Gaskiya Corporation in Zaria, which has also
published a weekly newspaper for over twenty-five
years.[3] Since 1969, much of this initiative has passed to
the Northern Nigerian Publishing Company, Zaria.

There follows a selection of the publications in English
or Hausa which are of value to students beginning the
study of Hausa.

2. *Grammars* of a language are of two types : reference
grammars and pedagogical (teaching) grammars. In

[1] Schön, J. F., *Grammar of the Hausa Language.* London : Church
Missionary House, 1862. *Dictionary* (same publisher), 1876.

[2] ' Linguistic Bibliography of Northern Nigeria ', *Journal of the
African Society*, XI, 1911–12, pp. 47–61, 213–230.

[3] First issued January, 1939, editor Abubakar Imam.

spite of certain modifications made in the present
grammar to make it usable as a pedagogical grammar, it
is basically an introductory reference grammar. It is
recommended that this book be used whenever possible
in conjunction with a good pedagogical grammar, plus a
native speaker of Hausa, for maximum effectiveness.

(a) *Pedagogical Grammars.* Two pedagogical grammars
can be recommended. The first will be most easily
usable with this book because of the similarity of
approach. Tape recordings are available for use with
each of these books.

Kraft, Charles H. and Marguerite G., *Spoken Hausa:
Introductory Course.* Los Angeles, University of
California Press, 1973.

Hodge, Carleton T., and Ibrahim Umaru, *Hausa
Basic Course.* Washington, D.C. : U.S. Government
Printing Office (for the Foreign Service Institute),
1963.

An earlier pedagogical approach which, though brief,
is useful (if obtainable) is H. L. Ogilvie, *Helps to the
Study of Hausa.* Jos : Sudan Interior Mission,
1942–1951.

(b) *Reference Grammars.* The majority of the grammars
of Hausa which have been published must be classified as reference grammars (although many, like the
present volume, provide vocabularies and exercises
to assist the beginning student).

   (i) Only one of these grammars provides any
       accurate and thoroughgoing representation of
       tone and vowel length. It also provides a more
       accurate treatment of Hausa grammar than any
       of its competitors and thus, in spite of grave
       defects in the way the book is organized must,
       be regarded as the best available :

Abraham, R. C., *The Language of the Hausa People*. London : University of London Press, 1959. This edition is a rearrangement of *A Modern Grammar of Spoken Hausa*, 1941.

(ii) Other reference grammars with which the student may come into contact are listed and briefly evaluated below.

Maxwell, J. Lowry, and Eleanor M. Forshey, *Yau da Gobe*. Jos : Niger Press, n.d.
A valuable, though traditional, outline presentation of Hausa grammar. It ignores tone and vowel length but is generally reliable and more convenient to use than most of the other reference grammars listed here.

Robinson, Charles H., *Hausa Grammar*. London : Routledge and Kegan Paul, 1925 (reprinted 1959).
Once the standard grammar of Hausa. Produced between 1897–1925 by one of the greatest of Hausa scholars. A brief treatment of Hausa grammar with no attention to tone or vowel length but containing some valuable cultural materials.

Taylor, F. W., *A Practical Hausa Grammar*, London : Oxford University Press, 1923 (reprinted 1959).
A more complete grammar than Robinson's. Among the more useful of the older grammars but not always accurate.

Migeod, F. W. H., *A Grammar of the Hausa Language*. London : Kegan Paul, 1914.
The most extensive of the older grammars.

(iii) Passing mention may also be made of the following grammars which because of age,

incompleteness or unreliability are of less value
than those already listed :

Miller, W. R., *Hausa Notes*. London : Church
Missionary Society, 1901.

Miller, E. P., *Wata Biyu* (*A Guide to Hausa*).
Jos : S. I. M. Bookshop, revised edition 1939.

Howeidy, A., *Concise Hausa Grammar*. Oxford :
George Ronald, 1953 and 1959.

Skinner, A. N., *Hausa for Beginners*. London :
University of London Press, 1958. 2nd edition,
1968.

Brauner, S., and M. Ashiwaju, *Lehrbuch der
Hausa-Sprache*. Leipzig : VEB Verlag Enzyklo-
padie, 1966.

3. *Dictionaries.* There are two good dictionaries of
Hausa : [4]

Abraham, R. C., *Dictionary of the Hausa Language*.
London : University of London Press, 1949 (reprinted
1962).

Bargery, G. P., *A Hausa–English Dictionary and
English–Hausa Vocabulary*. London : Oxford University
Press, 1934 (reprinted 1951).

Abraham's dictionary provides a more accurate tonal
analysis and marks tone and vowel length throughout.
It contains, however, no English to Hausa section. Both
dictionaries cover virtually the same ground.

A. N. Skinner's, *Hausa–English Pocket Dictionary :
Kamus na Hausa da Turanci* (London : Longmans,
Green and Company, 1959, revised 1968) and *An*

---

[4] The earlier dictionaries by Schön (1876) and Robinson (1900),
' good ' in their day, do not compare with Abraham or Bargery.

English–Hausa Dictionary (Zaria ; Gaskiya Corporation, 1966) are very much ' for the pocket '. Unfortunately, they either ignore or are untrustworthy in their representation of tone and vowel length.

A more useful book (although it does not represent tone or vowel length) is *Hanyar Tadi da Turanci,* published by Longmans, Green and Company in 1957 (by A. N. Skinner though no author is indicated). This book is subtitled *A Dictionary of English Conversation for Hausa Students* but is very useful as an English to Hausa guide, containing over 300 pages of ordinary and idiomatic Hausa expressions.

4. *Reading Materials in Hausa.* As mentioned above there is an abundance of such materials and more are being produced all the time. Of the hundreds of items that could be listed, the following is a small sampling.

Abraham, R. C., *Hausa Literature and the Hausa Sound System.* London : University of London Press, 1959.

The first two thirds of this volume is an unorganized collection of Hausa literature with English translations of varying quality. This and Kraft's, *Hausa Readings* are, however, the only published collections of Hausa literature which are marked for tone and vowel length.

Ainslie, Marian D., *Nijeriya.* London : Longmans, Green and Company and Zaria : Gaskiya Corporation, 1960.

A 90-page elementary school geography book.

Baker, R. L. and L. O. Musawa, *Oxford Hausa Reader*, series 1, 2, 3. London : Oxford University Press, 1957–58.

Three well illustrated primary school reading primers.

Bello, Alhaji, *Gandoki,* Zaria : Gaskiya Corporation, 1934. 4th edition 1968.

A 73-page historical novel.

Bamalli, Nuhu, *Mungo Park Mabudin Kwara*. Zaria :
Gaskiya Corporation, 1948 (reprinted 1955).
A 153-page account of Mungo Park's first and his last
journeys seeking the mouth of the Niger River.

Bamalli, Nuhu, *Bala da Babiya*. Zaria : Gaskiya
Corporation, 1950.
An 82-page elementary health book.

Court, J. W., ed., *Kungurus Kan Kusu*. London :
Longmans, Green and Co., 1958.
A short selection of fables in Hausa.

East, Rupert, and Abubakar Imam, *Ikon Allah*.
Zaria : Gaskiya Corporation, 1949 (reprinted 1952).
A nature study book of nearly 400 pages.

Edgar, Frank (vols I and II), and Malam Mamman
Kano (vols III, IV, V), *Dare Dubu da Daya* (five
volumes). Lagos : CMS Bookshop and Zaria : Gaskiya
Corporation, 1924–64.
The Arabian Nights in Hausa.

Johnston, H. A. S., ed., *A Selection of Hausa Stories*.
London : Oxford University Press (Oxford Library of
African Literature Series), 1966.

Kirk-Greene, A. H. M., and Yahaya Aliyu, *A Modern
Hausa Reader*, London : University of London Press,
1966.
A collection of speeches and newspaper reports
illustrating contemporary Hausa.

Kraft, C. H., *Hausa Reader*. Berkeley and Los Angeles :
University of California Press, 1973.
Cultural, geographical and historical texts in Hausa (all
marked for tone and vowel length).

Imam, Alhaji Abubakar, *Magana Jari Ce* (three
volumes). Zaria : Gaskiya Corporation, 1937–39.
5th edition 1960.

A good, full-length (over 650 pages) novel. A bit advanced for a beginner but excellent reading at a later stage. A classic of Hausa literature.

Maƙarfi, Abdullahi, *Namun Daji da Tsuntsaye*. Zaria : Gaskiya Corporation, 1958.
A 71-page description of several wild animals and birds of West Africa.

Mani, Abdulmalik, *Zuwan Turawa Nijeriya Ta Arewa*. London : Longmans, Green and Company, and Zaria : Gaskiya Corporation, 1957.
A 218 page history of the arrival of the British in Northern Nigeria.

Rimmer, E. M., *et al.*, *Zaman Mutum da Sana'arsa*. Zaria : Gaskiya Corporation, 1955.
A 200-page treatment of various customs and crafts of certain of the world's peoples.

Skinner, A. N., *Hausa Tales and Traditions*, vol. I. London : Frank Cass, 1969.
This is the first of three volumes giving for the first time an English translation of F. Edgar's classic three-volume collection of Hausa folktales published in 1911–13 as *Litafi na Tatsuniyoyi na Hausa*.

Skinner, A. N., *Hausa Readings*. Wisconsin University Press, 1968.
A collection of readings from Edgar in Hausa with notes. Some are in *ajami* (Arabic) as well as romanized script.

Tafawa Balewa, Alhaji Sir Abubakar, *Shehu Umar*. Zaria : Gaskiya Corporation, 1946 (reprinted 1955).
The first novel of the late Prime Minister of Nigeria (49 pages), dealing with the travels of Shehu Umar from Bornu to Arabia. An English translation by M. Hiskett was published by Longmans in 1967.

U

Miscellaneous story booklets published by Gaskiya Corporation and Northern Nigerian Publishing Company :

Ka Kara Karatu (47 pages of fables).

Ka Yi Ta Karatu (77 pages of fables).

Al'mara (29 pages of fables).

Karamin Sani (two booklets, 56 and 62 pages of helpful information for elementary school children).

Jiki Magayi (a 51-page novelette).

Littafi Na Karantawa (48 pages of fables).

Ka Koyi Karatu (a 30-page elementary reader)

Ruwan Bagaja (a major novel).

Idon Matambayi (elementary reader).

Labaru Na Dā Da Na Yanzu (a schools' favourite).

5. *Specialized Studies.* These include general historical and cultural background materials both in English and Hausa.

Ames, David, and King, Anthony, *Glossary of Hausa Music . . . in Social Contexts.* Northwestern University Press, 1971.

Dalziel, J. M., *A Hausa Botanical Vocabulary.* London, 1916.
The standard work on this topic.

Hassan, A., and S. Naibi, *Chronicle of Abuja.* Lagos : African Universities Press, 1962.
An excellently illustrated account of Hausa society in Abuja.

Hill, Polly, *Rural Hausa : A Village and a Setting.* Cambridge University Press, 1972.

Hogben, S. J., and A. H. M. Kirk-Greene, *The Emirates of Northern Nigeria.* London : Oxford University Press, 1966.
Detailed history of the Hausa kingdoms.

Kirk-Greene, A. H. M., ' Neologisms in Hausa : A Sociological Approach,' *Africa*, vol. XXXIII, 1963, pp. 25–44.

A treatment of many of the fascinating borrowings coming into Hausa recently through contact with European languages (primarily English).

—— A Preliminary Inquiry into Hausa Onomatology. Zaria : Ahmadu Bello University, 1964.

Three studies in the origins of personal, title and place names.

——, *Ai, Hausa Ba Dabo Ba Ne*, Ibadan : Oxford University Press, 1966.

A collection of 500 Hausa proverbs with translations and notes.

Madauci, Ibrahim, Yahaya Isa and Bello Daura, *Hausa Customs*. Zaria, N.N.P.C., 1968.

A useful exposition of Hausa customs, crafts, pastimes, etc. Published in English.

Rattray, R. S., *Hausa Folk-Lore, Customs, Proverbs*. Oxford : Clarendon Press, 1913 (reprinted 1968).

An important collection, mostly gathered in Northern Ghana.

Smith, Mary F., *Baba of Karo*. London : Faber and Faber, 1954 (reprinted 1964).

A valuable biography of a Hausa woman in English with an introduction to Hausa society by M. G. Smith.

Smith, M. G., *The Economy of a Hausa Community of Zaria*, London : Her Majesty's Stationery Office, 1955.

A detailed study of the economics of a Hausa village.

—— *Government in Zazzau*. London : Oxford University Press, 1960.

An excellent political analysis of a Hausa state, 1800–1950.

Taylor, F. W., and A. G. Webb, *The Customs of the Hausa People.* London : Oxford University Press, 1932. A useful collection of cultural texts in Hausa and English.

Tremearne, A. J. N., *Hausa Superstitions and Customs.* London : J. Bale, Sons, 1913 (reprinted Frank Cass 1970). A large collection in English of cultural materials.

Whitting, C. E. J., *Hausa and Fulani Proverbs.* Lagos : Government Printer, 1940 (reprinted by Gregg International, Farnborough, Hants, England, 1967). A major collection of 2000 Hausa and 600 Fulani proverbs with English translations.

6. *Technical Studies.* A few of the many technical studies in English are noted here for those who wish to go more deeply into Hausa study. The titles indicate the content.

Other important technical articles in English will be found in such journals as *African Language Studies, Journal of African Languages, Journal of West African Languages, Bulletin of the School of Oriental and African Studies, Studies in African Linguistics, Afrika und Übersee,* etc. There are, in addition, several prominent Hausa scholars who customarily write in languages other than English. Among these are D. Olderogge of Russia, C. Gouffé of France, J. Lukas of Germany, P. Zima of Czechoslovakia and N. Pilszczikowa of Poland. In 1972 the Nigerian Languages Centre of Abdullahi Bayero College, Kano, produced the first issue of an African languages review written in Hausa, *Harsunan Nijeriya.* The most complete recent listing of writings on Hausa is that compiled by D. W. Arnott for the revised edition (1970) of D. Westermann and M. A. Bryan, *The Languages of West Africa* (International African Institute).

Carnochan, J., ' Glottalization in Hausa,' *Transactions of the Philological Society,* 1952, pp. 78–109.

Carnochan, J., 'A Study of Quantity in Hausa,' *Bulletin of the School of Oriental and African Studies*, 1951, pp. 1032–1044

Greenberg, Joseph H., ' Arabic Loan-Words in Hausa,' *Word*, 1947, pp. 85–97.
—— 'Some Problems in Hausa Phonology,' *Language*, 1941, pp. 316–323.

Hodge, Carleton T., *An Outline of Hausa Grammar*, supplement to *Language*, 1947.

Kraft, Charles H., ' The Morpheme nǎ in Relation to a Broader Classification of Hausa Verbals,' *Journal of African Languages*, 1964, pp. 231–240.
—— *A Study of Hausa Syntax* (3 volumes). Hartford, Connecticut : Hartford Seminary Foundation Bookstore, 1963.

Newman, Paul, ' Ideophones From a Syntactic Point of View ', *Journal of West African Languages*, V, 1968, pp. 107–17.

Parsons, F. W., ' An Introduction to Gender in Hausa,' *African Language Studies I*, 1960, pp. 117–136.
—— 'The Operation of Gender in Hausa : The Personal Pronouns and Genitive Copula,' *African Language Studies II*, 1961, pp. 100–124.
—— ' The Operation of Gender in Hausa : Stabilizer, Dependent Nominals and Qualifiers, *African Language Studies IV*, 1963, pp. 166–207.
—— ' Suppletion and Neutralization in the Verbal System of Hausa ', *Afrika und Übersee*, LV, 1971, pp. 49–97.
——, ' The Verbal System in Hausa,' *Afrika und Übersee*, XLIV, 1960, pp. 1–36.

Schachter, Paul, ' A Generative Account of Hausa ne and ce ', *Journal of African Languages*, V, 1966, pp. 34–53.

PART FIVE

APPENDICES

Key to Exercises

Hausa to English Exercises : [1]

Lesson 5 :

1. It's water.
2. They are donkeys.
3. It's an elephant.
4. She's an old woman.
5. He's a European.
6. It's a bird.
7. He's (my) grandfather.
8. It's a rat.
9. He's a student.
10. He's a man.

Lesson 6 :

1. Who is it ?
2. It's a town.
3. He's not the chief.
4. It is a school.
5. It's a bucket.
6. It's not a compound.
7. They are not children.
8. It's me.
9. It is her.
10. It is us.

---

[1] It should be noted that there is often more than one possible translation for a given sentence. Only one translation (usually the most probable) is given here. The translations are designed to provide the most natural English equivalent of the Hausa rather than to be word for word literal renderings.

Lesson 7 :

1. They didn't go away.
2. I haven't eaten yet.
3. They didn't bring the book.
4. The girl didn't return.
5. Audu didn't come to school.

Lesson 8 :

1. Where is the chief's home ?
2. He's the chief's boy.
3. I brought Garba's lamp.
4. It is cat food.
5. The girl went to the schoolteacher's farm.

Lesson 9 :

1. The boy went to Kano with his mother.
2. Your teacher went to his farm this morning.
3. Why did you put your book on my chair ?
4. My horse entered your friend's town.
5. He brought my bicycle. He didn't bring yours.

Lesson 10 :

1. A (certain) boy fell into the water.
2. This river is the Niger.
3. You (have) put this spoon in this box.
4. Where is the chair ? There's the chair.
5. These people went to a certain town.

Lesson 11 :

1. There are two mangoes on the table.
2. Arithmetic is difficult. But I understand.
3. He put the banana in his mouth, he ate (it).
4. Where is the large box ? Bello has gone to his home
   with it.

5. How many guavas did you bring ? Ten.
6. Good heavens ! Audu has forgotten my name. This is not good.

Lesson 12 :

1. Don't do this work.
2. Don't let the girl eat this food.
3. Come and sit down (to a female).
4. Don't do thus.
5. Go out and close the door.

Lesson 13 :

1. I am hungry. Is there food ?
2. Did you bring that man ? Yes, here he is.
3. Isn't there a spoon here ? Yes (there is not).
4. Have the children gone to school ? Not yet.
5. Haven't you got ready ? No (on the contrary, we have got ready).
6. Here is Malam Garba's book. Where is mine ?

Lesson 14 :

1. What happened at Yakubu's house ?
2. The storm has passed now. Let's play.
3. Stop and tie up your loads.
4. His horse ran swiftly to the town.
5. He went to his friend's.

Lesson 15 :

1. Bello brought us meat.
2. Take them this book and return quickly.
3. Who gave you the eggs ? The trader at the side of the road.
4. She went to market, she bought an expensive yam.
5. You (*f.*) picked them up. You (*f.*) took them to your husband's home.

Lesson 16 :

1. I am very hungry. Because of this I will eat now.
2. We won't eat here.
3. What will you (*f.*) do ? I shall return to town after a while.
4. Will you tell me the news of your trip ?
5. Are you going to market today ? No, we're going to my friend's home.

Lesson 17 :

1. He fell into the water.
2. After the dance we will go to the chief's.
3. If he returns then I shall go.
4. He did his work like a boy.
5. Before I go he will come.
6. The guest put his shoes under my chair.

Lesson 18 :

1. I don't have (any) farming implements.
2. His father is coming now.
3. My wife is working very well on the farm.
4. The chief wants to come and talk to us tomorrow.
5. (My) wife has our food in her hut.
6. The people of that town don't dance.

Lesson 19 :

1. She is drinking water.
2. Does he open the door ? Yes, he opens (it).
3. Do they sell motor cars ? Yes, they sell (them).
4. This box is heavy.
5. This work is not difficult.

Lesson 20 :

1. The people who are coming will stay here a long time.
2. The one who came today left early.

3. There is no one whom they fear.
4. What was done at Kano the day before yesterday ?
5. I didn't see those that you want there.

Lesson 21 :

1. Where is the money I gave you yesterday ?
2. Which lorry will you go in ?
3. I saw a kind of dance that I hadn't seen before.
4. Whenever he comes I don't want to see him.
5. I won't buy anything at market today.

Lesson 22 :

1. Lorries killed many people last year.
2. People want doctors to do their work well.
3. Men are stronger than women.
4. Where are the compounds in which we left our loads yesterday ?
5. He sent me to the leading men of the town because they want(ed) me to talk to them.

Lesson 23 :

1. Some large aeroplanes landed at Kano.
2. Those looking for food obtained a little.
3. This little book is better reading than that big one.
4. Little children are playing in the old man's home.
5. He put on (his) big gown but didn't dance.

Lesson 24 :

1. During the rainy season this river filled to the brim with water.
2. All of us got up at the same time, we threw him outside.
3. When I saw him all of a sudden he mounted his horse (and) ran off.

4. Long ago there was an old man who prepared his farm at the edge of this road.
5. It is imperative that they get work right away. Will you give it to them ?

Lesson 25 :

1. They dismissed her from (her) work.
2. Sell it to me please.
3. Don't you (*pl.*) worry, nothing has happened yet.
4. Pour it in the basin. After that water the horse.
5. Why won't you reveal your secret from within your heart ?

Lesson 26 :

1. May God permit us to be successful in our trading. If this does not happen we'll have to borrow.
2. Let me increase my efforts in this work. Why, haven't you got tired ? Won't you leave (it) yet ?
3. I've never seen this type of dance. Let me try to do it. God forbid ! Good gracious, you won't be able to do it !
4. I talked to him last week but he hasn't returned this week.
5. In the past they rode horses but now they prefer cars. Is that so ? It's true.

Lesson 27 :

1. I had planned to go to his home (anyway) to greet him, then I heard the news and decided it would be best for me to tell him.
2. Before he (first) came I had worked here a long time.
3. When I came upon him immediately he broke into a run.
4. Is our food all gone ? No, there is a little left. Do you want me to cook some more ?
5. Will the Minister of Education give a speech at Gusau ? Yes, let's get ready and go.

Lesson 28 :

1. Why, I forgot to bring the food cooked. I brought it uncooked.
2. It will be best for you to wait here for now. Before you return again it will be foodtime.
3. We kept asking everywhere in town but we got no news of him.
4. Heavens! An amazing thing happened yesterday— the noise of an aeroplane frightened me so that I almost ran away!
5. I'm going to the canteen to buy tinned food, bottled beer and (some) other things that I need.

Lesson 29 :

1. I need to cut this cloth. Pick up the scissors and help me.
2. He's not a person of good character. He is trying to keep my friend from (obtaining) work.
3. When he had entered his market stall he sat down and started sewing.
4. I'll wait for him. That is, I shall wait here until he returns.
5. There are indications that you will have trouble here if you don't relocate your things right away.

Lesson 30 :

1. A snake bit the messenger but the doctor gave him medicine so that he got well.
2. He's not a Hausa, he's a Fulani. But in spite of this he speaks the Kano dialect (of Hausa) well.
3. Zaria is south-west of Kano. Katsina is to the north-west of it.
4. We had planned to work together but he was late. Because of this I lack anything to sell at market.
5. Moses is an expert. There is no one who can do this work except him alone. We should engage him instead of Audu.

English to Hausa Exercises : [2]

Lesson 5 :

1. Sūnā nè.
2. Sâ nē.
3. Bērāyē nè.
4. Bàhaushè nē.
5. Mātā nè.
6. Màcè cē.
7. Wàsā nè.
8. Zàkarà nē.
9. Gidā nè.
10. Watà nē.

Lesson 6 :

1. Makarantā cè.
2. Mùtûm nē.
3. Yârā nè.
4. Sarkī nè.
5. Shī kè nan.
6. Bà sâ ba nè, sānìyā cè.
7. Bà yârā ba nè.
8. Kudī nè.
9. Bà idò ba nè.
10. Bà kàsuwā ba cè.

Lesson 7 :

1. Mùtûm bài yi gōnā ba.
2. Bài zō dà sâfē ba.
3. Yārinyà bà tà tàfi gōnā ba.
4. Bàn yi aikì ba tùkùna.
5. Bà à kāwō kujèrā ba.

[2] It should be noted that there is often more than one possible translation for a given sentence. Only one translation (usually the most probable) is given here. The translations are designed to provide the most natural Hausa equivalent of the English rather than to be word for word literal renderings.

Lesson 8 :

1. Wannàn giɗan sarkī nè ?
2. Ùban yārò yā tàfi Kanò.
3. Mālàmin makarantā bài ci àbinci ba.
4. Ìnā àbincin dōkì ?
5. Gà sānìyar Audù.

Lesson 9 :

1. Uwātā dà ùbānā sun tàfi gidankà jiyà.
2. Ìnā sàbulùna ? Nā sâ shi cikin ɗākìna. Gà nākà.
3. Gidammù à Kanò nē. Ìnā nākà ?
4. Ùbantà yā fìta gàrī à kân hanyàr Kanò.
5. Yàushè àbōkīnā ya ci àbincinsà. Dà sāfē.

Lesson 10 :

1. Wannàn yārò àbōkīnā nè.
2. Kin sâ wancàn kujèrā nân.
3. Waɗànnân yârā. Waɗàncân yârā.
4. Bàn sanì ba tùkùna.
5. Nā tàfi gàrin càn.

Lesson 11 :

1. Yārinyà tā zaunà à kujèrā.
2. Nā yi kuskurè cikin lìssāfìna.
3. Yā kai kèkē zuwà gidansà.
4. Mun bi hanyà à bàkin kògī.
5. Kâi !, àkwai mùtûm takwàs cikin wancàn mōtà.

Lesson 12 :

1. Kadà kà buɗè tāgà !
2. Tsàya ! Shìga ! Zàuna !
3. Kì kāwō àbinci nân.
4. Bàri yà yi aikìnsà.
5. Kù zō kù ci àbincinkù à gidammù.

x

Lesson 13 :

1. Uwātā tā dāwō (nè) ? Ā'à, bà tà dāwō ba.
2. Bellò bài tàfi Kanò jiyà ba ? Ā'à, yā tàfi.
3. Àkwai aikì ? Ī, àkwai aikì dà yawà àmmā bābù kuɗī.
4. Àkwai ƙwai dà madarā nân ? Àkwai madarā, àmmā
   bābù ƙwai.
5. Nā ji yunwà. Kai fà ?

Lesson 14 :

1. Tā wucè ƙōfà.
2. Sun tàfi sù zaunà cikin inuwàr itàcē.
3. Yā fàru nân jiyà.
4. Audù yā kōmà gidā shēkaranjiyà.
5. Tā tàfi kàsuwā dà wuri.

Lesson 15 :

1. Yā gan nì ? Ī, àmmā bài san kà ba.
2. Yā sàmi nāmà. Tā dafà shi. Sun cī shì dà saurī.
3. Mun bar mangwàrò (gùdā) ukù cikin mōtàrsà. (Kà)
   tàfi kà sàmē sù.
4. Tā shiryà manà àbinci cikin inuwàr bàbban itàcē.
5. Yā sàyi kāyan aikì. Bàn san dàlīlì ba.

Lesson 16 :

1. Zā mù tàfi rawā à kàsuwā gòbe.
2. Bà zā kà tàfi makarantā ba.
3. Zā sù tàmbàyē kà kà bā sù kuɗī.
4. Ìnā zâ ka ? Zâ ni yāwò.
5. Gòbe Mālàm Bellò zâi tàfi Kanò. Zâi kāwō dōkìn
   ùbansà.

Lesson 17 :

1. Nā ga Yūsufù dà ùbansà à gidansù.
2. Kō nī kō ita zâi zō makarantā gòbe dà sāfē.

3. Nā nềmi àkwiyầ ƙàrƙashin tēbừr àmmā bàn gan tầ ba.
4. Ìdan nā dāwō watầ mài zuwầ sai ìn sầyē shì.
5. Ìdan kā yi minì aikì zā kà sầmi kuɗī dàgà gàrē nì (or dàgà wurīna).

Lesson 18 :

1. Sunầ màganầ tầre.
2. Yā yìwu yanầ Ìkkō yànzu.
3. Yanầ dà bầbban itầcē gàban gidansà.
4. Yanầ dà 'yan'uwā (gùdā) ukù à gidā.
5. Bầ ni dà shī. Don Allầ kadầ kà yi fushī !
6. Ìdan yanầ nan bà zân tầfi cikin jirgin ƙasā ba.

Lesson 19 :

1. Kōfầ tanầ bùɗe. Rùfē shì.
2. Tanầ kāwō ƙwaryầ.
3. Yanầ sầyen àbinci ? Ī, yanầ sầyē.
4. Bà tà hūrầ wutā ba ? Ā'ầ, tā hūrầ.
5. Yanầ tsầye dà kāyā mài nauyī à kânsầ.

Lesson 20 :

1. Tīcầ nē mukầ ganī.
2. Wancàn màcè tanầ aikì nân.
3. Yầushè kikà zō ?
4. Gầ yầrā waɗầndà zā sù tầfi cikin mōtầ.
5. Zā mù sầmē sù à wurîn dà mukầ gan sù jiyầ.

Lesson 21 :

1. Kā san shì nē ? Yanầ dà zàzzầɓī.
2. Ìnā ka tầfi dà mōtàrmù ?
3. Wàcè irìn rìgā nề ka kāwō dàgà kàntī ?
4. Inầ dà aikì dà yawầ kō'ìnā cikin gàrin nàn.
5. Cân nā ga sarkîn dà ya zō gàrī jiyầ.

Lesson 22 :

1. Àkwai màkàràntū dà yawà à ƙasàshen Afìrkà.
2. Hàusàwā sunà dà kùjèrū dà yawà cikin gidàjensù.
3. Waɗansu lìttàttàfai sunà dà tātsūniyōyī à cikī.
4. Bābù mōtōcī dà yawà à waɗansu ƙasàshē.
5. Maròƙā waɗàndà su kè nan jiyà bā sà nan yâu.

Lesson 23 :

1. Kanò bà tà kai Ìkkō girmā ba.
2. Rìgarsà ja-ja cè.
3. Dōkìnsà yā kai nàwa gudù.
4. Gàjèrū dà yawà sunà zàune à ɗàkì.
5. Faràrē sun fi baƙàƙē kyâu.

Lesson 24 :

1. Tāyà waddà na ganī sābuwā ful cè.
2. Gùdu maza-maza kà kāwō ruwā.
3. Zā tà shiryà àbinci yâu yâu.
4. Inà sô ìn tàfi gidānā tùkùn.
5. An jimà kàɗan zā mù kōmà gidàjemmù.

Lesson 25 :

1. Kâr kà zub dà shī ! Kàmā shì kà shìga.
2. Sun sayō itàcē.
3. Kā tabbàtā tā shā shì dukà ? Ī, tā shā.
4. Sàukar dà shī nân. Yànzu kwàntar dà shī.
5. Mun fisshē shì, mun tsayar dà shī.

Lesson 26 :

1. Nā zìyàrci gidan sarkī àmmā yā rigā yā tàfi.
2. Kâi, wancàn mùtûm yā cikà ƙaryā ! Sabò dà wannàn
   bā nà sônsà.
3. Anà ruwā dà yawà dà dàmunā. Hakà nē.

4. Bài daɗè à Nïjēriyà ba àmmā yā iyà Hausā kàmar jàkin Kanò.
5. Inà sô ìn ci bāshì dòmin ìn sàyi sābuwar mōtà.

Lesson 27 :

1. Waɗansu mafàsā sunà sô ìn gayà masù làbārìn gàrī.
2. Nā sàmē shì yanà aikì. Shī màkānīkì nē. Yā daɗè yanà gyāran mōtōcī.
3. Dà mā yā yàrda yà dākàtā nân har ìn zō, àmmā yànzu bàn san àbîn dà zâi yi ba.
4. Sarkī yā cê, kadà kà sākè zuwà gidansà. Yā fi kyâu kà sàmē shì à ōfìshinsà.
5. Yā iyà Hausā àmmā tanà masà wùyā ainù.

Lesson 28 :

1. Nawà-nawà nē gwēbà ? Kwabò-kwabò (nē), bâ ragì.
2. Câ na kè zā kà zō gòbe àmmā kā zō jiyà.
3. Àkwai abūbuwà màsu bā dà màmākì dà yawà à dūniyà yâu.
4. Yā fi kyâu à ci dàfaffen àbinci dà tàfàsasshen ruwā kadà à ji cïwò.
5. Ìdan bàn yi jarràbâwā ba bà zân cī tà ba.

Lesson 29 :

1. Kà ɗinkà minì kyàkkyāwar rìgā. Zâ ni rawā gòbe.
2. Inà sô kà tàimàkē nì ìn kau dà kèken ɗinkìnā zuwà wata bukkà.
3. Nī, kàm, zân jirā shì nân—wàtàkīlà zâi zō an jimà.
4. Bàn nūnà masà àgōgonkà ba. Wai, yā gan shì à hannunkà.
5. Bài ci ba tùkùna. Dom mè ? Dòmin nā hanà masà àbinci har kà dāwō.

Lesson 30 :

1. Shī màntau nè. Kadà kà gayà masà yà yi makà wani àbù.

2. Jìm kàɗan ma'àikàtā dukà sukà tàfi. Bàn san àbîn
   dà zân yi ba.
3. Kàwō mabūɗī nân. Bàri ìn būɗè ƙōfà.
4. Nā dākàtā kàɗan har makàɗā sukà fārà kasà kûnnē.
5. Inà tsàmmānì ìdan màtarsà tā rērà wāƙà sarkī zâi yi
   màmākì.

Translations of Dialogues and Fables

Lesson 4 :

B. Greetings at (your) coming, Isa.
I. Greetings.
B. How's (your) tiredness ?
I. There's no tiredness.
B. How's (your) work ?
I. (I'm) thankful for work.
B. What's the news ?
I. The news (is) only good.
B. Good.
I. Did (you) sleep well ?
B. Fine.
I. How's (your) family ?
B. Very well.
I. Good. (See you) tomorrow.
B. Good, may God take us (to tomorrow).
I. Amen.

Lesson 5 :

M. Greetings student.
A. Greetings teacher.
M. What's this ?
A. This is a donkey.
M. Okay, what's this ?
A. It's a bird.
M. What's this ?
A. It's a goat.
M. Okay, what's this ?
A. This is a sheep.
M. Good, until tomorrow.
A. Okay, may God take us (to tomorrow).

Lesson 6 :

Y. Greetings at your coming David.
D. Greetings.
Y. Did you sleep well ?
D. Very well.
Y. Who went to town ?
D. Audu.
Y. Has he returned ?
D. No, not until tomorrow.
Y. Good.

Lesson 7 :

B. How's (your) day (going) ?
G. Fine.
B. How's (your) tiredness ?
G. There's no tiredness.
B. Good.
G. Have you come well ?
B. Fine, nothing's wrong.
G. Is your family well ?
B. Very well.
G. Where's Bello ?
B. He went to Kano.
G. Good. Did he go to market ?
B. No, he didn't go to market.
G. Okay. (See you) later.
B. Okay. (See you) later.

Lesson 8 :

U. What is this called ?
A. It's a bicycle.
U. Whose is it ?
A. This is the bicycle of the chief's son.
U. Okay, where's Audu's bicycle ?
A. There it is in the hut.

U. Good, thank (you).
A. Okay.

Lesson 9 :

Ad. Is this compound yours ?
Ab. Yes, it's mine.
Ad. Where is your farm ?
Ab. There's my farm over there.
Ad. Good.
Ab. I finished planting yesterday.
Ad. Fine, when did you start ?
Ab. At the beginning of this month.
Ad. As for me, I haven't finished mine yet.
Ab. That's okay. I (have to) go now.
Ad. Okay, until another time.
Ab. Fine, may God take us (to another time).
Ad. Amen.

Lesson 10 :

K. Some people have come to our compound.
M. Good, I've brought food from market today.
K. Good. There's plenty of drinking water too.
M. The chief of the town has come.
K. (You're) right. He has come with an important man.
M. Is that man a chief also ?
K. Yes, his boy has brought a large box.
M. Good, what's in the box ?
K. I don't know.

Lesson 11 :

M. Two and three are how many ?
D. They are five.
M. That's right. How about six and seven ?
D. Thirteen.
M. Good. Four times two is how many ?

D. It's nine.

M. No ! You made a mistake.

D. (You're) right. It's only eight.

M. Okay. How many is six times three ?

D. Eighteen.

M. Good. Is this arithmetic difficult ?

D. No, it's not difficult.

M. Good.

Lesson 12 :

H. Jacob, greetings.

Y. Greetings.

H. Is your family well ?

Y. Very well. Have you come well ?

H. Fine. Nothing's wrong.

Y. Good. Enter, let's sit down.

H. Good. Gosh, the sun is hot today.

Y. (You're) right. Boy, bring drinking water !

H. I've come to greet you.

Y. Good. Thank (you). Have you come from market ?

H. No, I've come from home just now.

Y. Fine. Here's water to drink.

H. Good, thanks. I (have to) go now.

Y. Okay. Until another time.

H. Fine, until another time.

Lesson 13 :

M. Are there potatoes at market today ?

G. No, but there are a lot of yams.

M. Good. How much do yams cost ?

G. 1 shilling and 5 kobos to 2 shillings.

M. Wow they are expensive !

G. Not so ! They are all large.

M. That's all right. Are there also bananas ?

G. Yes there are, but not many.

M. Fine, how about guavas ?

G. A lot. There are also plenty of mangoes and citrus.
M. Good. Let's go and get (some).
G. Good, let's go.

Lesson 14 :

B. How much does a bicycle tyre cost ?
M. Well, there are three kinds. There are white, black and red.
B. Fine, how much does each cost ?
M. A white one is 1 naira, 6 shillings.
B. Wow, that's expensive !
M. But that's the best one.
B. How about a black one ?
M. 1 naira, 4 shillings.
B. What about a red one ?
M. The red ones are the least expensive at 1 naira, 2 shillings.
B. Good.

Lesson 15 :

B. Okay, I'll buy the white one for 1 naira, 4 shillings.
M. No sale. That's the price of a black one.
B. All right, how much is the real price ?
M. I reduce (the price) 3 kobos.
B. I increase (my price) by 5 kobos.
M. Come, come now sir !
B. Speak the truth.
M. Pay ₦1·55.
B. Okay, I offer (you) ₦1·50.
M. I'll agree to ₦1·52½.
B. Good, here's the money.

Lesson 16 :

A. Where are you going Kande ?
K. I'm going to the canteen to buy a new body cloth.
A. Why ?

K. To put on to go to the dance the day after tomorrow.
A. Good. Boy, your present body cloth is no good !
K. You're right. It has really got old.
A. Did your husband give you the money ?
K. No ! I sold (some) peanuts.
A. Okay.

Lesson 17 :

M. Greetings in (your) work Dogo.
D. Greetings at (your) coming.
M. How's (your) day (going) ?
D. Fine, nothing wrong.
M. Good.
D. Are you heading for town ?
M. No, I'm just out for a stroll.
D. Okay. Let's sit down and chat.
M. Okay. Here's (some) good shade.
D. Goodness, it's (really) hot today !
M. You're right, it's the time for it.
D. Right.
M. I hear you will go to Kano tomorrow.
D. Yes. I'll go by lorry in the morning.
M. Good, what will you do there ?
D. I'm going to sell my guinea corn in the market.
M. Good. Will you stay long in Kano ?
D. Yes, I'm going to look for work there.
M. Fine. When will you return (here) ?
D. Not until next month.
M. Good. I have to go now.
D. Okay. (See you) when I return from Kano.
M. Right, may you return safely.
D. Amen.

Lesson 18 :

J. I want to talk to the head of the house.
G. The head of the house isn't here today.

J. Okay, when will he return ?

G. Why, I don't know. He went to Lagos.

J. Did he go by aeroplane ?

G. No, by train.

J. How many days will he stay there ?

G. Oh it won't be more than a week.

J. Is he going to buy supplies there ?

G. Probably. But he went because his brother has died.

J. Will he most probably return next week ?

G. Yes.

J. When he returns tell him I need his help.

G. Okay, I'll tell him.

J. Good. (See you) later.

G. Okay, (see you) later.

Lesson 19 :

T. In schoolwork what is the most difficult for you ?

A. Well, only arithmetic gives me trouble.

T. Is that right ? What about English ?

A. Well, English is very difficult but arithmetic is more so.

T. Reading isn't difficult ?

A. No. It's easy. Reading is also (very) enjoyable.

T. Good. Do you read a lot ?

A. Yes indeed ! All the time.

T. But you can't do arithmetic ?

A. No, I can do (it) all right. But it is difficult.

T. Okay. Continue with your efforts.

Lesson 20 :

The Hyena, the Lizard and the Dog

In olden times there was a hyena. One day she was very hungry. So she arose and went out. She was looking for food when there was a lizard stealing beans. When she saw the lizard she caught him. She was about to eat him when she saw a dog.

So she said (to herself), ' Let me take the lizard home before I return to catch the dog.'

So she took the lizard home.

When she returned she didn't see the dog. While she was taking the lizard home the dog ran off into the bush.

When the hyena returned home she didn't see the lizard. While she was looking for the dog the lizard left the hyena's hole and went into the bush.

The hyena was amazed, she said, ' Why, whatever you seek in the world, if it is not your lot, you won't get (it) ! '

Lesson 21 :

S. (My) wife told me you are not well.
B. That's right.
S. What's bothering you ?
B. It's a headache.
S. Oh, (I'm) sorry ! Have you taken (some) medicine ?
B. Yes. The doctor gave me a shot.
S. Good. Is there also a fever ?
B. Formerly there was but it is better now.
S. Good. When did it hit you ?
B. Why it was yesterday, while I was (working on my) farm.
S. Well, I hope that God will make (you) better.
B. Amen.

Lesson 22 :

S. What are they doing in town ?
I. Why they're dancing—the market day dancing.
S. Good. What kind of dancing do they do ?
I. Every kind. There's no kind that they will not do.
S. Are there a lot of people there ?
I. There certainly are ! There are men and women, children and old folks.
S. Will they allow me to go and watch ?

I. Why certainly they'll agree ! Let's go together.
S. Good. Are you going to dance ?
I. Good heavens, I don't dance anymore. I'm too old !
S. That's okay.
I. How about you ? Do you want to try (this type of) dancing ?
S. No. *I* can't do your kind of dancing.
I. Okay, let's just stand and watch.
S. Fine.

Lesson 23 :

Everyone Has One Who Is Stronger Than He Is

One day a small bird caught a worm. He was about to eat it when the worm cried out saying, ' Please let me go ! '

The bird said, ' No. Why, I'm going to eat you, because I'm stronger than you are.'

So he picked up the little worm and ate it.

When he finished eating it a hawk saw him. So the hawk caught the little bird. As he was about to eat him the bird cried out saying, ' Be patient with me, let me go ! '

The hawk refused saying, ' Why, you are my food for today, because I'm stronger than you are.'

So the hawk ate the bird that had eaten the little worm.

Before the hawk had finished eating the bird a griffon fell upon him. So the hawk began to cry out, but the griffon didn't release him because she was stronger than he was.

After a little while the griffon flew up into the air. She didn't get very far (*lit.* stay long) before she felt an arrow in her body. Why, a certain hunter had seen her and killed her.

The griffon had come up against the one who was the strongest of all.

Lesson 24 :

L. Gosh, the rainy season is really upon us !

H. You're right. I went to the river this morning. I couldn't get across.

L. Is it full ?

H. It is completely full ! To the extent that the strength of the current made me fearful.

L. That's certainly something to fear. It is very swift.

H. (You're) right ! Why, sometimes it carries a person off.

L. That's so. If someone falls in he will die.

H. (You're) right ! This kind of a river is an evil thing.

L. Well, what shall we do ?

H. Why, we'll have to follow a different road.

L. But another road will be (very) long. Won't it ?

H. Yes. But there's no other way.

L. You're right. We have to go the long way.

H. Okay, let's go.

Lesson 25 :

U. You've returned from the city, have you ?

B. Yes, I returned the day before yesterday morning.

U. Fine. But I heard that there was trouble there.

B. That's for certain ! Wow ! Some compounds caught fire, it burned them up completely !

U. Gosh ! (Those) people are certainly unfortunate ! How about you ?

B. Why, I'm okay. It didn't come near where I was living.

U. Good ! Previously I had thought that perhaps it had come near where you were.

B. No. It didn't bother us at all. But some had a lot of trouble.

U. That's for certain.

B. Why, one day I met a friend of mine and asked him about the fire. He said their compound had burned completely.

U. Good heavens ! What did you do ?

B. Why, I had to fix him a place in my room.

U. Fine, but what happened to his family ?

B. Oh they stayed at another person's home.

U. Good ! When will they (be able to) start a new compound ?

B. They won't wait long. They'll gather the materials and start right away.

U. Good. May God help them.

B. Amen !

Lesson 26 :

Audu and Ali

Audu and Ali were travelling. They were on their way to market with (some) goods. All at once there was something at the side of the path. Ali picked it up and looked at it. Why it was a bag of money !

So Audu said, ' Gosh, we have fallen into luck today ! '

Ali said, ' What ? *We* have fallen into luck ? Or is it *I* who have fallen into luck ? '

Audu said, ' Okay, (have it your way), may God grant us safety.'

They continued on their way until they came to a forest. Then some highway robbers fell on them. Audu and Ali took off on the run. The robbers followed after them.

After awhile Ali got tired because of his heavy load. He said, ' Alas. Today we have fallen into misfortune.'

Audu said, ' What ? *We* have fallen into misfortune. Or is it *you* who has fallen into misfortune ? '

Lesson 27 :

The Fruitbat Doesn't Pay Taxes

One day the king of the animals called his representative (*wakili*) and said to him, ' Go everywhere in my country

Y

to the homes of all the animals and collect taxes from each of them.'

The *wakili* said, ' May you live long, I'll do it right away.'

So the *wakili* went all over the land and collected the tax from every home. But when he came to the home of the fruitbat (the latter) refused to pay the money.

' Why, I'm not an animal,' said the fruitbat. ' Well, is there any one of the subjects of the king of the animals who has wings like I have ? Is there any who can fly in the air like me ? Well, I'm not going to pay taxes to the king of the animals.'

That was that. The *wakili* of the king of the animals left him and returned to the palace and told the king. The king, for his part, thought a bit and said, ' Well, he's right. The fruitbat is not our kind, leave him alone.'

The next day the king of the birds called *his* representative (*wakili*) and sent him to collect taxes from every bird. When the *wakili* came to the fruitbat's home and asked him for the tax money, the fruitbat laughed at him saying, ' As for me, I won't pay him taxes.'

' Have you ever seen a bird with teeth,' he said. ' Or one who gives birth to its young alive and breast-feeds them ? Come, come ! I'm not a subject of the king of the birds ! '

When the *wakili* returned to the palace and told the king of the birds, they (all) agreed : the fruitbat is not a bird.

For this reason the fruitbat is betwixt and between : he isn't an animal, he isn't a bird.

Lesson 28 :

T. David !

D. Yes ?

T. Where are you going ?

D. I'm headed home. I've just now left work (and arrived here).

T. Fine. Where do you work ?

D. Well, I'm a clerk at a canteen.

T. Is that so ? I thought you were in school.

D. No. Last year I left (*i.e.* having completed) Primary School. I couldn't get into Secondary School.

T. Didn't you pass the examination ?

D. No, it was very difficult for me. But that's okay, since I've (been able to) get work.

T. Good. What kind of work do you do ?

D. Well, I have various jobs : sometimes I arrange goods, sometimes I sell goods, sometimes even the head clerk gives me paperwork to do.

T. Hm. Are most of your goods brought from European countries ?

D. Yes. But now they have started to make certain things in this country—like shoes, cloth, cement and bottled drinks.

T. Good ! Is it true that bottled drinks are only made from boiled water ?

D. Of course ! It's not like our own beer !

T. How about tinned food—is it all cooked ?

D. Yes. They say that they cook it when they prepare it.

T. Gracious ! It really is amazing how it is possible to cook a lot of food, put it in tins, and set it aside for even as much as five years !

D. You're right. Well, that's the way the world is now— it is full of amazing things.

T. Indeed it is.

Lesson 29 :

H. Greetings, tailor !

G. Why, Aaron ! Greetings in the (late) afternoon.

H. Greetings. How's (your) work today ?

G. Well, work never runs out.

H. Good. That's the way one wants it.

G. You're right. Are you (just) wandering in the market ?

H. No. I've been looking for your stall.

G. Oh. The other day I moved my things to this place.

H. Good. Before you were in a grass (mat) stall but this one is (made) of corrugated roofing (pan).

G. Right. I've been fortunate.

H. Good. Could you sew me some clothing ?

G. Well, it's my occupation ! What kind do you want ?

H. I need two (pair of) shorts and a big gown.

G. Fine. Did you bring (*lit.* come with) the material ?

H. Yes. Here's the khaki cloth for making the shorts and white cloth for making the gown. How much is the cost of sewing (it) ?

G. The whole job will be 45/——that is, 4 naira and 5 shillings.

H. Heavens ! that's too much ! If you don't agree (to do it) for 4 naira I'll (have to) look for someone else (to do it).

G. Okay, I agree. Leave the cloth there.

H. Good. When shall I come and get (it) ?

G. Not till tomorrow. I can't finish sewing them all today.

H. Okay, see you tomorrow.

G. Okay, until tomorrow.

Lesson 30 :

The Jackal Is The Chief of Schemers

One day a crow was wandering about. He was looking for something to eat. Then he saw a little piece of meat on the ground near a rock. He descended and picked it up in his mouth. He rose into the air with the meat in his mouth and landed in a tree.

Well, a jackal was watching him—he saw everything that the crow did. The jackal, for his part, was hungry.

He wanted to get the meat. So he worked out a scheme to get (it).

So the jackal went to the base of the tree, he greeted the crow. He said to him, ' Gosh, the other day I heard you singing a song. Your voice was very pleasant indeed. How long (will I have to wait until) I can hear your song again ? '

The crow listened (attentively). What the jackal said pleased him (very much). When he heard it he forgot about the thing in his mouth. He opened his mouth. He was about to (oblige by) singing a song.

That was that ! The meat fell down. The jackal picked (it) up and said, ' Thanks.' He went off with it. That's the end !

Hausa–English Vocabulary

This vocabulary includes all the words and most of the idiomatic expressions found anywhere in these lessons (with the exception of some of the less common forms listed in Lesson 39, section 7). Note that the alphabetical order in which the words are arranged is Hausa (that is with separate sections for **ɓ, ɗ, ƙ, sh, ts** and **'y**) rather than combining these letters with the most similar letter of the English alphabet as most Hausa dictionaries do.

Note : *the student is cautioned against assuming that he can learn the meaning of a word or construction by simply referring to the over-brief glosses provided in these short vocabularies. He should at least cross-check with one of the large dictionaries before attempting to make use of these items on his own.*

a, (impersonal p-a pronoun employed with **zã**)

à, (impersonal subjunctive p-a pronoun)

à, at, in

à kân, atop, on top of

à, (impersonal p-a pronoun employed after **bã**)

â, (impersonal future II p-a pronoun)

a'a, (exclamation of amazement)

ã'à, no

a'àhã, (exclamation of concern over misfortune)

àbin, (see **àbù**)

àbinci, food

àbōkī (*f.* **àbōkìyã ;** *pl.* **àbòkai**), friend

àbù (*pl.* **abūbuwà**), thing

— **àbîn dà,** what, the thing which

— **àbin màmākì,** a marvellous thing

— **àbinsà,** (about) his own business

— **àbin shâ,** something to drink

Àbūbakàr, (man's name)

ādalcì, justice, fairness, acting honestly

ādàlī (*pl.* **àdàlai**), just, honest, righteous (person)

Adàm, (man's name)

Ādàmū, (man's name)

àddā (*f.*) (*pl.* **addunà**), matchet

af/ap, (exclamation of surprised recognition)

Afrìl/Àfrīlù, April

āfù, (see **āhù**)

àgōgō (*pl.* **agōgunà**), watch, clock

Àgustà, August

āhù/āfù, 1½ kobos

ai, why, well (introductory exclamation)

aibǔ (*pl.* **aibōbī**), fault, blemish

àikā (**i/ē**), *v.* send (on errand)

aikì (*pl.* **ayyukà**), work

aikō, *v.* send here

ainù(n), very much, too

àjìyayyē (*f.* **àjìyayyiyā**; *pl.* **àjìyàyyū**), (something) set aside

ajìyē, *v.* set aside, put, place

akà, (impersonal relative completive p-a construction)

a kàn, (impersonal habitual p-a construction)

à kân, (see **à**)

àkàwū (*pl.* **akāwunà**), clerk

— **bàbban àkàwū,** head clerk

a kè, (impersonal relative continuative p-a construction)

àkwai, *v.* there is/are

àkwàtì (*pl.* **akwātunà**), box

àkwiyǎ (*f.*) (*pl.* **awākī**), goat

àl'ādǎ (*f.*) (*pl.* **àl'àdū**), custom, tradition

àladè (*pl.* **àlàdai**), pig

àlaikà sàlāmù/sàlâm, greetings (in reply to sàlāmù/sàlâm àlaikùn)

àlāmǎ/hàlāmà (*f.*) (*pl.* **àlàmai**), sign, indication

àlbarkà, no sale!

àlbarkàcī, kindness at the hands of, benefits received from

àlbishìrī, good news

Àlhajì, (title of one who has made the pilgrimage—**hajì**—to Mecca)

àlhamdù lillāhì, praise God!, fine! (an exclamation of gratefulness)

Àlhàmîs (*f.*), Thursday

àlhērì, kindness, liberality, favourable attitude

— **sai àlhērì,** (reply to **inā làbārì ?**), only good (news)

Àlī, (man's name)

alìf, 1000

Àliyù, (man's name)

àljīfū/àljīhū (*pl.* **aljīfunà**), pocket

àlkalàmī (*pl.* **alkalumà**), pen

àlƙālī (*pl.* àlƙàlai), judge
Allà, God
— allà ?, is that so ?
— allà !, it is true
àllō (*pl.* allunà) school-
slate, blackboard
àllurà (*f.*) (*pl.* àllùrai),
needle, inoculation
àlmājìrī (*f.* àlmājìrā ; *pl.*
àlmàjìrai), pupil, student
disciple
àmfànī, usefulness
àmin, amen, may it be so
Amìna, (woman's name)
amincì, reliability, friendship
Amirkà (*f.*), America
àmmā, but
amsà, *v.* or *n.* (*f.*) answer
an, (impersonal completive
aspect p-a pronoun)
— an jimà, after a while
(*lit.* one has waited
awhile)
anà, (impersonal continuative p-a construction)
— anà nan, after a while
angò, bridegroom
angwancì, being a bride-
groom, marriage-feast
ànīnī (*pl.* ànìnai), 1/10 of a
kobo, button
àrā (i/ē), *v.* borrow (other
than money)
arō, a loan, borrowing

àràhā, cheapness, inexpensiveness
— yā yi àràhā, it is in-
expensive
arbà, 4000
— yi arbà, *v.* happen on
unexpectedly
àrbà'in, 40
àrbàminyà, 400
arèwā, north
— arèwā masò gabàs,
north-east
— arèwā masò yâmma,
north-west
— arèwā sak, due north
arèwa, northward, to the
north
arzìkī/azzìkī, prosperity,
wealth
arzùtā, *v.* become pros-
perous
Àsabàr (*f.*), Saturday
asìbitì (*pl.* asibitōcī),
hospital
àsīrī (*pl.* àsìrai), secret
àshē, well !, oh !, really ?
àshìrin, 20
àttājìrī (*pl.* àttàjìrai),
wealthy trader,
merchant
Audù, (man's name)
aukà, *v.* fall on
àuku, *v.* happen
aunà, *v.* weigh, measure
àurā(i/ē), *v.* marry
aurē, marriage

àutā, youngest of several children

awà (f.) (pl. awōwī), hour

àyàbà (f.), banana(s)

bā, v. not be in the process of

bā/bâ, v. give

— bā dà, v. give

— bā dà màmākì, be amazing (lit. give amazement)

— ban tsòrō, causing (lit. giving) fear

bâ/bābù, v. there is no/not

— bâ kōmē, there's nothing (wrong), it doesn't matter

— bâ kyâu, it is not good

bà . . . ba, (negative particles employed with most p-a pronouns)

— bài . . . ba, (third person masculine singular negative particles)

— bàn . . . ba, (first person singular negative particles)

bà . . . ba, (negative particles employed with nouns, noun phrases, etc.)

bābà, paternal aunt

bàba, father, paternal uncle

bàbba (pl. mânyā), big (thing), important (thing), adult person

bābù, (see bâ/bābù)

bàdūkù (pl. dùkàwā), leather worker

bàɗi, next year

bàfādà/bàfādè (pl. fàdàwā), chief's servant, courtier

Bàfàransì (f. Bàfàransìyā ; pl. Fàrànsâi), Frenchman

Bàfilācè (f. Bàfilātà ; pl. Filànī), Fulani person

Bàhaushè (f. Bàhaushìyā ; pl. Hàusàwā), Hausa person

bài, (see bà . . . ba)

bàjimī, (see bìjimī)

Bàkanè/Bàkanò (f. Bàkanùwā ; pl. Kanāwā), Kano person

bàkī (pl. bākunà), mouth, edge

— bàkin hanyà, edge of the road

bakwài, seven

baƙī (f. baƙā ; pl. baƙàƙē), black (thing)

— baƙi-baƙi, blackish

— baƙī ƙirin/sidiƙ/sil, pitch-black, jet-black

— baƙin dājì, forest (lit. black bush)

Bàƙo, (man's name)

bàƙō (f. bàƙwā ; pl. bàƙī), guest, stranger

336 HAUSA

— **yi bàƙō,** have a guest
Bàlā, (man's name)
Bàlārabè (*f.* **Bàlārabìyā ;**
  pl. **Lārabāwā**), Arab
  person
bàlle, much more/less . . .
bàn, (see **bà . . . ba**)
bana, this year
bangō, wall, book cover
bàntē, loincloth
ban tsòrō, causing (*lit.* giving) fear, frightening
banzā, worthless (thing),
  uselessness
bappà, paternal uncle
barcī, sleep
bàra, last year
barì/bar, *v.* let, allow
barkà (*f.*), greetings
bàsarākè (*pl.* **sarākunà**),
  office-holder under a chief
bàtū, conversation, matter,
  affair
— **bàtun,** concerning, regarding
Bàtūrè (*f.* **Bàtūrìyā ;** *pl.*
  Tùràwā), European person
bāshì, debt, loan
— **ci bāshì,** *v.* incur a debt
Baucī (*f.*), the town of
  Bauchi
bàutā, slavery
bāwà (*f.* **bâiwā ;** *pl.* **bāyī**),
  slave
bāyā, the back

— **bāyan,** behind
— **bāyân dà,** after
— **bāyan gidā,** lavatory,
  toilet, faeces
bāya, backwards, to/to-
  wards the rear
bāyar, *v.* give
bazarā (*f.*), hot, muggy
  season just before the
  rains come
bèbàntakà (*f.*), being deaf
  and dumb
bēbē (*f.* **bēbìyā ;** *pl.* **bēbàyē**), deaf-mute
bègē, longing, hope
Bellò, (man's name)
bi, *v.* follow
bî, following (*v.n.* from **bi**)
bìjimī/bàjimī (*pl.* **bìjìmai/
  bàjìmai**), big bull
Bīnuwài (*f.*), Benue River
birì (*pl.* **birai**), monkey
birnī (*pl.* **birànē**), (walled)
  city
— **birnin Arèwā,** capital/
  most important city of
  the Northern Region
bìskitì (*pl.* **biskitōcī**), biscuit, cookie
bìsmillà, go ahead and start
  (whatever is to be done) !
bismìllāhì, (formula said
  on standing up, sitting
  down, starting work, beginning a meal, *etc.*)
biyā, *v.* pay

biyà, paying (verbal noun from **biyā**)

biyar, five

biyō, v. follow (here)

biyu, two

brōdì, (see **burōdì**)

bubbùgā, v. keep on beating (from **bugà**)

Būbà, (man's name)

bùdurwā (pl. **'yam mātā**), unmarried girl of marriageable age

būɗà, v. clear away, prepare, open

bùɗe, open

— **à bùɗe,** open

būɗè, v. open

bugà, v. beat

— **bugà mâi,** step on the gas, start a lorry/car

bùgā (i/ē), v. beat, thrash

bugè, v. beat and knock over/out

bugù, thrashing, beating

bùkātà (f.) (pl. **bùkàtū**), a need/requirement

bukkà (f.) (pl. **bukkōkī**), hut of grass (mats) or stalks, market stall

burōdì/brōdì bread, roll

būsà, v. blow

būshè, v. get dry

but, sudden action (an ideophone)

— **yā yi but,** he made a sudden leap

ɓācì, v. become spoiled

ɓàrāwò (pl. **ɓàràyī**), thief

ɓātà, v. spoil

ɓērā (pl. **ɓēràyē**), rat, mouse

ɓōye, hidden

— **à ɓòye,** hidden, in secret

ɓōyè, v. hide (something)

ɓutuk, stark naked (an ideophone)

— **yā fitō ɓutuk,** he came out naked

câ, thinking

—**câ ni/na kè,** I thought (that) . . .

can/cân/càn, there, that

cân, later

canjì, change

càsà'in, ninety

cē/cè, (see **nē**)

cê/cè, v. say

cêwā, saying, quote, that

ci, v. eat, win (a contest)

— **ci bāshì,** incur a debt

— **ci jarràbâwā,** pass a test

cî, eating

cī dà, (see **ciyar**)

cif, exactly (an ideophone)

— **ƙarfè ukù cif,** exactly three o'clock

cigàba, v. continue

cikà, v. fill

cìka, v. become full

— **yā cìka fal,** it is full to the brim

cìkakkē (*f.* cìkakkiyā ; *pl.* cìkàkkū), full

cikè, *v.* fill completely

cikì, stomach, pregnancy

— baƙin cikì, sadness (*lit.* black stomach)

— cikì yā ɗaurè, I am constipated (*lit.* stomach has become tied up)

— farin cikì, happiness

— yi cikì, become pregnant

cikī, inside

— (à) cikin, inside

cînyē, *v.* eat completely

cirè, *v.* pull out of

cirō, *v.* pull out of

cīshē, *v.* (form of ciyar)

città, four days hence

cīwò, illness, pain

— cīwòn cikì, stomach-ache

— cīwòn kâi, headache

ciyar/cī (dà), *v.* cause to eat, feed

cìyāwà (*f.*) (*pl.* cìyàyī), grass

cìzā (i/ē), *v.* bite

cōkàlī (*pl.* cōkulà), spoon

cūrì, ball (of something)

cùtā (*f.*), illness, disease, wound

cùtā (i/ē), *v.* injure, cheat

dà, with, and ; that (= wandà)

— kō dà, even though

dà, *v.* there is/are (= àkwai)

dà, if, when

dâ, in the past, formerly, previously

— dâ-dâ, long in the past

— dâ mā, it has been planned that, it is well known that, already

— tun dâ, from earliest times

dàban, different

dàbārà (*f.*) (*pl.* dàbàrū), plan, scheme

dabbà (*f.*) (*pl.* dabbōbī), (domestic) animal

daddàfā, *v.* keep on cooking (from dafà)

dàddarē, at night

daɗà, *v.* increase

daɗè, *v.* spend a long time

daɗèwā, spending a long time

— tun dà daɗèwā, from a long time ago

dādī, pleasantness

dafà, *v.* cook

dàfaffē (*f.* dàfaffiyā ; *pl.* dàfàffū), cooked

dàfu, *v.* be cooked

dàgà, from

dai, indeed, however, on the other hand (an insert)

daidai, correct, exactly

dājì, ' bush ' country, un-
inhabited land
— baƙin dājì, forest
dākàtā, v. wait for
dalà (f.) (pl. dalōlī), florin,
two shillings (= fàtakà)
dàlīlì (pl. dàlìlai), reason,
cause
dāmā (f.), chance, oppor-
tunity
— bâ dāmā, there's no
chance
dāma (f.), to the right
— dāma-dāma, so-so,
slightly (better)
— hannun dāma, right
hand/arm
dàmā, v. worry
dāmà, v. wet-mix
dàmu, v. be worried
dāmù, worrying
dàmunā/dàmanā/dàminā
(f.), rainy season
dàmuwā (f.), being wor-
ried/concerned
dangì, relatives
dànkalì, (sweet) potato(es)
dàrā (f.), fez
— hùlad dàrā, fez
darē, night
— dà (dàd) darē, at night
dàriyā (f.), laughter
Daudà, (man's name
= David)
dāwà (f.), guinea corn

dawà, ' bush ' country
(= dājì)
dāwō, v. return here
dāwôwā, returning here
dilā, jackal
dingà, v. keep on (doing)
dirēbà, driver
Dìzambà (f.), December
Dōgo, (man's name)
dōgō (f. dōguwā ; pl.
dōgàyē), tall, long
dòkā (i/ē), v. thrash, beat
dòkā (f.) (pl. dōkōkī),
order, rule
— ɗan dòkā (pl. 'yan dòkā),
N.A. policeman
dōkì (pl. dawākī), horse
dōlè, perforce, of necessity,
' must '
don, (see dòmin)
— don Allà, please, for
God's sake
— dom mè, why ?
dòmin/don, because of, in
order to
dōyà (f.), yam(s)
dōzìn, dozen
dūbà, v. look (at), inspect
dubū, 1000
duddùbā, look everywhere,
keep on looking (from
dūbà)
duhù/dufù, darkness
dukà/duk, every, all
— duk dà (hakà), in spite
of (this), nevertheless

— **duk ɗaya,** all the same
— **duk wandà,** anyone who
dūkà, v. beat, thrash
dūniyà (f.), world
dūtsè (pl. **duwàtsū**), stone, rock, mountain

ɗā (pl. **'yā'yā**), son
— **ɗan Adàm** (pl. **'yan Adàm**), person, human being (lit. son of Adam)
— **ɗan dòkā** (pl. **'yan dòkā**), N.A. policeman (lit. son of the orders/rules)
— **ɗan fārì,** firstborn son
— **ɗan jīkà,** great-grand-child
— **ɗan Kanò** (pl. **'yan Kanò**), native of Kano
— **ɗan sàndā** (pl. **'yan sàndā**), Government policeman (lit. son of a stick)
— **ɗan'ùbā** (pl. **'yan'ùbā**), half brother (lit. son of one's father)
— **ɗan'uwā** (pl. **'yan'uwā**), brother (lit. son of one's mother)
ɗagà, v. lift up, raise
ɗai-ɗai, one by one, singly
ɗākì (pl. **ɗākunà**), hut, room
ɗālìbī (pl. **ɗàlìbai**), student
ɗan, (see **ɗā**)
ɗanyē (f. **ɗanyā** ;   pl.

ɗanyū), raw/uncooked (thing)
ɗārī, coldness due to wind (usually *dry-cold* as opposed to **sanyī** = *damp-cold*)
ɗàrī, 100 ; ½k (= **sìsìn kwabò**)
ɗaukà (i/ē), v. take/pick up, carry
ɗaukè, v. pick up all of
ɗâukē, v. (rain) stop, remove
ɗaukō, v. carry here
ɗaurà, v. tie on to
ɗaurè, v. tie (completely/well) on to, tie up
ɗàure, tied up
— **à ɗàure,** tied up
ɗaya, one
— **ɗaya tak,** one only (i.e. no more, no less than one)
ɗàzu, just a little while ago
ɗēbō, v. dip out and bring (-ō form of **dībà**)
ɗēbè, v. remove, subtract
dībà, v. dip out, extract
ɗîn, the one in question
ɗin, particle used with numbers (see Lesson 11, section 5)
ɗinkà, v. make by sewing
ɗinkè, v. sew (up) completely)
ɗinkì, sewing
ɗìyā (f.), daughter (= **'yā**)

d̃òyī, stench, unpleasant odour

en'ĕ (*pl.* en'ĕ-en'ĕ), Native Administration (abbreviated N.A.)

fa, indeed, on the other hand (an insert)

fà ?, what about ?

Fàbrairù, February

fādà (*f.*), chief's residence/ audience chamber

fàdamà (*f.*) (*pl.* fadamōmī), marshy, swamp

fàdàwā, (see bàfādà)

fad̃à, quarrel, fighting, argument

fād̃à, *v.* fall into

fàd̃a (i/ē), *v.* say

fàd̃ā (*f.*), thing said, spoken words, conversation

fād̃ì, *v.* fall (down/on)

fād̃ō, *v.* fall down to someone

fàhimtà (i/ē), *v.* understand

fàhìmtaccē (*f.* fàhìmtacciyā ; *pl.* fàhìmtàttū), understood, intelligent

fal, completely (see cika)

fâm, 2 naira

fànsā (i/ē), *v.* redeem, ransom

fārà, *v.* start, begin

fàrā (*f.*) (*pl.* fàrī), locust, grasshopper

Fàransà (*f.*), France

Fàrànsâi, (see Bàfàransì)

fàrarrē (*f.* fàrarriyā ; *pl.* fàràrrū), having been begun

fārì, beginning, start (= farkō)

— na/ta fārì, the first (= na/ta farkō)

farī (*f.* farā ; *pl.* faràrē), white (thing), whiteness

— fari-fari, white-ish

— farī fat, snow-white

— farin cikì, happiness (*lit.* white stomach)

farkē/falkē (*pl.* fatàkē), itinerant trader

farkō, beginning, start (= fārì)

— na/ta farkō, the first (= na/ta fārì)

fartanyà (*f.*) (*pl.* fartan-yōyī), hoe

fàru, *v.* happen

fasànjà (*pl.* fasanjōjī), passenger

fàskarà (i/ē), *v.* be beyond doing, be impossible

fâs ōfìs, post office

fat, (see farī)

fātā, hoping (for)

fātà (*f.*) (*pl.* fātū), skin, hide

fàtakà, florin, two shillings (= dalà)

fâutā, *v.* cut up meat for sale

faye̱, *v.* be characterized by

fensìr(ī) (*pl.* **fensirōrī**), pencil

fi, *v.* surpass, exceed

— **nā fi sô ...,** I prefer ...

— **yā fi dukà ...,** it is the best in ...

yā fi ... kyâu, it is better than ...

— **yā fi kyâu,** it is better (that we do ...)

ficè, *v.* (see **wucè**)

fiffìkě (*pl.* **fìkàfìkai**), wing

fìffìtà, *v.* keep going out (from **fìta**)

Filànī, (see **Bàfilācè**)

fīlī (*pl.* **fīlàyě̱**), open country, space

firamàrě̱, primary school

fisshē, *v.* (form of **fitar**)

fìta, *v.* go out

fìtā, going out

fitar/fid (dà), *v.* take out, remove, depose, expel

fìtilà (*f.*) (*pl.* **fìtìlū**), lantern, lamp

fitō, *v.* come out

fitò, ferrying

fitō, guinea-corn beer

fitôwā, coming out (from **fitō**)

fitsārī, urine

ful, (see **sābō**)

furā (*f.*), a food made of cooked flour mixed with milk

fuskà (*f.*) (*pl.* **fuskōkī**), face

fushī, anger

— **yi fushī**, get angry

ga, (see **ganī**)

gà, *v.* here/there is ...

— **gà shi ...,** seeing that, indeed, for

— **sai gà ...,** then behold ...

gà/gàrē, in the presence of, regarding, in the possession of

gàbā, front

— **gàban**, in front of

gàba, in front

— **gàba daya**, all together, at once

gabàs, east

— **gabàs sak**, due east

gadà (*f.*), (permanent) bridge

gadō (*pl.* **gadàjē**), bed

gāfarà (*f.*), pardoning, forgiving ; excuse me !

gai dà, *v.* (see **gayar**)

gaishē, *v.* (form of **gayar**)

gaisuwā (*f.*), greetings

gājě, *v.* inherit

gàjērē (*f.* **gàjērìyā** ; *pl.* **gàjěrū**), short

Gàjēre, (man's name)

gajertà (*f.*), shortness

gàji, *v.* be tired

gàjiyǎ (*f.*), tiredness, fatigue

gamà, v. finish ; join together

Gàmbo, (man's name)

gàmu (dà), v. meet (with)

gānà, v. chat (confidentially)

gànannē (f. gànanniyā ;
pl. gànànnū), seen

gānè, v. understand

ganī/gan/ga, v. see

ganī, seeing

gāra, it would be better that

gàrā (f.), white ant(s),
termite(s)

Garbà, (man's name)

gàrī (pl. garūruwà), town

— gàrī yā wāyè, it has
dawned

gàrī, flour

garkè, herd of cattle

gàrmā (f.) (pl. garèmanī),
large type of hoe, plough

gāshì, hair, feathers

gàskē, real

— dà gàskē, extremely (see
also ƙwarai)

gàskiyā (f.), truth

gātà, three days hence

gàtarī (pl. gāturà), axe,
hatchet

gayà, v. tell (requires an
indirect object)

gayar/gai (dà), v. greet

— gayar minì dà, greet for
me . . .

gēmù, beard

gērō, millet

gidā (pl. gidàjē), home,
compound

— gidan saurō, mosquito
net

— mài gidā, head of the
house, husband

— uwar gidā, woman of
the house, (first) wife

giginyà (f.), deleb-palm

ginà, v. build (usually with
clay, brick or cement)

gìndī, base, bottom, but-
tocks

gìrbā (i/ē), v. reap, harvest

girbì, harvesting

girgijè (pl. gìzàgìzai), rain-
cloud

girmā, bigness, honour, importance

gishirī, salt

gīwā (f.) (pl. gīwàyē), elephant

giyà (f.), (native) beer

gòbarā (f.), catching fire

gòbe (f.), tomorrow

gōdè, v. thank

gòdiyā (f.), thanks, gratitude

— dà gòdiyā, with thank-
fulness

gōɗìyā (f.), mare

gōgà, v. rub, polish

gōgè, v. rub (completely)

gògu, v. be experienced,
has been rubbed

gōmà, ten

z

— **gōmà-gōmà**, ten apiece/
each

— **gōmà shâ ɗaya**, eleven

gōnā (*f.*) (*pl.* **gònàkī**), farm

gōrò, kolanut

gùdā, a unit

gudù, *v.* run

gudù (*pl.* **gùje-gùjē**), running (see also **gùje-gùjē**
below)

gùgā (*pl.* **gūgunà**), bucket
(of skin, gourd or metal)
for dipping from a well

gùje, speedily, on the run

— **à gùje**, on the run,
running

gùje-gùjē, running in track
and field competition

gùmī, perspiration

guntū (*pl.* **guntàyē**), short
(thing), fragment (of
something)

Gùsau (*f.*), (town in N.
Nigeria)

gwadà, *v.* measure, test

gwaggò, **gwàggō**, paternal
aunt, father's wife (not
one's mother), maternal
uncle's wife

gwàmmà, rather, it would
be better that . . .

gwangwan (*pl.* **gwangwàyē**), tin (of food)

gwànī (*f.* **gwànā** ; *pl.*
gwanàyē), expert

gwànintà (*f.*), skill

gwàuràntakà (*f.*), being
wifeless

gwaurō/gwamrō (*pl.*
gwauràyē), wifeless man,
bachelor

gwēbà, guava

gyàɗà (*f.*), groundnut(s),
peanut(s)

gyārà, *v.* repair

gyārā, a ' makeweight '
given by seller ; repairing

gyârtā, *v.* repair

gyàru, *v.* be repaired

habà, come now !, don't be
a fool !, nonsense !

haɓà (*f.*), chin

hadarì/hadirì, storm

hàɗu, *v.* meet, be joined

hagu/hagun, left-hand side

haifù (**i/ē**), *v.* give birth

hajì, the pilgrimage to
Mecca

hakà, thus, so

hakùntā, *v.* administer,
possess jurisdiction over,
give verdict

haƙōrī (*pl.* **haƙòrā**), tooth

hàƙurà, *v.* be patient

hàƙurī, patience, resignation

hàlakà, *v.* perish, die

hàlāmà, (see **àlāmà**)

halì, character, temperament

hàmsàminyà, 500

hàmsin, fifty

hanà, v. prevent, forbid, refuse

hàngā (i/ē), v. see afar off

hànkākà (pl. hànkàkī), crow

hankàlī, intelligence, sense ; careful

— à hankàlī, carefully

hannū (pl. hannàyē), arm (including hand), hand

hanyà (f.) (pl. hanyōyī), path, road, way

har, until, to the extent that

hàrājì, tax

hàrbā (i/ē), v. shoot

harbì, act of shooting

harshè (pl. harsunà), tongue, language

Hārūnà, (man's name = Aaron)

hàsārà, loss due to some unlucky incident, misfortune

Hasàn, (man's name)

hatsī, grain staple (i.e. guinea-corn or millet)

hau, v. mount, climb

hàukā, madness, insanity

Hausā (f.), the Hausa language, the Hausa people ; language

haushī, vexation, anger

hawā, mounting, riding on

hayā̀kī, smoke

hayè, v. mount, climb, cross over (e.g. a river)

hāzā wasàlàm(mù), (formula used at end of a letter = yours faithfully)

huɗu, four

hùlā (f.) (pl. hūlunà), cap, hat

hūrà, v. blow on, light (fire)

hūtà, v. rest

hūtàwā (f.), resting

hūtū, resting, holiday, vacation

ī, yes

— ī mànà, yes indeed !

ì/yì ta yâu, today week

ìdan/in, if, when

idò (pl. idànū), eye, sight

— idòn sanì, acquaintance

igiyà (f.) (pl. igiyōyī), rope, string

Ìkko, Lagos

ilmì/ilìmī, knowledge, education

Ìmâm, (man's name, from lìmân, Muslim priest)

in, (see ìdan)

— in shā Àllā(hù), if God wills

ìn, (first person singular subjunctive p-a pronoun)

— ìn ji . . ., according to, quote . . ., says . . .

inà, (first person singular
  continuative p-a con-
  struction)
ìnā, where ?
ìndà, (place) where
  (= wurîn dà)
Ingìlà (f.), England
innà/ìnnā/iyà, mother,
  maternal aunt
inuwà (f.), shade
in shā Àllā(hù), (see in)
irì, kind, sort, seed
— irì-irì, various kinds, all
  kinds
Ìsā, (man's name = Jesus)
ìsa, v. be sufficient, reach
  (a place)
ìsasshē (f. ìsasshiyā ; pl.
  ìsàssū), enough, sufficient
iskà (f. or m.), wind, air
isō, v. arrive (here)
Ishāƙù, (man's name
  = Isaac)
ita, she (third feminine
  singular independent
  pronoun)
itàcē (pl. itātuwà), tree,
  piece of wood, twig,
  wood
iyà, v. be able to . . .
— yā iyà Hausā, he can
  speak Hausa well
iyà, (see innà)
iyā/iyàkā (f.), boundary,
  limit
— iyā gìndī, (one's) waist

ìyālì, man's wife/wives and
  children, one's household
iyàwā (f.), ability
iyàyē, parents
iyò, swimming

jā (pl. jājàyē), red (thing)
— ja-ja, reddish
— jà wur/jir/zur, bright
  red, scarlet
jā, v. pull, drag, draw
jàkā (f.) (pl. jakunkunà),
  bag, ₦200
jàkī (f. jàkā ; pl. jākunà),
  donkey
Jànairù, January
Jànhôl/Jàn hwâl, John
  Holt canteen
jàrfā (f.), tattoo marks
jarràbâwā (f.), school
  examination
— ci jarràbâwā, pass an
  examination
— yi jarràbâwā, take an
  examination
jārùmī (f. jārùmā ; pl.
  jàrùmai), brave person
Jàtau, (man's name—
  usually given to light-
  skinned person)
jāwō, v. pull (here), drag
  (toward speaker)
jàyayyà (f.), controversy,
  dispute
jē, v. go to
— jè ka, go away !

jêfā̀, v. throw
jềfā (i/ē), v. throw at
ji, v. hear, sense, feel
— ji ƙai, v. have mercy, be sympathetic
— ji yunwà̠, v. be hungry
jî̠, hearing, feeling
— jîn ƙai, mercy, sympathy
jībi, day after tomorrow
jībì̠, meal, feast
jīfā̀, throwing at
jīkà̠ (pl. jīkōkī), grandchild
jīkanyà̠, granddaughter
jìkī (pl. jikunà̠), body
jimà̠, v. spend quite a time at
— an jimà̠, (see an)
— jìm kàɗan, after a little while
sai an jimà̠, see you later
jinī, blood
jir, (see jā)
jirā, v. wait for
jirà̠, waiting for
jirgī (pl. jirà̠gē), boat, canoe, ship
— jirgin ƙasā, railway train
— jirgin samà̠, aeroplane
jirif, kerplunk ! (an ideophone)
— ùngùlū tā sàuka jirif, the vulture landed kerplunk
jitā̀, v. wear, put on (clothing)

jìtu, v. be on good terms, get along well
jiyà̠ (f), yesterday
jìyayyà̠ (f.), being on good terms
Jumma'à̠ (f.) Friday
Jun, June
jūnā, each other
jùrum, be despondent (an ideophone)
— sun yi jùrum, they stood despondently
jūyà̠, v. turn

ka, (second singular masculine relative completive p-a pronoun and the form employed after zâ, bâ, jè)
— ka kàn, (second singular masculine habitual p-a construction)
— ka kề, (second singular masculine relative continuative p-a construction)
ka/kà, (second singular masculine object pronoun)
kā, (second singular masculine completive p-a pronoun)
kâ, (second singular masculine future II p-a pronoun)

kà, (second singular masculine p-a pronoun used
with **bā**)

kà, (second singular masculine subjunctive p-a pro-
noun)

-kà, (second singular masculine possessive pro-
noun)

kàbēwà (*f.*) (*pl.* **kàbèyī**),
pumpkin

kadà/kâr, do not, lest (followed by subjunctive)

kàdai, (used with **sànnu**
and **barkà** as below)

— **sànnu/barkà kàdai**
(reply to **sànnu/barkà**),
hello (in reply)

Kadunà, Kaduna

kaɗà, *v.* beat a drum

kaɗai, only

kàɗan, a few, a little,
slightly

— **kàɗan-kàɗan,** very
slightly

kafà, *v.* establish, build,
erect, set up

kàfìn/kàfin, (= **kàmìn**)

kàfu, *v.* be established

kai, you (masculine singular independent pro-
noun)

kai, *v.* carry, take to, reach,
be enough, be equal to

kâi (*pl.* **kāwunà**), head, top

— **à kân,** on top of

— **kân,** atop

— **kân sarkī,** postage
stamp

kâi, self

— **nī dà kâina,** I myself

kàkā (*f.*), harvest season

kàkā (*pl.* **kàkànī**), grandfather, grandmother

ka kàn, (see **ka**)

ka kè̀, (see **ka**)

kākàrē, *v.* become jammed

kàkī, khaki cloth

kakkaràntā, *v.* read in
succession

kakkāwō, *v.* keep on
bringing

kal, (see **farī**)

kālā, gleaning

kallō, looking at

kàm, indeed, on the other
hand (an insert)

kam (see **kullè**)

kāmà, *v.* catch, seize

— **cīwò yā kāmà ni,** I've
become ill (*lit.* illness has
caught me)

— **yā kāmà hanyà,** he went
on his way

kàmā, similarity

— **kàmar,** like . . .,
about . . ., as if . . .

kāmàwā, catching

kàmìn/kàmin, before (followed by subjunctive)

kāmō, *v.* catch and bring
here

kàn, (particle employed with habitual aspect— see **ka kàn,** *etc.*)

kân, (see **kâi**)

kanà, (second singular masculine continuative p-a construction)

Kananci, the Kano dialect of Hausa

Kanāwā, (see **Bàkanè**)

Kànde, (woman's name)

Kanò, Kano

kàntī (*pl.* **kantunà**), shop selling (primarily) imported goods

kâr, (see **kadà**)

kàràmbànī, meddlesomeness, nuisance

karàntā, *v.* read, study

kàràtū, reading, studying, education

kàrɓā (i/ē), *v.* receive

kàrē (*pl.* **karnukà**), dog

— **kàren mōtà,** motor boy (*lit.* motor dog)

karyè, *v.* (stick) snap, break

kasà, *v.* arrange in heaps, pile

— **kasà kûnnē,** prick up (one's) ears, pay attention

kāsà, *v.* fall short (in amount, ability, *etc.*)

kashè, *v.* kill

kàshègàrī, on the next day

kāshī, excrement, faeces

kaskō, small, earthenware, bowl-shaped vessel

kàsuwā (*f.*) (*pl.* **kāsuwōyī**), market

kau/kawad (dà), *v.* remove to another place

kawài, only, merely

kāwō, *v.* bring

kāwôwā (*f.*), bringing

kāwù/kàwū (*pl.* **kàwùnai**), maternal uncle (see **rāfànī**)

kāyā (*pl.* **kāyàyyakī**), load, outfit, belongings

— **kāyan aikì,** tools, implements of one's work

kàzā (*f.*) (*pl.* **kàjī**), hen

kē, you (*f.*) (second singular feminine independent pronoun)

kè, *v.* be in process of, be at (specialized verbal employed in relative continuative aspect)

— **kè nan,** it is (emphasizes the phrase or clause which precedes it)

kèkē (*pl.* **kēkunà**), bicycle, machine

— **kèken dinkì,** sewing machine

kēwàyā, *v.* go around place

kēwàyē, *v.* go roundabout way, go around place, encircle

ki, (second singular feminine p-a pronoun employed after **zâ, bâ, jè**)

— **ki kàn,** (second singular feminine habitual p-a construction)

— **ki kè,** (second singular feminine relative continuative p-a construction)

ki/kì, (second singular feminine object pronoun)

kì/kyà, (second singular feminine p-a pronoun employed after **bā**)

-kì, (second singular feminine possessive pronoun)

kibiyà (*f.*) (*pl.* **kibiyōyī**), arrow

kikà, (second feminine relative completive p-a pronoun)

ki kàn, (see **ki**)

ki kè, (see **ki**)

kikkirā, *v.* keep calling

kin, (second singular feminine completive p-a pronoun)

kinà, (second singular feminine continuative aspect construction)

kirā, *v.* call

kirāwō, *v.* call (here)

kirkì, excellence, good character, honesty

kīshìyā (*f.*) (*pl.* **kīshiyōyī**), co-wife

kìwò, (animal) seeking food, grazing ; (person) tending animal

kō, or, whether, perhaps, (question particle), (prefix converting an interrogative nominal into an indefinite nominal)

— **kō dà,** even, even though, even if

kòfī, coffee

kògī (*pl.* **kōgunà**), river

kō'inā/kòinā, wherever

kòmà, *v.* return (there)

kōmar (dà), *v.* return, restore

kōmē, everything, anything, whatever

— **kōmē dà kōmē,** everything

kōmō, *v.* return here

kōnawà, however many

kōrè (*f.* **kōrìyā** ; *pl.* **kwârrā**), grass-green, emerald-green

— **kōrè shar,** bright green

kōwā, everyone

— **kōwā dà kōwā,** everyone

kōwàccē, (see **kōwànnē**)

kōwàcè, (see **kōwànè**)

kōwàɗannē, (see **kōwànnē**)

kōwàɗannè, (see **kōwànè**)

kōwànè (*f.* **kōwàcè** ; *pl.* **kōwàɗannè**), every, any

kōwǎnēnè/kōwǎnē nè (*f.* **kōwǎcēcè/kōwǎcē cè**), everyone, whoever

kōwǎnnē (*f.* **kōwǎccē** ; *pl.* **kōwàɗànnē**), everyone

kōyàushè/kōyàushe, whenever

kōyàyà, however

kū, (second plural independent pronoun)

ku, (second plural p-a pronoun employed with **zâ, bâ, jè**)

— **ku kàn**, (second plural habitual p-a construction)

— **ku kè**, (second plural relative continuative p-a construction)

ku/kù, (second plural object pronoun)

kù, (second plural subjunctive p-a pronoun)

kǔ, (second plural p-a pronoun employed with **bā**)

-kù, (second plural possessive pronoun)

kudù, south, southwards

— **kudù sak**, due south

kuɗī, money

— **kuɗin ƙasā**, tax (= **hàrājì**)

kujèrā (*f.*) (*pl.* **kùjèrū**), stool, chair

kūkā, weeping, crying

kūkà (*f.*) (*pl.* **kūkōkī**), baobab tree, pods or leaves

kukà, (second plural relative completive p-a pronoun)

ku kàn, (see **ku**)

ku kè, (see **ku**)

kùlā (dà), *v.* pay attention (to), take notice (of)

kullè, *v.* lock

— **nā kullè ƙōfà kam**, I locked the door tightly

kullum/kullun, always

kumā, also

kun, (second plural completive p-a pronoun)

kunà, (second plural continuative p-a construction)

kùnkurū (*pl.* **kunkurà**), turtle, tortoise

kûnnē (*pl.* **kunnuwà**), ear

kūrā (*f.*) (*pl.* **kūràyē**), hyena

kurùm (*f.*), silence ; only (= **kawài**)

kusa, nearness, closeness

— **kurkusa/kusa-kusa**, very close, ever closer

kusa, *v.* approach, get near

kuskurè, mistake, error, missing the mark in shooting

kùwā, indeed, as for . . ., however, on the other hand (an insert) kwā̂, (second plural future II p-a pronoun)

kwā̀, (second plural p-a pronoun employed with bā)

kwabồ (pl. kwàbbai), kobo

kwàɗàyī, keen desire, greed

kwàɗō (pl. kwàɗī), frog, padlock

kwàikwayà (i/ē), v. imitate

kwal, (the form of kwāna employed before lāfiyà)

kwalabā/kwalbā (f.) (pl. kwalàbē), glass bottle, crowbar

kwānā (pl. kwànàkī), night-time, a twenty-four hour day (when counting days)

— kwānā biyu, a long time (lit. two days)

— kwānā gōmà, ten days

kwāna/kwal, v. spend the night

— nā kwāna biyu à wurîn, I spent a long time there

kwānồ (pl. kwānōnī), any metal bowl or basin, headpan, roofing pan

kwântā, v. lie down, (wind, dispute, etc.), subside, (mind) be at rest

kwantar (dà), v. cause to lie down

Kwârà (f.), Niger River

kwāsà, v. dip out

kwāshè, v. collect and remove (all of)

kwatà (f.), quarter

kwatàntā, v. compare, give a rough idea, imitate

kyà̂, (second singular feminine future II p-a pronoun)

kyà̀, (second singular feminine p-a pronoun employed with bā)

kyàkkyāwā (m. or f.) (pl. kyāwà̀wā) good, handsome, beautiful, (often = mài kyâu)

kyar, difficulty (used only with dà as below)

— dà kyar, with difficulty

kyâu, goodness (usually to the sight), handsomeness, beauty

— dà kyâu, good, handsome beautiful (lit. possessing goodness)

ƙàdangarè (pl. ƙàdàngàrū), lizard

ƙàhō/ƙàfō (pl. ƙàhồnī), horn (of animal), horn for blowing

ƙai, (see ji ƙai)

ƙà̀ƙà̀, how ? (= yàyà)

ƙàƙƙarfā (pl. ƙarfàfā), strong

ƙalau/lau, very spotlessly

ƙanè (f. ƙanwà̀ ; pl.

ƙannē), younger sibling
(= brother or sister)

ƙànƙanè (f. ƙànƙanùwā ;
pl. ƙanānà), small
(thing), a little

ƙanƙantà (f.), smallness

ƙan'wà (f.), younger sister
(see ƙanè)

ƙārā (f), crying out, complaint to one in authority

ƙārà, v. increase, repeat
(doing something)

ƙàramī (f. ƙàramā ; pl.
ƙanānà), small (thing)

ƙārè, v. be complete, finish

ƙarfè (pl. ƙaràfā), metal ;
o'clock

— ƙarfè biyu, two o'clock

ƙarfī, strength

ƙàrƙashī, under-side

— ƙàrƙashin, under-
neath . . .

ƙàru, v. be increased, make
progress

ƙaryā (f.) (pl. ƙàryàce-
ƙàryàcē), a lie, untruth,
falseness

ƙasā (f.) (pl. ƙasàshē),
earth, soil, country,
district

— nan ƙasā, here in this
country

ƙasà, on the ground, downward

— ƙasà-ƙasà, slightly
downward

ƙàshī (pl. ƙasūsuwà), bone

ƙauyè (pl. ƙauyukà), vil-
lage, rural area

ƙētàrā, v. step/cross over

ƙētàrē, v. cross (road, river,
border)

ƙi, v. refuse, dislike

ƙî, refusal, hatred

ƙirin, (see baƙī)

ƙìyayyà (f.), mutual hatred

ƙōfà (f.) (pl. ƙōfōfī), doorway

ƙòƙarī, (praiseworthy)
effort, (worthy) attempt

ƙōnà, v. burn

ƙōnè, v. burn (completely),
become burned

— yā ƙōnè ƙùrmus, it's
completely burned up

ƙōtà (f.) (pl. ƙōtōcī), handle
of, e.g. axe, hoe

ƙùrmus, (see ƙōnè)

ƙùrùnƙus, here ends the
fable/matter

ƙwai, egg(s)

ƙwarai, very much

— ƙwarai dà gàskē, very
much indeed

ƙwaryā (f.) (pl. ƙôrē),
gourd bowl

ƙyālè, v. ignore, take no
notice of

ƙyēyà (f.), back of the head

làbārì (pl. làbàrū), news,
information

— bâ làbārì, without warning

laɓàɓā, v. walk stealthily, sneak up on

laccà, (political) speech

lādā, reward, wages

Lādì/Lādì, (see Lahàdì)

lāfiyà (f.), health, well-being, safety

làfìyayyē (f. làfìyayyiyā; pl. làfìyàyyū), healthy, sound

Lahàdì/Lādì (f.), Sunday

lâifī (pl. laifōfī), fault, crime

— bâ lâifī, that's all right (lit. there's nothing wrong)

— lâifin kânsà, his own fault

lālàcē, v. become spoiled, deteriorate

lallē, for sure

Làràbā (f.), Wednesday

Lārabāwā, (see Bàlārabè)

lattì, lateness

lau, (see ƙalau)

launì (pl. launōnī), colour

Lawàl, (man's name)

lēbùrà (pl. lēburōrī), labourer

lēɓè (pl. lēɓunà), lip

lèmō/lèmū, citrus (fruit or tree)

likità (pl. likitōcī), doctor

lìnzāmì (pl. lìnzàmai), bit, bridle

lissāfì, act of reckoning up, arithmetic, accounting

littāfì (pl. littàttàfai), book

Lìttìnîn/Àttànîn (f.), Monday

lōkàcī (pl. lòkàtai), time

lōtò, time

— lōtò-lōtò, from time to time

m, well (an exclamation indicating thoughtful consideration of a matter)

mā/ma, as for . . ., on the other hand, however (an insert)

mâ, (first plural future II p-a pronoun)

ma-/wà, to/for (indirect object indicator)

ma'àikàcī (f. ma'aikacìyā; pl. ma'àikàtā), worker

ma'àikī (pl. ma'àikā), messenger

ma'ajī (pl. mà'àjìyai), storehouse

ma'aunā (f.) (pl. mà'àunai), place where grain is sold

ma'aunī (pl. mà'àunai), any measure, scales

mabūɗī (pl. màbùɗai), key

màcè (f.) (màta- ; pl. mātā), woman, wife

— **tamàcè/tamàtā**, female
(*lit.* pertaining to
woman)

macìjī (*pl.* **màcìzai**), snake

madafā/madafī (*pl.* **màdàfai**), kitchen, cooking-
place

mādàllā, splendid, fine,
thank you

madarā (*f.*), (fresh) milk

madìnkī (*f.* **madinkìyā** ;
pl. **madìnkā**), tailor

madaurī (*pl.* **màdàurai**),
thing used for tying

mafàshī (*pl.* **mafàsā**), highway robber

mafì/mafìyī (*pl.* **mafìyā**),
in excess of, superior to

màganà (*f.*) (*pl.* **màgàngànū**), word, thing said

māgànī (*pl.* **māgungunà**),
medicine

— **shā māgànī**, take
medicine

magàyī, informer

magirbī (*pl.* **màgìrbai**),
(type of harvesting tool
shaped like a **fartanyà**)

magwajī (*pl.* **màgwàdai**),
measuring rod

mahàifī (*f.* **mahaifìyā** ; *pl.*
mahàifā), parent

mahàrbī *pl.* **mahàrbā**),
hunter, one who shoots

mahàucī (*pl.* **mahàutā**),
butcher, meat-seller

mahàukàcī (*f.* **mahaukacìyā** ; *pl.* **mahàukàtā**),
madman, insane person

mahautā (*pl.* **màhàutai**),
place where meat is sold

mahukuntā (*pl.* **màhùkùntai**), law court

mahùƙùrcī (*f.* **mahuƙur-
cìyā** ; *pl.* **mahùƙùrtā**),
patient/long suffering
person

mai (**dà**), (see **mayar**)

mài (*pl.* **màsu**), possessor
of . . ., characterized
by . . .

— **mài gidā**, head of the
house, husband

— **mài tēbùr**, small market
trader who (usually)
displays his goods on a
table

— **mài zuwà**, that which is
coming (*e.g.* **satī mài
zuwà** = next week)

mâi, oil, fat, grease, petrol

— **mân shānū**, cream,
butter

màimakon, instead of . . .

maishē, (form of **mayar**)

majèmī (*pl.* **majèmā**),
tanner

majì/majìyī (*f.* **majiyìyā** ;
pl. **majìyā**), hearer,
feeler, one who hears/
feels

makà, to/for you (*m. sing.*)
(indirect object pronoun
construction)

makàɗī (*pl.* makàɗā),
drummer

makaɗī (*pl.* màkàɗai),
drum-stick

màkāhò/màkāfò (*f.*
makaunìyā ; *pl.* màkàfī),
blind person

màkānīkì (*pl.* màkànìkai),
mechanic

màkarà, *v.* be/come late,
dally

makarantā (*f.*) (*pl.*
makarantōcī), school

màkàrau, person who is
customarily late, dila-
tory person

makì/mikì, to/for you (*f.
sing.*), (indirect object
pronoun construction)

mākò, week (= sātī)

— mākòn gòbe, next week

— mākòn jiyà, last week

makòyī (*f.* makōyìyā; *pl.*
makòyā), learner,
apprentice

makù/mukù, to/for you
(*pl.*), (indirect object
pronoun construction)

maƙàryàcī (*f.* maƙarya-
cìyā ; *pl.* maƙàryàtā),
liar

màƙōgwàrō, throat, wind-
pipe

mālàm(ī) (*f.* mālàmā ; *pl.*
màlàmai), teacher, Mr.

mālamancī, (playful term
coined to refer to the
mixture of Hausa and
English which people
fluent in both languages
employ in informal con-
versation)

màmā, (woman's) breast(s),
Mother

màmākì (*pl.* màmàkai),
being surprised, amaze-
ment

Mammàn, (man's name)

mân, (see mâi)

manà/mamù, to/for us (in-
direct object pronoun
construction)

mànà, indeed ! (an exple-
tive)

— ī mànà, yes indeed !

mangwàrò, mango(es),
mango tree

manì, (see minì)

mântā (dà), *v.* forget

màntaccē (*f.* màntacciyā ;
pl. màntàttū), forgotten
(thing), forgetful person

màntau, forgetful person

mânyā, (see bàbba)

— mânya-mânyā, impor-
tant people

maràbā, welcome !,
welcoming

màràicē, (late) evening

— dà màràicē, in the (late) evening

maràs (*pl.* maràsā), lacking in

maràshī (*f.* marashìyā ; *pl.* maràsā), lacking in

Māris (*f.*), March

maròɓī (*f.* maróɓìyā ; *pl.* maròɓā), beggar, one who is requesting/ pleading

martabà̀ (*f.*) (*pl.* marta-bōbī), high rank

Maryamù̀, Mary

masà̀/mishì, to/for him (in-direct object pronoun construction)

māshì (*pl.* māsū), spear

masò̀/masòyī (*f.* masōyìyā; *pl.* masò̀yā), one who likes/loves

māsū, (see māshì)

masù̀/musù̀, to/for (indirect object pronoun con-struction)

màsu, (see mài)

matà̀, to/for her (indirect object pronoun con-struction)

mātā/màta-, (see màcè)

matsà̀, *v.* squeeze/pinch to-gether, bother

màtsu, *v.* be under pressure

mawàdà̀cī (*f.* mawadācìyā ; *pl.* mawàdà̀tā), wealthy person

mayar/mai (dà), *v.* put back, return (a thing to its place), change into, regard as

Māyù̀ (*f.*), May

mazā, (see mijì̀, namijì̀)

maza, quickly

— maza-maza, very quickly

mè̀/mènē/mènēnè̀, what (is it) ?

mètan (*f.*), 200

m̀hm̂, greetings (in reply to a greeting)

mijì̀ (*pl.* mazā), husband

mikì, (see makì)

mīkìyā (*f.*), Ruppell's griffon (a large scaven-ger bird)

mìlyân, million

minì/manì, to/for me (in-direct object pronoun construction)

mìnistà̀ (*pl.* ministōcī), government minister

minshārī, snoring

mishì, (see masà̀)

m'm̂, (expression of sym-pathetic concern)

mōtà̀ (*f.*) (*pl.* mōtōcī), auto-mobile, lorry

mòtsī, movement, motion

mū, (first plural inde-pendent pronoun)

mu, (first plural p-a pronoun employed with zā, bā)

— **mu kàn,** (first plural habitual p-a construction)

— **mu kè̌,** (first plural relative continuative p-a construction)

mu/mù, (first plural object pronoun)

mǔ, (first plural p-a pronoun employed with **bā**)

-mù, (first plural possessive pronoun)

mūgǔ (*f.* **mugunyà** ; *pl.* **miyàgū**), bad/evil (person or thing)

mùgùntā (*f.*), badness, wickedness

mukà, (first plural relative completive p-a pronoun)

mu kàn, (see **mu**)

mu kè̌, (see **mu**)

mukù, (see **makù**)

mun, (first plural completive p-a pronoun)

munà, (first plural continuative p-a construction)

munāfùkī (*f.* **munāfùkā** ; *pl.* **mùnàfùkai**), hypocrite

murfǔ/murhǔ (*pl.* **muràfū**), the three stones which form the indigenous cooking-place, stove

muryà (*f.*) (*pl.* **muryōyī**), voice

Mūsā, Moses

musù, (see **masù**)

mutù, *v.* die

mùtûm/mùtumǐ (*pl.* **mutànē**), man, person

mutuncì, manliness, self-respect

mùtùntakà (*f.*), human nature

mwâ, (first plural future II p-a pronoun)

mwǎ, (first plural p-a pronoun employed with **bā**)

na/-n (*f.* **ta/-r**), of, pertaining to (the referential)

— **na/ta biyu,** the second one

na, (first singular relative completive p-a pronoun)

— **na kàn** (first singular habitual p-a construction)

— **na/ni kè̌,** (first singular relative continuative p-a construction)

nā, (first singular completive p-a pronoun)

nā-/nà̌- (*f.* **tā-/tà̌-**), belonging to (prefixed to possessive pronouns to form the independent possessive pronouns)

nâ, (first singular future II p-a pronoun)

nà, first singular p-a pronoun employed with **bā)**

-nà, be in the process of, be
at (specialized verbal
employed in continua-
tive aspect construc-
tions)

-na/-nā (*f.* **-ta/-tā**), my
(first singular possessive
pronoun)

na'àm, (particle of assent
or interest), yes

nà'am, (reply to a call),
yes ?, what ?

naɗà, *v.* wind (a turban),
fold (a cloth), appoint (a
person to office)

naɗêwā, folding, winding,
appointing

nàɗu, *v.* be folded up, be
wound, be appointed

nai, 9d

nairà, 1 naira

nākà/tākà, yours (*m. sing.*)
(independent possessive
pronoun)

na kàn, (see **na**)

na kè, (see **na**)

nākì/tākì, yours (*f. sing.*)
(independent possessive
pronoun)

nākù/tākù, yours (*pl.*) (independent possessive
pronoun)

nāmà (*pl.* **nāmū**), (wild)
animal, meat, flesh

namijì (*pl.* **mazā**), male,
brave man

nan/nân/nàn, this/these,
that/those, here/there

— **nan dà nan,** immedi-
ately, at once

— **nan gàrī,** in this town

— **nan ƙasā,** in this country

nànnēmà, *v.* look all over
for

nāsà/tāsà, his (independent
possessive pronoun)

nāsù/tāsù, theirs (independent possessive pronoun)

nātà/tātà, hers (independent possessive pronoun)

nauyī, heaviness

— **dà nauyī,** heavy

nawà, how much/many ?

— **nawà-nawà,** how much
each/apiece

nàwa/tàwa, mine (independent possessive pronoun)

nē/nè (*f.* **cē/cè**), is, was

nēmā, seeking, looking for

nèmā (i/ē), *v.* seek, look for

nèmammē (*f.* **nèmammiyā** ;
pl. **nèmàmmū**), sought

nènnēmà, (= **nànnēmà**)

nēmō, *v.* seek and bring
here

nēsà, far away (= **nīsa**)

ngō/ungō, take hold (of
what I am handing you) !

nī, (first singular independent pronoun)

ni/nì, (first singular object pronoun)

Nìjērìyà (f.), Nigeria

ni kè, (see na kè under na)

nīsā, distance

nīsa, afar

— dà nīsa, far away

nōmā (f.), v. farming

nòmā (i/ē), v. till a farm

Nūhù, Noah

nūnà, v. show

nùna, v. become ripe

nutsè/nitsè, v. vanish

Nùwambà (f.), November

ōfìs/ōfìshī, office

òhō, what do I care !, I don't know or care

Òktōbà (f.), October

rabà, v. divide, separate

rabì, half

ràbō, one's lot, sharing out, share

ràbō/ràbuwā (f.), separation

ràbu (dà), v. part from, separate

rāfànī (pl. ràfànai), maternal uncle (= kāwù)

ragà, v. reduce

ragè, v. reduce, remain

ragì, reduction

— bâ ragì, there is no reduction (in price)

râi (pl. rāyukà), life

— rânkà yà daɗè, may you live long ! (lit. may your life last a long time)

ràkē, sugarcane

rāmì (pl. rāmunà), hole (in ground, wall, earth-floor)

rân, (see râi or rānā)

rānā (f.), sun, heat of sun, day

— rân nan, (on) a certain day, the other day

— ran Tàlātà, Tuesday

rānī, the dry season

rasà, v. lack, be unable to

rashì, lack

— rashìn sanì, ignorance, lack of knowledge

ràsît/ràsitì, receipt

ràsu, v. die, be in short supply

rātsè, v. swerve, stray (from road)

rawā (f.) (pl. ràye-ràyē), dancing, a dance

rawànī (pl. rawunà), turban

ràwayà (f.), yellow

— ràwayà-ràwayà, yellow-ish

rērà, v. sing

— rērà wāƙà, sing a song

rigā/rìgāyà, v. (have) already done, precede

rìgā (f.) (pl. rìgunà), gown, robe, shirt, coat

rìgàkafì, prevention

rìgāyầ, v. (see rigā)

rījìyā (f.) (pl. rījiyōyī), a well

rìk̃à, v. keep on doing

rìk̃è, v. hold

ròk̃à (i/ē) v. request, beseech

ròk̃ō, v. a request, requesting

rōmō, broth

rubùtā, v. write

rùbùtū, writing, act of writing

rufầ, v. cover, close

rufè̃, v. cover (up/over), close, conceal

ruwā, water, rain

— ìnā ruwāna ?, what do I care ?

— ruwan samầ, rain

— ruwan shầ, drinking water

sâ (f. sānìyā ; pl. shānū), bull

sâ, v. put, place, appoint

sâ/swâ, (third plural future II p-a pronoun)

sà/swà/sù̃, (third plural p-a pronoun employed with bā)

-sà, (third singular possessive pronoun)

sā'à (f.), good luck, hour, time

— sā'àd dà, when . . .

— sā'àn nan, then . . .

sàbà'in, seventy

sābō (f. sābuwā ; pl. sầbầbbī), new (thing)

— sābō ful, brand new

sabò dà/sabòdà, because of

sầbulù̃, soap

sādà̃, v. cause to meet

sầdu (dà), v. meet (with)

sāfè̃, morning

— dà sāfè̃, in the morning

sāfiyā (f.), morning

sai (dà), v. (see sayar)

sai, except, then, unless, only, until, must (etc.)

— sai kà cê, as if (lit. you must say)

— sai kà ganī, you'll have to see it (to believe it)

Sà'ìdù̃, (man's name)

sak, exactly (with directions—see arè̃wā)

sàk̃ā (i/ē), v. release (i.e. from prison, marriage, etc.)

sakandàrè̃, secondary school

sāk̃è̃, v. change

— sàk̃è fàɗā, (please) repeat (what you) said

Sakkwato, Sokoto

sàlāmù/sàlâm àlaikùn, greetings ! (called from outside the compound)

sallà (f.), Muslim prayers, festival

sallàmā, *v.* agree to sell at price offered

samā̀, sky

samà, upward

— **samà-samà,** slightly upward

sàmā/sāmù (i/ē), *v.* obtain, get, come upon

Sambò, (man's name)

sàmmakō, making an early start

sāmō, *v.* get and bring here

sāmù, *v.* (see **sà̀mā**)

sà̀mu, *v.* occurred, be obtainable

sàna'à̀ (*f.*) (*pl.* **sana'ō'ī**), (one's) trade, occupation, profession

sànannē (*f.* **sànanniyā ;** *pl.* **sànànnū**), known

sanar (dà), *v.* cause to know

sanasshē, *v.* (form of **sanar**)

sàndā (*pl.* **sandunā̀**), stick, force

— **ɗan sàndā** (*pl.* **'yan sàndā**), Government Policeman

sànē, knowledgeable

Sānī, (man's name)

sanì/san, *v.* know

sānìyā (*f.*), cow (see **sā̀**)

sànnu, greetings !, slowness, carefulness

— **sànnu dà aikì,** greetings in (your) work

— **sànnu dà zuwā̀,** greetings at (your) coming

— **sànnu sànnu,** greetings

— **sànnu-sànnu,** slowly

santsī, slipperiness

sanyī, damp coldness

sarkī (*pl.* **sarākunā̀**), chief, king

sassāfē, very early morning

— **dà sassāfē,** in the very early morning

sàssayā̀, *v.* keep on buying

sassayar, *v.* keep on selling

sassàyē, *v.* keep on buying until (one) has bought all of

sātà̀ (*f.*), stealing

sà̀tā (i/ē), *v.* steal

sātī, week, Saturday, (= **mākò**), weekly wages

— **sātī mài zuwā̀,** next week

— **sātī wandà ya wucè,** last week

Sàtumbà (*f.*), September

sàu, times (used with numbers, *e.g.* **sàu ukù** = three times)

sàuka, *v.* descend, get down from, arrive (at)

saukar (dà), *v.* lift down, bring/put down

saukō, *v.* come down (from)

saukà̀ƙē, = **sawwàƙē**

sauƙī, easiness

— dà sauƙī, easily, less bothersome, (illness) be better

— yanà dà sauƙī, it (e.g. illness, tiredness) is better

— yā yi sauƙī, it got better

saurā, remainder

saura, v. remain, be left over

sauràyī (pl. sàmàrī), young man

saurī, quickness

— dà saurī, quickly

sâwā, putting (verbal noun from sâ)

sawwàƙē, reduce completely, make (e.g. illness) better

sàyā (i/ē), v. buy

sayar/sai (dà), v. sell, cause to buy

sayârwā, selling

sayè, v. buy all of

sàyē, buying

sayō, v. buy and bring here

sàyu, v. be bought (completely)

sh-, (see sh section following this section)

sidiƙ, (see baƙī)

sifìrī, zero

sil, (see baƙī)

simintì/sumuntì, cement

sirdì (pl. siràdā), saddle, seat (of bicycle, motorcycle)

sìsì, 5 kobos

— sìsìn-kwabò, ½ kobo (= ɗàrī)

— sìsì-sìsì/sī-sìsì, 5 kobos apiece/each

sìttin, sixty

sō, v. want, like, love

sô, wanting, liking, loving

sōmà, v. begin, start

sòsai, well, correctly, exactly

sòyayyà (f.), mutual affection

su, (third plural p-a pronoun employed with zâ, bâ)

— su kàn, (third plural habitual p-a construction)

— su kè, (third plural relative continuative p-a construction)

sū, (third plural independent pronoun)

su/sù, (third plural object pronoun)

sù, (third plural subjunctive p-a pronoun)

sũ, (see sà)

-sù, (third plural possessive pronoun)

sukà, (third plural relative completive p-a pronoun)

su kàn, (see su)

sukàr(ì), sugar

su kè, (see su)

sùkùkù, despondently (an ideophone)

— yanà zàune sùkùkù, he was sitting despondently

sulè (*pl.* sulūluwà), shilling

Sulè, (man's name)

Sùlèmānù, (man's name)

sun, (third plural completive p-a pronoun)

sunà, (third plural continuative p-a construction)

sūnā (*pl.* sūnàyē), name, price

— sâ sūnā, set the price (of an article)

sùnkwìye, bent over, stooped

— à sùnkwìye, bent over, stooped

sùrukā/sùrùkuwā (*f.*), mother-in-law

sùrukī (*f.* sùrukā ; *pl.* sùrùkai), (father)-in-law ; *pl.* in-laws

sùrūtù, loud (senseless) chattering

swâ, (see sâ)

swà/sù/sà, (see sà)

shā, *v.* drink

— shā māgànī, take medicine

— shā wàhalà, have trouble

shā (dà), (see shāyar)

shâ, drinking ; and (with numbers 11–19 only)

shàfā (i/ē), *v.* wipe, affect a person

shāhò (*pl.* shāhunà), hawk

shâidā, *v.* bear witness, inform

shakkà (*f.*), doubting

— bâ shakkà, doubtless, without doubt

shar, (see kōrè)

shārè, *v.* sweep

shàrī'à (*f.*) (*pl.* sharī'ō'ī), administration of justice, law, court

shāshē, (form of shāyar)

shāyar/shā (dà), *v.* water (an animal), cause to drink

shègàntakà (*f.*), impudence, rascality

shēgè (*f.* shēgìyā ; *pl.* shègū), bastard, illegitimate child

shēgè !, damn it !, you bastard !

shèkarà (*f.*) (*pl.* shèkàrū), year

shēkaràn città, five days hence

shēkaranjiyà, day before yesterday

shēƙà, *v.* winnow, pour out

— shēƙà dà gudù, take to (one's) heels

shi, (third singular masculine p-a pronoun employed with zâ, bâ)

shī, (third singular masculine independent pro-
noun)

shī kḕ nan, that's that,
that's the end of the
matter

shi/shì, (third singular
masculine object pro-
noun)

shidà, six

shiga, *v.* enter (there), go in

shigā, entering (there)

shigḕ, *v.* pass by (= **wucḕ**)

shigō, *v.* enter (here), come
in

shin/shîn, could it be ?, I
wonder . . .

shìnkāfā (*f.*), rice

shirū, silence

— **shiru-shiru,** quietness,
taciturnity

shiryà, *v.* prepare ; settle
quarrel

shūɗì (*f.* **shūɗìyā ;** *pl.*
shūɗɗā), blue (thing)

shūkà, *v.* sow, plant seed

shūkà, planting, crops

ta, in the process of,
through

ta, (third singular feminine
relative completive p-a
pronoun and the p-a
pronoun employed with
zâ, bâ)

— **ta kàn** (third singular

feminine habitual p-a
construction)

— **ta kḕ,** (third singular
feminine relative con-
tinuative p-a construc-
tion)

ta/tà, (third singular feminine object pronoun)

tā, (third singular feminine
completive p-a pronoun)

tâ, (third singular feminine
future II p-a pronoun)

tà, (third singular feminine
subjunctive p-a pro-
noun)

tǎ, (third singular feminine
p-a pronoun employed
with **bā**)

ta/-r, (see **na/-n**)

— **ta bìyar,** the fifth (see
also **na/-n**)

tabbàtā, *v.* be sure (that),
confirm

tàbbàtaccē (*f.* **tàbbàtac-
ciyā ;** *pl.* **tàbbàtàttū**),
confirmed, proven (fact
or person)

tabbatar (dà), *v.* make certain, confirm

tabɗì, (expression of utter
amazement)

taɓà, *v.* touch ; have ever/
previously done

tàɓà kunnē, great grandchild

tādì, chatting

tàfasà, v. (water, etc.) boils

tàfàsasshē (f. **tàfàsasshiyā** ; pl. **tàfàsàssū**), boiled

tàfi, v. go (away)

— **tàfi àbinkà !,** scram

tàfī, palm of the hand, sole of the foot

tàfiyà (f.), travelling, going

tāgà (f.) (pl. **tāgōgī**), window (hole)

tàimakà (i/ē), v. help

tàimakō, help, act of helping

tak, (see **ɗaya**)

tākà, v. tread on, walk along

tākà, (see **nākà**)

tàkàlmī (pl. **tākalmà**), sandal, shoe, boot

ta kàn, (see **ta**)

takàrdā (f.) (pl. **tàkàrdū**), paper, (small) book

ta kè, (see **ta**)

tākì, (see **nākì**)

tākù, (see **nākù**)

takwàs, eight

talàkà (pl. **talakāwā**), common person

Tàlātà (f.), Tuesday

tàlàtin, thirty

Talle, (man's name)

tamàtā, female

tàmànin, eighty

tàmbayà (i/ē), v. ask

tàmbayà (f.) (pl. **tamba-yōyī**), question, act of asking

tāmù, (see **nāmù**)

tanà, (third singular feminine continuative p-a construction)

tàntàmbayà, v. keep on asking

tarà, nine

tārà, v. gather, collect

tàre (dà), together (with)

tarō, 2½ kobos

tàru, v. be gathered together

tāsà (f.) (pl. **tāsōshī**), metal bowl or basin ; pl. dishes

tāsà, (see **nāsà**)

tāsù, (see **nāsù**)

tashà/tēshà (pl. **tashōshī**), (railway) station

tāshì, v. get up, start out (on a journey), stand up

tātà, (see **nātà**)

tàttàɓà kunnè, great-great grandchild

tattàkē, v. trample under foot

tàtsūnìyā (f.) (pl. **tātsūni-yōyī**), fable

taurī, hardness, toughness

tàwa, (see **nàwa**)

tàwadà (f.), ink

tāyà (f.) (pl. **tāyōyī**), tyre

tayà, v. make an offer (in bargaining)

tēbùr(ī) (pl. **tēburōrī**), table, shovel

tēshà, (see **tashà**)

tīcà (*pl.* tīcōcī), teacher

tīlàs, perforce, of necessity

tìnjim, abundantly, in large numbers (an ideophone)

— mutànē tìnjim, a large number of people

tȭ/tȍ, well, okay

ts-, (see the ts- section following this section)

tufà (*pl.* tufāfì), clothes

tùkùna, not yet, first

tukunyā (*f.*) (*pl.* tukwànē), cooking-pot

tùlū (*pl.* tūlūnà), pitcher

tun, since

tunà, *v.* remember

tùnànī, reflecting, remembering, regret, apprehensiveness

tunkìyā (*f.*) (*pl.* tumākī), sheep

tūrà, *v.* push

Tūrai (*f.*), Europe

tūrè, *v.* push/knock over

tūsà (*f.*), breaking wind

tuwō, guinea-corn or millet mush (the staple food of Northern Nigeria)

tsàdā (*f.*), expensiveness

— yanà dà tsàdā = yā yi tsàdā, it is expensive

tsāfì, fetish, idol

tsai (dà), (see tsayar)

tsakà/tsakiyà (*f.*), centre, middle

— tsakàr tsàkānī, betwixt and between

tsàkānī, between

tsallē, jumping

— tsàlle-tsàllē, jumping events in track and field matches

tsàmmānì, thinking, thought

tsawō, length

tsayà, *v.* stand (up), stop, wait

tsayar/tsai (dà), *v.* cause to stand/stop/wait

tsàye, stopped, standing

— à tsàye, in a standing position, stopped

tsincè, *v.* pick up, select, find (thing)

tsìnī (*pl.* tsīnàyē), sharp point

tsìntā (i/ē), *v.* select, pick up

tsintsiyā (*f.*) (*pl.*) tsintsiyōyī), broom, type of thatching grass

tsìrārà (*f.*), nakedness, naked

tsit, silence (an ideophone)

— yā yi tsit, he kept silent

tsōhō/tsōfō (*f.* tsōhuwā; *pl.* tsòfàffī), old (person or thing)

— tsōfon hannū, experienced person, ' an old hand '

tsòrō, fear

tsūfa, *v.* become old

tsūfā, becoming old, ageing

tsuntsū (*f.* tsuntsuwā ; *pl.* tsuntsăyē), bird

tsūtsā (*f.*) (*pl.* tsūtsōtsī), worm

ùbā (*pl.* ùbànnī), father

ukù, three

Ùmarù, (man's name)

ungō, (see ngō)

ùngùlū (*f.*) (*pl.* ùngùlai), vulture

Ùsmân, (man's name)

uwā (*f.*), mother

— uwargidā, woman of the house, (first) wife

wā̃ (*f.* yā̃ ; *pl.* yâyyē), elder sibling (brother or sister) (= yǎyā)

wà, (see ma-/wà)

wǎ/wǎnē/wǎnēnè̃ (*pl.* su wà), who (is it) ?

— wǎnē shī ?, who does he think he is ?

waccàn, (see wancàn)

wàccē, (see wànnē)

wàcē/wàcēcè̃, (feminine of wǎnē/wǎnēnè̃)

wàcè, (see wànè)

wadai, curse (an exclamation)

— Allà wadankà, may God curse you !

waddà, (see wandà)

wadàncân, (see wancàn)

wadàndà, (see wandà)

wadànnân, (see wannàn)

wàdànnè, (see wànè)

wàdànnē, (see wànnē)

wadansu, (see wani)

wàhalà̃ (*f.*), trouble

wai, it is said, quote, rumour has it that . . .

wàiwàye, turning the head round to look

wajē, direction

— wajen, toward/to a person or place, in the presence of a person (= wurin)

wàje, outside

wākē, bean(s)

wàkīlì (*pl.* wàkìlai), representative

wākà̃ (*f.*) (*pl.* wākōkī), song, poem

wancàn (*f.* waccàn ; *pl.* wadàncân), that, that one

wàncan (*f.* wàccan ; *pl.* wàdàncan), the one in question

wandà/wândà (*f.* waddà ; *pl.* wadàndà), that which, which, who

— duk wandà, whoever

wàndō (*pl.* wandunà), pair of trousers

Wānè (*f.* Wancè ; *pl.* Su wānè), So-and-so

wànē/wànēnè, (see wà)

wànè (f. wàcè ; pl.
　　wàɗannè), which ?

wani (f. wata ; pl.
　　waɗansu), some (one), a
　　certain (one), a, another

wankè, v. wash (body,
　　clothes, pot, etc.)

wannàn (pl. waɗànnân),
　　this, this one

wànnē (f. wàccē ; pl.
　　wàɗànnē) which one ?

wànzāmì (pl. wànzàmai),
　　barber, tatooer

wàrhakà, at this time . . .

warkà, v. recover from
　　illness

warkar (dà), v. cure

warkè, v. recover from
　　illness, cure

wàsā (pl. wàsànnī), playing,
　　joking, dancing

wasàlàm, (see hāzā)

wàsīƙà (f.) (pl. wàsìƙū),
　　letter

wasu, (form of waɗansu)

wàshègàrī, (= kàshègàrī)

wata, (see wani)

watà (pl. wàtànnī), moon,
　　month

— watà mài zuwà, next
　　month

— watàn gòbe, next month

— watàn jiyà, last month

— watàn dà ya wucè, last
　　month

wàtàkīlà/watakīlà/kīlà,
　　probably, perhaps,
　　maybe (but probable)

wàtò, that is . . .

wātsè, v. become scattered

wāwā (pl. wāwàyē), fool

— wāwan barcī, heavy/
　　sound sleep

wayà (f.) (pl. wayōyī),
　　wire, telegraph, tele-
　　gram, telephone

— gidan wayà, post office
　　(where telegrams may be
　　dispatched)

wāyè, v. become light

— gàrī yā wāyè, it dawned

wàyō, cleverness, trickiness

wâyyô, alas ! (exclamation
　　of despair)

— wâyyô Allà, alas !

— wâyyô nī, woe is me !

wejì/wajì, wedge

wòfī (pl. wōfàyē), useless
　　(thing or person), empty

wōhò, booing

— sun bī sù wōhò-wōhò,
　　they followed them
　　booing

wucè, v. pass by (= ficè,
　　shigè)

wuƙā (f.) (pl. wuƙàƙē),
　　knife

wunì/yinì, v. spend the day

wunì/yinì, period of day-
　　light

wur, (see jā)

wurgằ, v. throw
wurgar (dà), v. throw
(violently)
wurgō, v. throw here
wurì (pl. kudī), cowry shell
(formerly used as money)
wurī (pl. wurằrē), place
— dà wuri-wuri, very
early, very promptly
— wurin, toward/to a per-
son or place, in the
presence of a person
(= wajen)
— (tun) dà wuri, promptly,
early
wutā (f.), fire
wuyằ (pl. wuyōyī), neck
wùyā (f.), difficulty

'y-, (see separate section for
'y- following this section)
ya, (third singular masculine relative completive
p-a pronoun)
— ya kàn, (third singular
masculine habitual p-a
construction)
— ya kè̀, (third singular
masculine relative con-
tinuative p-a construc-
tion)
yā̀, (third singular masculine completive p-a pro-
noun)
yā̀, v. come
— yā kà, come !

yâ, (third singular masculine future II p-a pro-
noun)
yâ, (see wâ)
yà̀, (third singular masculine subjunctive p-a pro-
noun)
yằ, (third singular masculine p-a pronoun em-
ployed with bā)
yaddà/yâddà, how, the way
in which
yādì, yard (measurement),
(European) cloth
ya kàn, (see ya)
ya kè̀, (see ya)
Yàƙubù, Jacob
yâmmā, west, (late) afternoon
— yâmmā sak, due west
yâmma, westward
yanà̀, (third singular
masculine continuative
p-a construction)
yankà̀, v. slaughter (animal), cut in two ; set (a
time) ; give verdict (in a
court case)
yankā, butchering
yankè̀, v. (= yankà̀)
— yankè shàrī'à̀, pro-
nounce judgement (in a
court case)
yankè̀wā (f.), cutting,
butchering, etc. (from
yankè̀)

yànzu, now
— har yànzu, still, up to the present
— yànzu-yànzu, right away
yar/yā (dà), v. throw away, discard
yàràntakà (f.), childishness, childhood
yàrda, v. agree, consent
yàrdā (f.), agreement, consent
yārinyà (f.), girl
yārò (pl. yârā), boy
yātsà (pl. yātsōtsī), finger
yâu, today
— yâu-yâu, this very day, today for sure
yàushè/yàushe, when ?
yâuwā/yâuwa, fine, splendid (reply to greeting)
yawà, abundance
— dà yawà, much, many
yāwò, strolling, wandering
yàyā, (see wâ)
yàyà, how ?
yayyafī, drizzle
yi, v. do, make
— yi ta yî, set about doing
yì, (see ì)
yî, doing, making
yinì, (see wunì)
yìwu, v. be possible
Yūlì, July
Yūnì, June

yunwà (f.), hunger, famine
— ji yunwà, be/go hungry
Yūsufù, Joseph

'yā (f.), daughter (= dìyā)
— 'yā màcè (pl. 'yam mātā), young woman
— 'yar cikī, type of gown
— 'yar fārì, firstborn daughter
— 'yar'ùbā, half-sister
— 'yar'uwā, sister
'yan, (see dā)
— 'yan kasā, inhabitants of a country
'yā'yā, (see da)
'Yòlà, Yola (a town near the Cameroun border)

zā, v. (specialized verbal employed as future I aspect particle), will
zâ, v. will go
zāfī, heat, pain
— yā yi zāfī, it was hot/painful
zâi, he will (third singular masculine form of future I p-a construction)
zàkarà (pl. zàkàrū), rooster, cock
zākī, sweetness
zalbè, common grey heron
zama, v. be, become, live
zamā, being, living

zāmànī (*pl.* zàmànai),
period of time
— zāmànin dâ, in olden
times
zambàr, 1000
— zambàr dubū, 1 000 000
zân, I will (first singular
form of future I p-a
construction)
zanè (*pl.* zannuwà, body-
cloth, cloth
zārè, *v.* unsheath (sword),
pull out (*e.g.* foot from
mud, stirrup, shoe, *etc.*)
zarè, *v.* snatch, grab
Zāriyà (*f.*), Zaria
zaunà, *v.* sit down, settle
(in a place)
zaunar (dà), *v.* cause to sit/
settle
zàune, seated
— à zàune, seated
zāwò, diarrhoea
zàzzàɓī, fever, malaria
Zazzaganci, the dialect of
Zaria (Zazzàu)
Zazzàu, Zaria

zīnārìyā (*f.*), gold
zìyārà (*f.*), visiting
zìyartà (i/ē), *v.* visit
zō, *v.* come
zōbè (*pl.* zôbbā), ring
zōmō (*pl.* zōmàyē), rabbit
zubà, *v.* pour
zubar/zub (dà), *v.* pour/
throw away
zubè, *v.* pour away (all of),
abort (pregnancy)
zūcìyā (*f.*) (*pl.* zūciyōyī),
heart
zùmùntā (*f.*), relationship
(by blood or marriage),
good relationship
zur, (see jā)
zūrà, *v.* start up quickly
— zūrà dà gudù, take to
(one's) heels
zùriyà/zùri'à (*f.*),
descendants
zuwà, coming ; towards
— zuwà gà . . ., to . . . (formula employed at start
of letter)

English–Hausa Vocabulary

Note : *when using the English–Hausa sections, it is recommended that the student cross-check entries with the Hausa–English section, a large dictionary and, if possible, with some occurrence of the words/constructions in context. It is very easy to be misled into wrong usage by the over-brief indications of the meanings provided in short vocabularies like this one.*

ability, **iyàwā** (*f.*)

able, be, *v.* **iyà**

according to, **ìn ji . . .,
wai . . .**

acquaintance, **idòn sanì**

adding up, **lìssāfì**

administer, *v.* **hakùntā**

adult, **bàbba** (*pl.* **mânyā**)

aeroplane, **jirgin samà**

affair, **bàtū**

affect, *v.* **shàfā (i/ē)**

affection (mutual), **sòyayyà**
(*f.*)

after, **bāyân dà**

afternoon (late), **yâmmā,
là'asàr**

ago, short while ago, **ɗazu**

agree, *v.* **yàrda**

air, **iskà** (*m.* or *f.*)

alas !, **wâyyô** !

all, **dukà**

all together, **gàba ɗaya**

allow, *v.* **barì/bar**

along, get along well, *v.*
jìtu

already planned or known,
dâ mā

already, to have (done), *v.*
rigā, *v.* **rìgāyà**

all right, that's all right,
bâ lâifī

also, **kumā**

although, **kō dà, kō dà shi/
ya kè**

always, **kullum/kullun**

amazement, **màmākì**

amen, **àmin**

America, **Amirkà** (*f.*)

and, **dà, kumā**

anger, **haushī**

angry, be, **yi fushī**

animal (domestic), **dabbà**
(*f.*) (*pl.* **dabbōbī**)

— (wild), **nāmà** (*pl.* **nāmū/
nāmōmī**)

answer, *v.n.* (*f.*) **amsà**

ants, white, **gàrā** (*f.*)

any, **kōwànè** (*f*. **kōwàcè** ; *pl*. **kōwàɗànnè**)
anyone who, **duk wandà**
anything, **kōmē**
appoint, *v*. **naɗà**
apprentice, **makồyī**
approach, *v*. **kusa**
April, **Afrìl**
Arab, **Bàlārabḕ** (*f*. **Bàlārabìyā** ; *pl*. **Lārabāwā**)
argument, **faɗà**
arithmetic, **lìssāfì**
arm, **hannū** (*pl*. **hannằyē**)
arrogance, **tàƙamā** (*f*.)
arrow, **kibiyằ** (*f*.) (*pl*. **kibiyōyī**)
as, **kàmar**
as for, **kàm**, **mā/ma**
as if, **sai kà cḗ**, **kàmar**
ask, *v*. **tàmbayằ (i/ē)**
at, **à**
attempt, **ƙồƙarī**
attention, pay, *v*. **kùlā (dà)**, **kasà kûnnē**
audience chamber (of chief), **fādà** (*f*.)
August, **Àgustà**
aunt (paternal), **bābà** ; **gwaggồ/gwàggō**
— (maternal), **innà/ìnnā/iyà** ; **gwaggồ/gwàggō** (maternal uncle's wife)
axe, **gằtarī** (*pl*. **gāturà**)

bachelor **gwaurō/gwamrō** (*pl*. **gwaurằyē**)
back, **bāyā**
— backwards, **bāya**
back of the head, **ƙyēyằ** (*f*.)
bad, **mūgū̀** (*f*. **mugunyằ** ; *pl*. **miyằgū**)
bad, go, *v*. **lālằcē**
badness, evil, **mùgùntā** (*f*.)
bag, **jàkā** (*f*.) (*pl*. **jakunkunà**)
ball **cūrì** ; **ƙwallō**
banana(s), **àyàbà** (*f*.)
baobab tree, **kūkà** (*f*.) (*pl*. **kūkōkī**)
barber, **wànzāmì** (*pl*. **wànzằmai**)
bastard, **shēgḕ** (*f*. **shēgìyā** ; *pl*. **shḕgū**)
be, *v*. **zama**, **nē/cē**
bean(s), **wākē**
bear child, *v*. **haihù (i/ē)**
bear witness, *v*. **shâidā**
beard, **gēmū̀**
beat, *v*. **bugà**, *v*. **bùgā (i/ē)**, *v*. **dồkā (i/ē)**
beat (drum), *v*. **kaɗà**,
beating, thrashing, **dūkà**
beautiful, **kyàkkyāwā** (*pl*. **kyāwằwā**)
because (of), **dồmin/ɗon**
because of, **sabò dà/sabòdà**
become, *v*. **zama**
bed, **gadō** (*pl*. **gadằjē**)
beer, corn, **fìtō**, **giyà** (*f*.)
before, **kằmìn/kằfìn**

beggar, marồƙī (*f.* marō-
ƙìyā ; *pl.* marồƙā)

begin, *v.* sōmằ, *v.* fārà

beginning, farkō, fārì

behind, bāyan

belongings, kāyā (*pl.*
kāyàyyakī)

bent over, sùnkwìye

Benue River, Bīnuwài (*f.*)

beseech, *v.* rồƙā

better than, fi . . . kyâu

better, it would be, gāra,
gwàmmà

between, tsàkānī

betwixt and between,
tsakàr tsàkānī

bicycle, kềkē (*pl.* kēkunằ)

big, bàbba (*pl.* mânyā)

bigness, girmā

bird, tsuntsū (*f.* tsuntsuwā ; *pl.* tsuntsằyē)

biscuit, bìskitì (*pl.*
biskitōcī)

bite, *v.* cìzā (i/ē)

black, baƙī (*f.* baƙā ; *pl.*
baƙàƙē)

— blackish, baƙi baƙi

— jet-black, baƙī ƙirin/
sidiƙ/sil

blackboard, àllō (*pl.* allunằ)

blemish, aibù (*pl.* aibōbī)

blind person, màkāhồ/
màkāfồ (*f.* makaunìyā ;
pl. màkàȓī)

blood, jinī

blow, *v.* būsằ

blow on, *v.* hūrằ

blue, shūdì (*f.* shūdìyā ;
pl. shûɗɗā)

boat, jirgī (*pl.* jirằgē)

body, jìkī (*pl.* jikunằ)

boil, *v.* tàfasà

— boiled, tàfàsasshē

bone, ƙàshī (*pl.* ƙasūsuwằ)

book, littāfì (*pl.* lìttàttàfai)

— book cover, bangō

borrow (other than
money), *v.* àrā (i/ē)

bottle, kwalabā/kwalbā (*f.*)
(*pl.* kwalằbē/kwalabōbī)

bottom, gìndī

boundary, iyằkā (*f.*)

bowl, kwānồ (metal) (*pl.*
kwānōnī), kaskō
(earthenware)

box, àkwằtì (*pl.* akwātunằ)

boy, yārồ (*pl.* yârā)

brave person, jārùmī (*f.*
jārùmā ; *pl.* jàrùmai)

bread, burōdì/brōdì

break (a stick), *v.* karyề

breasts, màmā

bride, amaryā (*f.*)

bridegroom, angồ

bridge, gadà (*f.*)

bridle, lìnzāmì (*pl.*
lìnzằmai)

bring, *v.* kāwō

broom, tsintsiyā (*f.*) (*pl.*
tsintsiyōyī)

broth, rōmō

brother, ɗan'uwā (pl.
 'yan'uwā)
brother, half, ɗan'ùbā (pl.
 'yan'ùbā)
brother, younger, ƙanè (pl.
 ƙânnē)
bucket, gùgā (pl. gūgunà)
build, v. ginà, v. kafà
bull, sâ (f. sānìyā ; pl.
 shānū), bìjimī/bàjimī (pl.
 bìjìmai)
burn, v. ƙonà, v. ƙonè
bush, dājì
but, àmmā
butcher, mahàucī (pl.
 mahàutā)
butchering, yankā
butter, mân shānū
buttocks, gìndī
button, ànīnī (pl. ànìnai)
buy, v. sàyā (i/ē)

calabash, ƙwaryā (f.) (pl.
 ƙôrē)
call, v. kirā
canoe, jirgī (pl. jiràgē)
cap, hŭlā (f.) (pl. hūlunà)
care, what do I ?, inā
 ruwāna ?
carefully, à hankàlī
carry, v. ɗaukà (i/ē)
cat, kyânwā (f.) (pl.
 kyanwōyī)
catch, v. kāmà
cause, dàlīlì (pl. dàlìlai)
cement, simintì/sumuntì

centre, tsakiyà/tsakà (f.)
certain, be, v. tabbàtā
chair, kujèrā (f.) (pl.
 kùjèrū)
chance, dāmā (f.)
change, v. sākè
change, canjì
character, halī
— good, kirkì
characterize, v. fayè
chase away, v. kòrā (i/ē)
chat, v. gānà
chattering, sŭrūtù
chatting, tāɗì
cheap, it is, yā yi àràhā
cheapness, àràhā
cheat, v. cùtā (i/ē)
chief, sarkī (pl. sarākunà)
child, yārò (f. yārinyà ;
 pl. yârā)
childishness, yàràntakà (f.)
chin, haɓà (f.)
citrus, lèmō/lèmū
city, birnī (pl. birànē)
clan, zùriyà (f.)
clerk, àkàwū (pl. akāwunà)
— head clerk, bàbban
 àkàwū
cleverness, wàyō
climb, v. hau, v. hayè
close, v. rufè
close (to), kusa (dà)
cloth (body), zanè (pl.
 zannuwà)
— (imported), yādì
clothes, tufāfì (sing. tufà)

cloud (rain), **girgijè** (*pl.* **gìzàgìzai**)

coffee, **kòfī**

coldness (dry), **ɗārī**

— coldness (damp), **sanyī**

collect, *v.* **tārà**

colour, **launì** (*pl.* **launōnī**)

come, *v.* **zō**

coming, **zuwà**

come out, *v.* **fìtō**

commoner, **talàkà** (*pl.* **talakāwā**)

compare, *v.* **kwatàntā**

complaint, **kūkā, ƙārā** (*f.*)

concerning, **bàtun**

confirm, *v.* **tabbàtā**

— confirmed, **tàbbàtaccē**

continue, *v.* **cigàba**

controversy, **jàyayyà** (*f.*)

conversation, **tāɗì, bàtū**

cook, *v.* **dafà**

cooked, **dàfaffē**

— be cooked, *v.* **dàfu**

cooking-pot, **tukunyā** (*f.*) (*pl.* **tukwànē**)

corn (guinea), **dāwà** (*f.*), **hatsī**

correct(ly), **daidai, sòsai**

country, **ƙasā** (*f.*) (*pl.* **ƙasàshē**)

courtier, **bàfādà/bàfādè** (*pl.* **fàdàwā**)

cow, **sānìyā** (*f.*)

co-wife, **kīshìyā** (*f.*) (*pl.* **kīshiyōyī**)

cowrie shell, **wurì** (*pl.* **kuɗī**)

crime, **lâifī** (*pl.* **laifōfī**)

cross, *v.* **ƙētàrē, hayè**

crow, **hànkākà** (*pl.* **hànkàkī**)

crowing (of cock), **cārā** (*f.*)

crying, **kūkā**

cunning, **wàyō**

cure, *v.* **warkar (dà)**, *v.* **warkè**

custom, **àl'ādà** (*f.*) (*pl.* **àl'àdū**)

dance, **rawā** (*m.* or *f.*) (*pl.* **ràye-ràyē**)

darkness, **duhù/dufù**

daughter, **'yā** (*f.*), **ɗiyā** (*f.*)

dawn, **àsubà/àsùbāhì/ sùbāhì**

dawn, *v.* **gàrī yā wāyè**

day (period of daylight), **rānā** (*f.*)

— (twenty-four hours), **kwānā** (*f.*) (*pl.* **kwànàkī**)

day after tomorrow, **jībi**

day before yesterday, **shēkaranjiyà**

deaf and dumb, **bèbàntakà** (*f.*)

deaf-mute, **bēbē** (*f.* **bēbìyā** ; *pl.* **bēbàyē**)

dear, it is, **yā yi tsàdā**

debt, **bāshì**

— incur a debt, *v.* **ci bāshì**

December, **Dìzambà** (*f.*)

depose, *v.* **fìtar/fìd dà**

descend, *v.* **sàuka**

descendants, zùriyầ (f.)
despondent, jùrum
despondently, sùkùkù
deteriorate, v. lālầcē
diarrhoea, zāwồ
die, v. mutù, v. ràsu, v.
 hàlakà
different, dàban
difficulty, wùyā (f.)
— with difficulty, dà kyar
dip out, v. kwāsầ ; ɗēbō
direction, wajē
disciple, àlmājìrī (f. àlmā-
 jìrā ; pl. àlmầjìrai)
disease, cùtā (f.)
dish, tāsầ (f.) (pl. tāsōshī)
dislike, v. ƙi
dispute, jầyayyầ (f.)
distance, nīsā
divide, v. rabầ
do, v. yi
doctor, likitầ (pl. likitōcī)
dog, kàrē (pl. karnukầ)
donkey, jầkī (f. jầkā ; pl.
 jākunầ)
door, ƙōfầ (f.) (pl. ƙōfōfī)
doubt, shakkầ (f.)
— doubtless, bâ shakkầ
dozen, dōzìn
drink, v. shā
driver, dirēbầ
drizzle, yayyafī
drummer, makàɗī (pl.
 makàɗā)
drum stick, makaɗī (pl.
 màkàɗai)

dry, v. būshè
dry season, rānī

each other, jūnā
ear, kûnnē (pl. kunnuwầ)
early (very), dà wuri-wuri,
 tun dà wuri
early start (of a trip),
 sầmmakō
earth, country, ƙasā (f.)
 (pl. ƙasầshē)
easiness, saukī
east, gabàs
easy, it is, yanầ dà saukī
eat, v. ci
— eat up, v. cînyē
edge, bầkī (pl. bākunầ)
education, ilmì/ilìmī
effort, àniyầ/niyyầ (f.),
 ƙồƙarī
egg(s), ƙwai
elder brother, wâ (pl.
 yâyyē)
— elder sister, yâ (f.) (pl.
 yâyyē)
elephant, gīwā (f.) (pl.
 gīwầyē)
end, v. ƙārè
England, Ingìlà (f.)
enter (there), v. shìga
— (here), v. shigō
erect, v. kafầ
error, kuskurè
establish, v. kafầ
estimate, v. kwatàntā
Europe, Tūrai (f.)

European person, Bàtūrè
(f. Bàtūrìyā ; pl.
Tùràwā)
evening, late, màràicē
ever, to have, v. taɓà
every, kōwànè (f. kōwàcè ;
pl. kōwàɗannè)
everyone, kōwā
everything, kōmē
evil, mūgù (f. mugunyà ;
pl. miyàgū), mùgùntā (f.)
exact(ly), sòsai, daidai
examination, jarràbâwā
(f.)
— to pass an examination,
ci jarràbâwā
— to take an examination,
yi jarràbâwā
excel, v. fi
except, sai
excrement, kāshì
excuse me !, gāfarà
expel, v. fitar/fid dà
expensiveness, tsàdā (f.)
experienced person, tsōfon
hannū
expert, gwànī (f. gwànā ;
pl. gwanàyē)
extremely, ƙwarai dà
gàskē
eye, idò (pl. idànū)

fable, tàtsūnìyā (f.) (pl.
tātsūniyōyī)
face, fuskà (f.) (pl.
fuskōkī)

fairness, ādalcì
fall short, v. kāsà
fall v. fāɗì
— fall into, v. fāɗà
— fall on, v. aukà
family, ìyālì, zùriyà (f.)
famine, yunwà (f.)
far away, dà nīsa
farm, gōnā (f.) (pl. gònàkī)
v. yi nōmā ; v. nòmā (i/ē)
— farmer, manòmī (pl.
manòmā)
— farming, nōmā
father, bàba, ùbā (pl.
ùbànnī)
father-in-law, sùrukī
fault, lâifī (pl. laifòfī), aibù
(pl. aibōbī)
fear, tsòrō
feast, jībì
feather(s), gāshì
February, Fàbrairù
feed, v. ciyar/cī dà
feel, v. ji
female, tamàtā
ferrying, fitò
fetish, tsāfì
fever, zàzzàɓī
few, kàɗan
fez, dàrā (f.)
fighting, faɗà
fill, v. cikà
fine !, yâuwā/yâuwa !
finish, v. gamà, ƙārè
find (by chance), v. tsìntā
(i/ē), v. tsincè

finger, **yātsà** (*pl.* **yātsōtsī**)

finish, *v.* **ƙārè**

fire, **wutā** (*f.*), **gòbarā** (*f.*)

first, **na/ta farkō**

five kobos, **sīsì**

florin, **fàtakà, dalà** (*f.*) (*pl.* **dalōlī**)

flour, **gàrī**

fold, *v.* **naɗà**

follow, *v.* **bi**

food, **àbinci**

fool, **wāwā** (*pl.* **wāwàyē**)

forest, **baƙin dājì**

forget, *v.* **màntā**

— forgetful person, **màntau**

formerly, **dã̀**

fourth day hence, **città**

fragment, **guntū** (*pl.* **guntàyē**)

France, **Fàransà** (*f.*)

Frenchman, **Bàfàransì** (*f.* **Bàfàransìyā** ; *pl.* **Fàrànsâi**)

Friday, **Jumma'à** (*f.*)

friend, **àbōkī** (*f.* **àbōkìyā** ; *pl.* **àbòkai**)

friendship, **amincì**

frightening, **ban tsòrō**

frog, **kwàɗō** (*pl.* **kwàɗī**)

front, **gàbā**

— in front, **gàba**

— in front of, **gàban**

Fulani person, **Bàfilācè** (*f.* **Bàfilātà** ; *pl.* **Filànī**)

full, become, *v.* **cìka**

gather, *v.* **tārà**

— be gathered, **tàru**

get, *v.* **sāmù**

get down, *v.* **sàuka**

get up, *v.* **tāshì**

girl, **yārinyà** (*f.*) (*pl.* **'yam mātā**)

girl (nubile), **bùdurwā**

give, *v.* **bā/bâ**, *v.* **bāyar**

give back, *v.* **mayar/mai(dà)**

gleaning, **kālā**

go, *v.* **tàfi**, *v.* **jē**

go around, *v.* **kēwàyā**

go out, *v.* **fìta**

goat, **àkwiyà** (*f.*) (*pl.* **awākī**)

God, **Allà/Allàh**

gold, **zīnārìyā** (*f.*)

good !, **dà kyâu** !

— goodness, **kyâu**

goodness ! good heavens ! **tabɗì** !

gown, **rìgā** (*f.*) (*pl.* **rīgunà**)

grab, *v.* **zarè**

grandchild, **jīkà** (*pl.* **jīkōkī**)

granddaughter, **jīkanyà**

grandfather, **kàkā** (*pl.* **kàkànī**)

grandmother, **kàkā** (*pl.* **kàkànī**)

grass, **cìyāwà** (*f.*) (*pl.* **cìyàyī**)

grasshopper, **fàrā** (*pl.* **fàrī**)

gratitude, **gòdiyā** (*f.*)

grazing, **kīwò**

grease, **mâi**

great-grandchild, tàɓà kunnē

— great-great-grandchild, tàttàɓà kunnē

greed, kwàɗàyī

green, kōrè (f. kōrìyā ; pl. kwārrā)

— bright green, kōrè shar

greet, v. gayar/gai dà

greetings, gaisuwā (f.), barkà (f.)

ground, on the, ƙasà

groundnut(s), peanut(s), gyàɗā (f.)

guava, gwēɓà

guest, bàƙō (f. bàƙwā ; pl. bàƙī)

hair, gāshì

half, rabì

half-kobo, sīsìn kwabò, ɗàrī

half-sister, 'yar'ùbā

hand, hannū (pl. hannàyē)

hand, on the other, ɗai, fa, mā

handle (hoe, axe), ƙōtà (f.) (pl. ƙōtōcī)

handsome, kyàkkyāwā (pl. kyāwàwā)

happen, v. fàru, v. àuku

— happen on, v. yi arbà

happiness, farin cikì

hardness, taurī

harvest, v. gìrbā (i/ē)

harvest season, kàkā (f.)

hat, hùlā (f.) (pl. hūlunà)

hatchet, gàtarī (pl. gāturà)

hatred, ƙiyayyà (f.), ƙî

Hausa person, Bàhaushè (f. Bàhaushìyā ; pl. Hàusàwā)

hawk, shāhò (pl. shāhunà)

head, kâi (pl. kawunà)

— headache, cīwòn kâi

health, lāfiyà (f.)

— healthy, làfìyayyē

heap up, v. kasà

hear, v. ji

heart, zūcìyā (f.) (pl. zūciyōyī)

heat, zāfī

heaven, samà

heaviness, nauyī

heels, take to one's, v. sheƙà/zūrà dà gudù

help, v. tàimakà (i/ē)

— help, tàimakō

hen, kàzā (f.) (pl. kàjī)

herd (of animals), garkè

here, nan/nân/nàn

here is . . ., gà . . .

heron, zalɓè

hide, v. ɓōyè

hide, skin, fātà (f.) (pl. fātū)

highway robber, mafàshī (pl. mafàsā)

hoe, fartanyà (f.) (pl. fartanyōyī); gàrmā (f.) (pl. garèmanī)

hold, v. riƙè
hole, rāmì (pl. rāmunà)
honesty, kirkì
honour, girmā
hoping, fātā, bègē
horn, ƙàhō/ƙàfō (pl. ƙàhònī)
horse, dōkì (pl. dawākī)
hospital, asìbitì (pl. asibitōcī)
hot season, bazarā (f.)
hour, awà (f.) (pl. awōwī)
house, gidā (pl. gidàjē)
— householder, mài gidā
how, yaddà/yâddà
how ?, ƙàƙà ?, yàyà ?
how many ?/how much ? nawà ?
however, dai
however, kōyàyà
however many, kōnawà
human being, ɗan Adàm (pl. 'yan Adàm)
human nature, mùtùntakà (f.)
hundred, ɗarī
hunger, yunwà (f.)
hungry, be, v. ji yunwà
hunter, mahàrbī (pl. mahàrbā)
husband, mijì (pl. mazā), mài gidā
hut, ɗākì (pl. ɗākunà)
hut, made of grass, bukkà (f.) (pl. bukkōkī)

hyena, kūrā (f.) (pl. kūràyē)
hypocrite, munāfùkī (f. munāfùkā ; pl. mùnāfùkai)

idol, tsāfì
if, ìdan/in, dà
ignorance, rashìn sanì
ignore, v. ƙyālè
illness, cīwò, cùtā (f.)
imitate, v. kwàikwayà (i/ē), v. kwatàntā
immediately, nan dà nan, yànzu-yànzu
important people, mânya-mânyā
impossible, be, v. fàskarà (i/ē)
impudence, shègàntakà (f.)
in, (à) cikin, à
increase, v. ƙārà
indeed, kàm
indication, àlāmà/hàlāmà (f.) (pl. àlàmai)
inexpensiveness, àràhā
information, làbārì (pl. làbàrū)
informer, magàyī
inhabitants, 'yan ƙasā
inherit v. gàdā, v. gājè
injection, àllurà (f.) (pl. àllùrai)
injure, v. cùtā (i/ē)
ink, tàwadà (f.)
inside, cikì, (à) cikin

instead of, **màimakon**

intelligence, **hankàlī**

iron, **ƙarfè**

jackal, **dilā**

jam, v. **kākàrē**

joking, **wàsā** (*pl.* **wàsànnī**)

journey, **tàfiyà** (*f.*)

judge, **àlkālī/àlƙālī** (*pl.*
 àlkàlai/àlƙàlai)

judgement, pronounce, v.
 yankè shàrī'à

July, **Yūlì**

jumping, **tsallē**

June, **Yūnì, Jun**

just person, **ādàlī** (*pl.*
 àdàlai)

justice, **ādalcì, shàrī'à** (*f.*)

Kano person, **Bàkanè/
 Bàkanò** (*f.* **Bàkanùwā**;
 pl. **Kanāwā**)

keep on (doing), v. **dingà,
 v. riƙà**

key, **mabūdī** (*pl.* **màbùɗai**)

khaki cloth, **kàkī**

kill, v. **kashè**

kind, **irì**

— all kinds, **irì-irì**

kindness, **àlhērì, àlbarkàcī**

king, **sarkī** (*pl.* **sarākunà**)

kitchen, **madafā/madafī**
 (*pl.* **màdàfai**)

knife, **wuƙā** (*f.*) (*pl.*
 wuƙàƙē)

knock over, v. **tūrè**

know, v. **sanì/san**

knowledge, **ilmì/ilìmī**

known, **sànannē**

kobo, **kwabò** (*pl.* **kwàbbai**)

kolanut, **gōrò**

labourer, **lēbùrà** (*pl.*
 lēburōrī)

lack, v. **rasà, rashì**

Lagos, **Ìkko**

lamp, **fitilà** (*f.*) (*pl.* **fitilū**)

language, **harshè** (*pl.*
 harsunà)

lantern, **fitilà** (*f.*) (*pl.*
 fitilū)

late, be, v. **màkarà**

latecomer, **màkàrau**

lateness, **lattì**

later, till, **sai an jimà**

laughter, **dàriyā** (*f.*)

lavatory, **bāyan gidā**

lawcourt, **shàrī'à** (*f.*) (*pl.*
 sharī'ō'ī), **mahukuntā**
 (*f.*) (*pl.* **màhùkùntai**)

lay down, v. **kwantar** (**dà**)

learner, **makòyī** (*f.* **makōyìyā**; *pl.* **makòyā**)

leather worker, **bàdūkù** (*pl.*
 dùkàwā)

left, **hagū**

— to the left, **hagu**

length, **tsawō**

lest, **kadà/kâr**

let, allow, v. **barì/bar**

letter, **wàsīkà/wàsīkà** (*f.*)
 (*pl.* **wàsìƙū**)

liar, **maƙàryàcī** (*f.*
　maƙaryacìyā ; *pl.*
　maƙàryàtā)
lie, **ƙaryā** (*f.*) (*pl.* **ƙàryàce-**
　ƙàryàcē)
lie down, *v.* **kwântā**
life, **râi** (*pl.* **rāyukà**)
lift, *v.* **ɗagà**
light (fire), *v.* **hūrà**
like, *v.* **sō**
like, **kàmar**
limit, **iyàkā** (*f.*)
lip, **lēɓè** (*pl.* **lēɓunà**)
little, **ƙàramī** (*f.* **ƙàramā** ;
　pl. **ƙanānà**), **ƙànƙanè** (*f.*
　ƙànƙanùwā ; *pl.*
　ƙanānà)
— a little, **kàɗan**
live, *v.* **zama**
lizard, **ƙàdangarè** (*pl.*
　ƙàdàngàrū)
load, **kāyā** (*pl.* **kāyàyyakī**)
loan (money), **bāshì**
— (not money), **arō**
lock, *v.* **kullè**
locust, **fàrā** (*f.*) (*pl.* **fàrī**)
loincloth, **bàntē**
long, **dōgō** (*f.* **dōguwā** ; *pl.*
　dōgàyē)
look (at), *v.* **dūbà**
— look everywhere, *v.*
　duddūbā
look for, *v.* **nèmā** (i/ē)
looking at, **kallō**
lot, **ràbō**
love, *v.* **sō**

luck, **sā'à** (*f.*)
lunatic, **mahàukàcī** (*f.*
　mahaukacìyā ; *pl.*
　mahàukàtā)

machine, **kèkē** (*pl.* **kēkunà**)
madman, **mahàukàcī** (*f.*
　mahaukacìyā ; *pl.*
　mahàukàtā)
madness, **hàukā**
make, *v.* **yi**
malaria, **zàzzàɓī**
male, **namijì** (*pl.* **mazā**)
man, **mùtûm** (*pl.* **mutànē**)
mango(es), **mangwàrò**
many, **dà yawà**
March, **Mārìs** (*f.*)
mare, **gōɗìyā** (*f.*)
market, **kàsuwā** (*f.*) (*pl.*
　kāsuwōyī)
marriage, **aurē**
marriage feast, **angwancì**
marry, *v.* **àurā** (i/ē)
marsh, **fàdamà** (*f.*) (*pl.*
　fadamōmī)
matchet, **àddā** (*f.*) (*pl.*
　addunà)
matter, **bàtū**
matter, it doesn't, **bâ kōmē**
May, **Māyù** (*f.*)
meal, **jībì**
measure, *v.* **gwadà**, *v.* **aunà**
measuring stick, **magwajī**
　(*pl.* **màgwàdai**)
meat, **nāmà**

mechanic, màkānīkì (pl. màkànìkai)

meddlesomeness, kàràm-bànī

medicine, māgànī (pl. māgungunà)

meet, v. hàɗu, v. sàdu

— (with), v. gàmu (dà)

memory, tùnànī

merchant, àttājìrī (pl. àttàjìrai)

mercy, jîn ƙai

— have, v. ji ƙai

merely, kawài

metal, ƙarfè (pl. ƙaràfā)

middle, tsakiyà/tsakà (f.)

milk, madarā (f.)

millet, gērō

million, zambàr dubū, mìlyân

minister, mìnistà (pl. ministōcī)

misfortune, hàsārà (f.)

mistake, kuskurè

Monday, Lìttìnîn (f.)

money, kuɗī

monkey, birì (pl. birai)

month, watà (pl. wàtànnī)

— last month, watàn jiyà, watàn dà ya wucè

— next month, watàn gòbe, watà mài zuwà

moon, watà (pl. wàtànnī)

morning, sāfè, sāfiyā (f.)

mother, màmā (f.), uwā (f.)

mother-in-law, sùrukā (f.)

motor, mōtà (f.) (pl. motōcī)

— motor boy, kàren mōtà

mount, v. hau, v. hayè

mountain, dūtsè (pl. duwàtsū)

mouse, ɓērā (pl. ɓēràyē)

mouth, bàkī (pl. bākunà)

Mr., mālàm (f. mālàmā ; pl. màlàmai)

much, dà yawà

multitude, tulì

must, dōlè, tīlàs

nakedness, tsìrārà (f.)

name, sūnā (pl. sūnàyē)

namely, wàtò

nape of the neck, ƙyēyà (f.)

Native Administration, en'è (pl. en'è-en'è)

near (to), kusa (dà)

necessity, of, tīlàs

neck, wuyà (pl. wuyōyī)

need, bùkātà (f.) (pl. bùkàtū)

needle, àllurà (f.) (pl. àllùrai)

new, sābō (f. sābuwā ; pl. sàbàbbī)

— brand new, sābō ful

news, làbārì (pl. làbàrū)

— I have good news, àlbishìrī

nevertheless, duk dà hakà

next, mài zuwà

next day, kàshègàrī
Niger River, Kwârà (f.)
night, darē
— at night, dà (dàd) darē
night, spend the, v. kwāna
ninepence, nai
no, ā'à
nonsense !, habà
north, arèwā
— due north, arèwā sak
— north-east, arèwā masò
gabàs
— northward, arèwa
— north-west, arèwā masò
yâmma
not, bà ... ba, bà ... ba
notice, take notice of, v.
kùlā (dà)
November, Nùwambà (f.)
now, yànzu
nuisance, kàràmbànī

obtain, v. sāmù/sàmā (i/ē)
occupation, sàna'à (f.) (pl.
sana'ō'ī)
October, Òktobà (f.)
of, na/ta, -n/-r
of course !, mànà !
offer (bargaining), v. tayà
office, ōfìs (pl. ōfìsōshī)
oil, mâi
old, tsōfō/tsōhō (f. tsō-
fuwā ; pl. tsòfàffī)
— become old, v. tsūfa
one, ɗaya, gùdā
— one only, ɗaya tak

once, at, nan dà nan
only, kaɗai, kawài, kurùm
open, v. būɗè
opportunity, dāmā (f.)
or, kō
order, dòkā (f.) (pl.
dōkōkī)
order, in order to, dòmin/
don
outside, wàje
padlock, kwàɗō (pl. kwàɗī)
pain, cīwò, zāfī
palm tree (deleb), giginyà
(f.)
palm (of hand), tàfī
paper, takàrdā (f.) (pl.
tàkàrdū)
parent, mahàifī (f. mahai-
fīyā ; pl. mahàifā)
parents, iyàyē
parents-in-law, sùrùkai
part from, v. ràbu dà
pass (by), v. wucè, v. shigè
— exam, v. ci
passenger, fasànjà (pl.
fasanjōjī)
path, hanyà (f.) (pl.
hanyōyī)
patience, hàƙurī
patient, be, v., hàƙurà
pay, v. biyā
peasant, talàkà (pl.
talakāwā)
pen, àlkalàmī (pl. alka-
lumà)
pencil, fensìr (pl. fensirōrī)

perforce, dōlè, tīlàs

perhaps, wàtàkīlà/wata-kīlà/kīlà

perish, v. hàlakà

person, mùtûm (pl. mutànē)

perspiration, gùmī

petrol, mâi

pick up, v. ɗaukà (i/ē)

pig, àladè (pl. àlàdai)

pile, v. kasà

pilgrimage, hajì

pinch, v. matsà

pitcher, tùlū (pl. tūlūnà)

place, wurī (pl. wuràrē)

place, v. ajìyē, v. sâ

plan, dàbārà (f.) (pl. dàbàrū)

plant, v. shūkà

plate, tāsà (f.) (pl. tāsōshì)

play, playing, wàsā (pl. wàsànnī)

please, don Allà

pleasantness, dāɗī

plenty, yawà

plough, gàrmā (f.) (pl. garèmanī)

pocket, àljīfū/àljīhū (pl. aljīfunà)

poem, wāƙà (f.) (pl. wāƙōƙī)

policeman (Government), ɗan sàndā (pl. 'yan sàndā)

— (N.A.), ɗan dòkā (pl. 'yan dòkā)

polish, v. gōgà

porridge, tuwō

possible, be, v. yìwu

post office, gidan wāyà, fâs ōfìs

pot (cooking), tukunyā (f.) (pl. tukwànē), kaskō

potato(es), dànkalì

pound, ₦2, fâm (f.)

pour, v. zubà

— pour away, v. zubar/zub (dà)

praise God!, àlhamdùlìllāhì

prayers (Muslim), sallà

prefer, v. fi sô

pregnancy, cikì

prepare, v. shiryà

prevent, v. hanà

prevention, rìgàkafì

previously, dâ

primary school, firamàrè

probably, wàtàkīlà

profession, sàna'à (f.) (pl. sana'ō'ī)

prosperity, arzìkī/azzìkī

prosperous, become, v. arzùtā

pull, v. jā, v. jāwō

pull out, v. cirè, v. zārè

pumpkin, kàbēwà (f.) (pl. kàbèyī)

punishment, hòrō

pupil, àlmājìrī (f. àlmā-jìrā ; pl. àlmàjìrai)

push, v. tūrà

— over, v. tūrè

put, v. ajìyē, v. sâ

put down, v. **saukar (dà)**
put on (clothes), v. **jità**

quarrel, **faɗà**
quarter, **kwatà** (f.)
question, **tàmbayà** (f.) (pl. **tambayōyī**)
quickly, **maza, dà saurī**

rabbit, **zōmō** (pl. **zōmàyē**)
rain, **ruwan samà**
rainy season, **dàmunā** (f.)
raise, v. **ɗagà**
rank, high, **martabà** (f.)
ransom, v. **fànsā** (i/ē)
rat, **ɓērā** (pl. **ɓēràyē**)
raw, **ɗanyē** (f. **ɗanyā** ; pl. **ɗanyū**)
read, v. **karàntā**
reading, **kàràtū**
really ?, **àshē ?**
reap, v. **gìrbā** (i/ē)
reason, **dàlīlì** (pl. **dàlìlai**)
receipt, **ràsitì, ràsît**
receive, v. **kàrɓā** (i/ē)
recently, **ɗazu**
recover (illness), v. **warkà**, v. **warkè**
red, **jā** (pl. **jājàyē**)
— reddish, **ja-ja**
— bright red, **jà wur/jir/zur**
redeem, v. **fànsā** (i/ē)
reduce, v. **ragè**, v. **sawwàƙē**, v. **saukàƙē**
reduction, **ragì**
refuse, v. **ƙi**
regarding, **bàtun**

relationship, **zùmùntā** (f.)
relatives, **dangì**
reliability, **amincì**
remain, v. **saura**
— remainder, **saurā**
remedy, **māgànī**
remember, v. **tunà**
— remembering, **tùnànī**
remove, v. **kau/kawad dà** ; **ɗēbè**, v. **kwāshè**, v. **fitar/fid dà**
repair, v. **gyārà**, v. **gyârtā**
repeat (word), **sàkè fàɗā**
replace, v. **mayar/mai (dà)**
representative, **wàkīlì** (pl. **wàkìlai**)
request, v. **ròƙā** ; (n.) **ròƙō**
rest, **hūtū**, v. **hūtà**
— resting, **hūtàwā** (f.)
restore, v. **kōmar dà**
return (here), v. **dāwō**
— (there), v. **kōmà**
reward, **lādā**
rice, **shìnkāfā** (f.)
riding, **hawā**
right, to the, **dāma** (f.)
righteous person, **ādàlī** (pl. **àdàlai**)
ring, **zōbè** (pl. **zôbbā**)
ripen, v. **nùna**
river, **kògī** (pl. **kōgunà**)
road, **hanyà** (f.) (pl. **hanyōyī**)
rock, **dūtsè** (pl. **duwàtsū**)
roofing pan (material), **kwānò** (pl. **kwānōnī**)

room, ɗākì (pl. ɗākunà)
rope, igiyà (f.)
rub, v. gōgà
rule, dòkā (f.) (pl. dōkōkī)
rumour has it that . . ., wai
run, v. gudù
— running, gudù

saddle, sirdì (pl. siràdā)
sadness, baƙin cikì
safety, lāfiyà (f)
said, it is said that . . ., wai
sale, no !, àlbarkà
salt, gishirī
same, all the, duk ɗaya
sandal, tàkàlmī (pl. tākalmà)
Saturday, Àsabàr (f.), Sātī
say, v. cê, v. fàɗā (i/ē)
saying, cêwā
scales, ma'aunī
scheme, dàbārà (f.) (pl. dàbàrū)
school, makarantā (f.) (pl. màkàràntū, makarantōcī)
— school-slate, àllō (pl. allunà)
seated, à zàune
secondary school, sakandàrè
secret, in, à ɓòye
see, v. ganì/gan/ga
see from afar, v. hàngā (i/ē)
seed, irì
seek, v. nèmā (i/ē)

seize, v. kāmà
self, kâi
self-respect, mutuncì
sell, v. sayar/sai dà
send, v. àikā (i/ē)
sense, hankàlī
separate, v. rabà
separation, ràbō/ràbuwā (f.)
September, Sàtumbà (f.)
set aside, v. ajìyē
settle (in place), v. zaunà
sew, v. ɗinkà
— sewing, ɗinkì
sewing machine, kèken ɗinkì
shade, inuwà (f.)
share, ràbō
sharp point, tsìnī (pl. tsìnàyē)
sheep, tunkìyā (f.) (pl. tumākī)
ship, jirgī (pl. jiràgē)
shoe, tàkàlmī (pl. tākalmà)
shoot, v. hàrbā (i/ē)
— shooting, harbì
short, gàjērē (f. gàjērìyā ; pl. gàjērū)
— shortness, gajertà (f.)
shop, kàntī (pl. kantunà)
shovel, shēbùr, tēbùr (pl. shēburōrī, tēburōrī)
show, v. nūnà
shut, v. rufè
sign, àlāmà/hàlāmà (f.) (pl. àlàmai)

silence, **shirū**

similarity, **kàmā**

sing a song, v. **rērà wāƙà**

singly, **ɗai-ɗai**

sister, **'yar'uwā**

— older, **yàyā**

— younger, **ƙanwà**

sit down, v. **zaunà**

skill, **gwànintà** (f.)

skin, **fātà** (f.) (pl. **fātū**)

sky, **samà**

slaughter, v. **yankà**, v. **yankè**

slave, **bāwà** (f. **bâiwā** ; pl. **bāyī**)

— slavery, **bàutā**

sleep, **barcī**

— (sound), **wāwan barcī**

slightly, **kàɗan**

slipperiness, **santsī**

smallness, **ƙanƙantà** (f.)

smoke, **hayāƙī**

snake, **macìjī** (pl. **màcìzai**)

snap, v. **karyè**

snatch, v. **zarè**

sneak up on, v. **laɓàbā**

snoring, **minshārī**

soap, **sàbulù**

so-so, **dāma-dāma**

so-and-so, **wānè** (f. **wancè** ; pl. su **wānè**)

sole (foot), **tàfī**

son, **ɗā** (pl. **'yā'yā**)

song, **wāƙà** (f.) (pl. **wāƙōƙī**)

soon, **an jimà**

sort, **irì**

— all sorts, **irì-irì**

south, **kudù**

sow, v. **shūkà**

space, **fīlī** (pl. **fīlàyē**)

spear, **māshì** (pl. **māsū**)

speech (political), **laccà** (f.)

speech, **màganà** (f.) (pl. **màgàngànū**)

spend a long time, v. **daɗè**

spend a time, v. **jimà**

spend one day, v. **wunì/yinì**

splendid !, **yâuwā/yâuwa** !

spoil, v. **ɓātà**

spoon, **cōkàlī** (pl. **cōkulà**)

squeeze, v. **matsà**

stamp (postage), **kân sarkī**

stand up, v. **tāshì**, v. **tsayà**

stark naked, **ɓutuk**

start, v. **sōmà**, v. **fārà**

start out, v. **tāshì**

station, **tashà/tēshà** (pl. **tashōshī**)

steal, v. **sàtā** (i/ē)

stench, **ɗòyī**

stick, **sàndā** (pl. **sandunà**)

still, **har yànzu**

stomach, **cikì**

— stomach ache, **cīwòn cikì**

stone, **dūtsè** (pl. **duwàtsū**)

stool, **kujèrā** (f.) (pl. **kùjèrū**)

storehouse, **ma'ajī** (pl. **mà'àjìyai**)

stop, v. **tsayà**

storm, **hadarì/hadirì**

story, làbārì (pl. làbàrū)

stove (stone), murfǔ/
murhǔ (pl. muràfū)

stranger, bàƙō (f. bàƙwā ;
pl. bàƙī)

stray, v. rātsè

strength, ƙarfī

strolling, yāwò

strong, ƙàƙƙarfā (pl.
ƙarfàfā)

student, ɗālìbī (pl. ɗàlìbai),
àlmājìrī (f. àlmājìrā ;
pl. àlmàjìrai)

study, v. karàntā

— studying, kàràtū

subdue, v. dannè

sufficient, be, v. ìsa

— sufficient, ìsasshē

sugar, sukàr

sugarcane, ràkē

sun, rānā (f.)

Sunday, Lahàdì/Làdì (f.)

sunset, màgàribà

superior to, mafī/mafìyī
(pl. mafìyā)

sure, be, v. tabbàtā

sure, for, lallē

surpass, v. fi

surprise, màmākì (pl.
màmàkai)

swamp, fàdamà (f.) (pl.
fadamōmī)

sweep, v. shārè

sweetness, zāƙī

swerve, v. rātsè

swimming, iyò

table, tēbùr (pl. tēburōrī)

tailor, maɗìnkī (pl.
maɗìnkā)

tall, dōgō (f. dōguwā ; pl.
dōgàyē)

tanner, majèmī (pl.
majèmā)

tattoo marks, jàrfā (f.)

tax, hàrājì

teacher, mālàm (f.
mālàmā ; pl. màlàmai),
tīcà (pl. tīcōcī)

tear, v. tsāgà

telegram, wayà (f.) (pl.
wayōyī)

telephone, wayà (f.) (pl.
wayōyī)

tell, v. gayà

ten kobos, sulè (pl.
sulūlukà)

tenth, of a penny, ànīnī
(pl. ànìnai)

termites, gàrā (f.)

test, examination, jarrà=
bâwā (f.)

test, v. gwadà

thank, v. gōdè

— thanks, gòdiyā (f.)

— thank you, nā gōdè

that, can/cân/càn

that, wancàn (f. waccàn ;
pl. waɗàncân)

theft, sātà (f.)

then, sā'àn nan

there, can/cân/càn

there is/are, v. àkwai, v. dà

there is no/not, v. bābù/bâ
thief, 6àrāwò (pl. 6àràyī)
thing, àbù (pl. abūbuwà)
thinking, tsàmmānì, câ
third, sulùsī
this, these, nan/nân/nàn
thought, tsàmmānì
thousand, alìf, dubū,
  zambàr
thrash, v. bùgā (i/ē)
thrashing, bugù
three days hence, gātà
throat, màƙōgwàrō
through, ta
throw, v. jē̃fà, v. wurgà
throw at, v. jè̃fā (i/ē)
throw away, v. yar/yā dà
throwing at, jĩfà
Thursday, Àlhàmîs (f.)
thus, hakà
tie, v. ɗaurè
till a farm, v. nòmā (i/ē)
time, lōkàcī (pl. lòkàtai),
  lotò, sā'à (f.)
— from time to time, lōtò-
  lōtò
times, sàu
times, in olden, zāmànin dâ
tin, gwangwan (pl.
  gwangwàyē)
tired, be, v. gàji
tiredness, gàjiyà (f.)
today, yâu
— today week, ì ta yâu
together (with), tàre dà
toilet, bāyan gidā

tomorrow, gòbe (f.)
tongue, harshè (pl.
  harsunà)
tools, kāyan aikì
tooth, haƙōrī (pl. haƙòrā)
top, kâi
top, on top of, à kân
tortoise, kùnkurū (pl.
  kunkurà)
touch, v. ta6à
toughness, taurī
toward, wajen, zuwà
town, gàrī (pl. garūruwà)
trade, sàna'à (f.) (pl.
  sana'ō'ī)
trader (itinerant), farkē/
  falkē (pl. fatàkē)
tradition, àl'ādà (f.) (pl.
  àl'àdū)
train, jirgin ƙasā
trample, v. tattàkē
travel, tàfiyà (f.)
tread on, v. tākà
tree, itàcē (pl. itātuwà)
trouble, wàhalà (f.)
— have trouble, shā
  wàhalà
trousers, wàndō (pl.
  wandunà)
truth, gàskiyā (f.)
Tuesday, Tàlātà (f.)
turban, rawànī (pl.
  rawunà)
turn, v. jūyà
tyre, tāyà (f.) (pl. tāyōyī)

uncle (maternal), **kāwŭ/
kàwū** (*pl.* **kàwùnai**),
rāfằnī (*pl.* **rằfằnai**)

— (paternal), **bappà/bàba**

uncooked, **ɗanyē** (*f.* **ɗanyā**;
pl. **ɗanyū**)

underneath, **ƙàrƙashin**

understand, *v.* **fàhimtằ
(i/ē)**, *v.* **gānẹ̀**, *v.* **ji**

unit, **gùdā**

unless, **sai**

unsheath, *v.* **zārẹ̀**

until, **har, sai**

upward, **samà**

urine, **fìtsārī**

usefulness, **àmfằnī**

useless (thing), **wòfī** (*pl.*
wōfằyē)

vanish, *v.* **nutsẹ̀/nitsẹ̀**

very much, **ƙwarai, ƙwarai
dà gàskē, ainù(n)**

village, **ƙauyẹ̀** (*pl.*
ƙauyukà)

visit, *v.* **zìyartà (i/ē)**

voice, **muryằ** (*f.*) (*pl.*
muryōyī)

voyage, **tàfiyằ** (*f.*)

vulture, **ùngùlū** (*f.*) (*pl.*
ùngùlai)

waist, **iyā gìndī**

wait for, *v.* **jirā**, *v.* **dākàtā**

wall, **bangō**

wandering, **yāwò**

want, *v.* **sō**

wash, *v.* **wankẹ̀**

watch, **àgōgō** (*pl.* **agōgunà**)

water, **ruwā**

— drinking water, **ruwan
shâ**

water-pot, **tùlū** (*pl.* **tūlūnà**)

way, **hanyằ** (*f.*) (*pl.*
hanyōyī)

way, by way of, **ta**

wealth, **arzìkī/azzìkī**

wealthy person, **mawàdàcī**
(*f.* **mawadācìyā** ; *pl.*
mawàdàtā)

wear, *v.* **jità**

wedge, **wejì/wajì**

Wednesday, **Làràbā** (*f.*)

week, **mākò, sātī**

weeping, **kūkā**

weigh, *v.* **aunà**

welcome !, **maràbā** !

well, **rījìyā** (*f.*) (*pl.* **rījiyōyī**)

well !, **àshē** !

well . . ., **tô/tò** . . .

well-being, **lāfiyằ** (*f.*)

west, **yâmmā**

— westward, **yâmma**

wet-mix, *v.* **dāmằ**

what about ?, **fà ?**

whatever, **kōmē**

when, **lōkàcîn dà, sā'àd dà**

when ?, **yàushè ?/yàushe**

whenever, **kōyàushè/
kōyàushe**

where ?, **ìnā ?**

— where, **ìndà**

wherever, **kō'ìnā/kōìnā**

whether, kō
which, wandà (f. waddà ;
    pl. waɗàndà)
which ?, wànè ? (f. wàcè ;
    pl. wàɗànnè)
while, after a, an jimà, jìm
    kàɗan
white, farī (f. farā ; pl.
    faràrē)
— snow-white, farī fat
who, whom, wandà (f.
    waddà ; pl. waɗàndà)
who ?, wà/wànēnè ? (pl. su
    wà ?)
whoever, duk wandà
whoever, kōwànēnè (f.
    kōwàcēcè)
why ?, dom mè ?
why !, ai !
wife, màcè (pl. mātā), uwar
    gidā
— father's wife (not one's
    mother), gwaggò/
    gwàggō
win, v. ci
wind, iskà (m. or f.)
wind, v. naɗà
wind, breaking, tūsà (f.)
window, tāgà (f.) (pl.
    tāgōgī)
wing, fiffikè (pl. fìkàfìkai)
winnow, v. shēƙà
wipe, v. shàfā (i/ē)
with, dà
woe is me !, wâyyô nī !

woman, màcè/màta- (f.)
    (pl. mātā)
I wonder . . . ?, shin/
    shîn . . . ?
wood, itàcē (pl. itātuwà)
word, màganà (f.) (pl.
    màgàngànū)
work, aikì (pl. ayyukà)
worker, ma'àikàcī (f.
    ma'aikacìyā ; pl.
    ma'àikàtā)
worm, tsūtsà (f.) (pl.
    tsūtsōtsī)
worry, dāmù, v. dằmā
worthlessness, banzā
wound, cùtā (f.)
write, v. rubùtā
writing, rùbùtū

yam(s), dōyà (f.)
yard, yādì
year, shèkarà (f.) (pl.
    shèkàrū)
— last year, bàra (f.)
— next year, bàɗi (f.)
— this year, bana (f.)
yellow, ràwayà (f.)
yes, ī, na'àm, nà'am ?
yesterday, jiyà (f.)
yet (not yet), tùkùna
youngest (of children), àutā
youth, sauràyī (pl. sàmàrī)

zero, sifìrī